The JUGGLER and the KING

THE JEW AND THE CONQUEST OF EVIL

An Elaboration of the Vilna Gaon's Insights Into the Hidden Wisdom of the Sages

by

Aharon Feldman

FELDHEIM
Jerusalem / New York

ISBN No. 0-87306-557-3

2 3 4 5 6 7 8 9 10

Phototypeset at Targum Press

Distributed by
Philipp Feldheim, Inc.
200 Airport Executive Park
Spring Valley, NY 10977
(914) 356-2282/(800) 237- 7149

In Israel:
Lahav Publications
c/o Kornfeld
Sanhedria Murchevet 116D
Jerusalem
(02)822058

Printed in Israel

איכה יועם זהב ישנא הכתם הטוב

DEDICATED

TO THE MERIT OF THE SOUL
OF MY BELOVED AND PRECIOUS MOTHER

SHEINA GOLDIE FELDMAN ע"ה

לע"נ
אמי מורתי הכ"מ

מרת שינא גאלדא בת הרב חיים יואל ע"ה

שהשיבה נשמתה לבוראה בירושלים ת"ו
בש"ק ח' שבט, תש"ן

Who taught her children to love Torah and Mitzvos
Who was a living ideal of a Jewish mother and wife
Who during her lifetime rarely had a selfish thought

תנו לה מפרי ידיה ויהללוה בשערים מעשיה
תנצב"ה

מכתב תהלה

Letter of Approbation

Rabbi CHAIM P. SCHEINBERG
KIRYAT MATTERSDORF
PANIM MEIROT 2
JERUSALEM, ISRAEL

הרב חיים פנחס שיינברג
ראש ישיבת "תורה אור"
ומורה הוראה דקרית מטרסדורף
ירושלים טל. 521513

בס"ד
ירושלים ת"ו,
שילהי אב, תש"נ

אתא לקדמנא הרה"ג הר"ר אהרן פלדמן שליט"א ר"ם ומנהל רוחני בישיבת כנסת בית אהרן פעיה"ק ירושלים ובידו באור מקיף על פירושי הגר"א לאגדות רבב"ח וסבי דבי אתונא בב"ב ובבכורות, שבהם הרבה מיסודות הדת בעניני יצ"הר תלמוד תורה ומעלת עם ישראל, וכתב הרב הנ"ל את הדברים בשפת האנגלית וסידרם בסדר נאות והרחיב בהם הדיבור באופן שיהיו שווים לכל נפש, וכל זה לזכות אלה מאחב"י שקשה עליהם הלימוד בלשון הקודש ושמושפעים מהשפעות זרות כדי ליישר את דיעותיהם ולהעיר את לבם לעבודת ה' התמימה, וגם עשה כן למען כבוד התורה להראות קבל עם את עומק חכמת חז"ל ואיך שכלכלו דבריהם הנשגבים בדברי חידות ומשלים.

ואם כי לא עיינתי בגוף הספר, איתמחי גברא כת"ח מובהק וכמרביץ תורה ברבים בשנים רבות בשיעוריו ובספריו, ורבים מהרעיונות שמציע בספרו זה כבר הציע בפני תלמידיו בשבת תחכמוני בישיבה הנ"ל ובזמן שהי' ר"ם ומנהל דישיבת אור שמח פה, ותועלתם היתה מרובה וראוי לקבעם בדפוס, ואשר על כן לפעלא טבא אמינא יישר והנני מברכו שיצליח להוציא לאור ספר זה ועוד ספרים כהנה וכהנה לזכות בהם את הרבים ובזכות הרבצת התורה ובמיוחד תורת הגר"א נזכה מהרה לבגו"צ ולזמן ועידן שנאמר עליו ומלאה הארץ דעה כמים לים מכסים.

החותם למען כבוד התורה ולומדי'

חיים פינחס שיינברג

איכה יועם זהב ישנא הכתם הטוב

DEDICATED

TO THE MERIT OF THE SOUL
OF MY BELOVED AND PRECIOUS MOTHER

SHEINA GOLDIE FELDMAN ע"ה

לע"נ
אמי מורתי הכ"מ

מרת שינא גאלדא בת הרב חיים יואל ע"ה

שהשיבה נשמתה לבוראה בירושלים ת"ו
בש"ק ח' שבט, תש"ן

Who taught her children to love Torah and Mitzvos
Who was a living ideal of a Jewish mother and wife
Who during her lifetime rarely had a selfish thought

תנו לה מפרי ידיה ויהללוה בשערים מעשיה
תנצב"ה

מכתב תהלה

Letter of Approbation

Rabbi CHAIM P. SCHEINBERG
KIRYAT MATTERSDORF
PANIM MEIROT 2
JERUSALEM, ISRAEL

הרב חיים פנחס שיינברג
ראש ישיבת "תורה אור"
ומורה הוראה דקרית מטרסדורף
ירושלים טל. 521513

בס"ד
ירושלים ת"ו,
שילהי אב, תש"נ

אתא לקדמנא הרה"ג הר"ר אהרן פלדמן שליט"א ר"ם ומנהל רוחני בישיבת כנסת בית אהרן פעיה"ק ירושלים ובידו באור מקיף על פירושי הגר"א לאגדות רבב"ח וסבי דבי אתונא בב"ב ובבכורות, שבהם הרבה מיסודות הדת בעניני יצ"הר תלמוד תורה ומעלת עם ישראל, וכתב הרב הנ"ל את הדברים בשפת האנגלית וסידרם בסדר נאות והרחיב בהם הדיבור באופן שיהיו שווים לכל נפש, וכל זה לזכות אלה מאחב"י שקשה עליהם הלימוד בלשון הקודש ושמושפעים מהשפעות זרות כדי ליישר את דיעותיהם ולהעיר את לבם לעבודת ה' התמימה, וגם עשה כן למען כבוד התורה להראות קבל עם את עומק חכמת חז"ל ואיך שכלכלו דבריהם הנשגבים בדברי חידות ומשלים.

ואם כי לא עיינתי בגוף הספר, איתמחי גברא כת"ח מובהק וכמרביץ תורה ברבים רבות בשנים בשיעוריו ובספריו, ורבים מהרעיונות שמציע בספרו זה כבר הציע בפני תלמידיו בשבת תחכמוני בישיבה הנ"ל ובזמן שהי' ר"ם ומנהל דישיבת אור שמח פה, ותועלתם היתה מרובה וראוי לקבעם בדפוס, ואשר על כן לפעלא טבא אמינא יישר והנני מברכו שיצליח להוציא לאור ספר זה ועוד ספרים כהנה וכהנה לזכות בהם את הרבים ובזכות הרבצת התורה ובמיוחד תורת הגר"א נזכה מהרה לבגו"צ ולזמן ועידן שנאמר עליו ומלאה הארץ דעה כמים לים מכסים.

החותם למען כבוד התורה ולומדי'

חיים פנחס שיינברג

Table of Contents

Table of Scope of Chapters*

* Decimal numbers represent Sections (sub-chapters); whole numbers represent Chapters; roman numerals represent Parts.

III. The Yetzer Hara: General Topics

IV. The Yetzer Hara: Specific Aspects

V. Torah and Its Study

About This Book

Thirty years ago, at a street stand in Bnei Brak, I first came upon the slim Hebrew volume which forms the basis of this book. I was unaware at the time how momentous an occasion this was for me, for very few books have had so major an impact on my thinking. The book, פירוש על כמה אגדות ("Explanation of Several Aggaddos"),[1] is a commentary by the Vilna Gaon ("the genius of Vilna")[2] on two passages of Talmudic Aggadata,[3] the Rabba bar Bar-Chanah stories and the Savvei DeVei Atuna riddles.[4] They consist of fantastic stories and cryptic debates which constitute what are probably the most enigmatic parts of the entire Talmud.

Many commentators have attempted to elucidate these sections of Aggadata, but none of their attempts approach the Vilna Gaon's explanations. According to him, these passages are literally a guide to the Jewish view of God, life and history, discussing why man was created; what motivates him; how he can recognize and overcome the evil within himself; what the purpose of the Jewish people is; why Jews have suffered throughout history; what the function of the

1 First edition: Vilna, 5560 (1800); reprinted in an improved edition with some additional material, Koenigsburg, 5622 (1862); and reprinted in the Koenigsburg edition format many times since then.

2 Rabbi Eliahu of Vilna (5480-5554/1720-1794), also known by the acronym, "the GRA."

3 See next section, "An Overview of Aggadata," §§ 1-3, for a definition of this term.

4 Bava Basra 73a-74b and Bechoros 8b, respectively. There are several variations from the standard Talmud texts in the Vilna Gaon's citations. The Gaon's readings are generally based on those given in *Ein Yaakov*, the classic omnibus of Talmudic Aggadata.

Era of Mashiach (the Messiah) will be; and many other such seminal concepts. It is far from an exaggeration to say that no Jew can fully understand himself or the world around him without having studied the wisdom contained in the Gaon's book.

As with everything else the Gaon wrote, the interpretations ring true and clear. They give the student a palpable feeling that he is privy to the exact meaning behind the symbols of the Aggadata. The meaning flows out of the text into the interpretation; the interpretations do not, as is sometimes the case, force themselves into the text. The most convincing proof of their accuracy is the manner in which the Gaon demonstrates that the symbols employed in these Aggadata are consistent with the way they are used in other contexts in the Talmud, in the Midrashim, and in the Scriptures. This would lead us to accept the interpretations even if we did not know who wrote them; still more is this the case when we know that they come from the Vilna Gaon's own hand.

* * *

To delineate properly the greatness of the Vilna Gaon would take a whole volume in itself. Suffice it to say that most Torah scholars since his time agree that he was the greatest teacher of Torah in recent centuries, perhaps even since the time of the Rishonim.[5] His unusual talents were recognized even while he was a child; there was no teacher great enough to teach him after he turned seven, and his teacher until then was the author of the standard commentary on the Jerusalem Talmud, *Penei Moshe*. One of his recorded *chiddushim,*[6] an explanation of a difficult passage of the Talmud, was composed when he was nine years old;

5 The towering figures of the early Medieval period.

6 "New thoughts": insights or interpretations into a matter of Jewish learning that have never before been suggested.

when he was twelve he solved a problem in astronomy affecting the laws of *Kiddush HaChodesh* (the determination of the lunar month) whose solution had eluded the rabbis of his time. While still a young man he was recognized as a major authority, even though he lived in a generation of Torah giants. He spent his lifetime in virtually uninterrupted devotion to Torah, sleeping only two hours a day and eating only enough to sustain his body. He mastered every area of Torah learning and wrote definitive commentaries on them all, from the *Shulchan Aruch* (the Code of Jewish Laws) to the most abstruse passages of the Kabbalah. Everything he taught or wrote is considered authoritative and is carefully analyzed and studied to this day.

In his lifetime he wrote over seventy works of Torah commentary in a distinctively concise style in which a few brief words illuminate an entire subject. In addition, he was also an expert in nearly all secular wisdom of his time, for he felt that such knowledge enhanced the understanding of many aspects of Torah and Kabbalah; he even left several volumes which deal with mathematics and astronomy.[7] This, despite the fact that he would study non-Torah wisdom only during those times when Jewish law forbids one to occupy his mind with thoughts of Torah.

* * *

The Gaon's Aggadic commentaries in this volume are not easy to understand. They are written in the same terse, concise style as his other writings, and they are supported by hundreds of allusions to Scriptural and Talmudic sources.[8]

Although most of the Gaon's writings are standard texts for Torah scholars throughout the world, the present commentary, because of its cryptic nature, is one of his least

7 Personal testimony of the Vilna Gaon's children in the Introduction to the Hebrew text of this book.

8 Its brevity of expression can be demonstrated by the fact that the original commentary by the Vilna Gaon occupies only some twenty pages.

studied works. This is unfortunate, because, as stated above, it elucidates many of the ideas most basic to Judaism.

This English Rendition

Since I discovered this book, I have often tried teaching it to others, and I have never met a serious student who was not greatly moved by it. In particular I have found that it is a uniquely effective vehicle for introducing the basic ideas of Judaism to those who have had no previous exposure to Torah. This fact made me decide to translate it into English for the benefit of a large segment of Jewry who would have no other access to these concepts.

To arrive at the decision to translate was easy; the act of translation was vastly more difficult than could have been imagined at the start. Understanding the original Hebrew was not always an easy task, and translating it compounded the problem: the words are few; the ideas are not readily fathomable; the allusions are not always easy to understand, or, at times, even to locate.

With the help of God the work slowly took shape. Other writings of the Gaon helped illuminate some of the more cryptic passages. Ideas in the classic Aggadic commentaries of the Maharal of Prague,[9] Maharsha,[10] and Rabbi Moshe Chaim Luzzatto[11] helped shed light on various obscure passages. Ultimately, a cogent presentation of nearly the entire volume took form.

In rendering this text into English I was guided by two objectives. First, of course, I wanted this book to be an accurate rendition of the Gaon's ideas. Second, to allow the maximum effect on the reader, I wanted it to be as interesting and as readable as possible.

9 Rabbi Yehudah Loeve, Rabbi of Prague in the late 16th century.

10 Rabbi Shemuel Eliezer Eidels, late 17th-century Poland.

11 Known as "Ramchal," a classic expounder of Jewish thought of 18th-century Italy.

In line with the first objective, I did my best to arrive at a true understanding of the meaning of the text. There are many chapters whose explanation was fashioned only after uncounted reviews of the text over the course of many years.

To reach my second objective of maximum readability, I did not attempt a verbatim translation, or even a paraphrase. In order to make the ideas as clear as possible, I expanded liberally on the original text, and even re-arranged its original order. I elaborated extensively on some of the more difficult concepts, and, when I felt it was necessary, added explanations of related Aggadata, based on the Gaon's other commentaries, or, in one or two places, the commentaries of the Maharal of Prague. These are documented in the footnotes.

I divided the various stories and riddles into chapters; three of the Talmudic passages were divided into two chapters each because each consists of two separate ideas. The order of the stories and riddles is the same as in the original text, except for the first story, which is third in the original text but first here, due to the key message it presents.

An examination of the Hebrew text will show that not every passage has been rendered into English. Two "chapters" have been omitted,[12] as well as many passages within the translated chapters. This is due to one or more of the following reasons: 1) The concepts dealt with are foreign to the English reader and would have required lengthy and involved explanations beyond the scope of an introductory work such as this. 2) The main ideas expressed have already been incorporated (at least in my opinion) into other chapters.[13] 3) I was not able to fathom the full meaning of the text.[14] 4) The omitted passage is based upon exegeses (*derashot*) of the Hebrew text which would be difficult to follow,

12 The first of the Savvei DeVei Atuna debates, as well as the debate following "Of Eggs and Cheese," beginning, in the Hebrew text, with "רציצא."

13 This is the reason the first of the debates was omitted.

14 Parts of Chapter 18, "Of Eggs and Cheese," and the debate following it were omitted for this reason.

or even meaningless, in translation.

The basic meaning and function of Aggadata will be discussed in "An Overview of Aggadata," which immediately follows; but to give a clearer definition of its function, an appendix has been added containing R. Moshe Chaim Luzzatto's discussion of Aggadata, his *Ma'amar Al HaHaggados,* some of whose ideas will be cited below.

The Koenigsburg edition of the Vilna Gaon's commentary has been reproduced at the end of the book. Consulting it after studying the English rendition will introduce the scholarly reader to the compact, incisive style of the Vilna Gaon's commentaries, as well as granting him a dimension of understanding which is impossible to achieve in translation.

* * *

I am well aware that my intentions, however noble they may be, are no guarantee of success. It would be presumptuous to claim that I have arrived at the Gaon's true intention in every chapter and every detail. Consequently, this work should in no way be taken as the last word on the Gaon's interpretations, and any ideas or interpretations which the reader does not find acceptable should be attributed to my poor understanding rather than to the Gaon's commentary. I shall be thankful to anyone who will apprise me of any such shortcomings.

The Name of This Book

The Gaon explains that the juggler in the first story in this book represents a man who has devoted himself entirely to materialism. Like a juggler who concerns himself with nothing else but throwing one ball after the other, materialistic man lives exclusively to juggle activities which afford him gratification. His life is a constant switch between the pursuit of fleshly pleasures and of status and prestige. The

King of the universe observes all this with disappointment, for He created him for nobler ends. Finally, He passes judgment on the juggler's antics.

The Jew's purpose on earth is to control the juggler within himself and to direct himself not towards folly but towards accomplishing the goals set for him by the King of Kings. Success in this struggle means another step towards perfection both for each individual and for all of mankind. For it is the essence of the Jew's function in this world to bring mankind to the recognition that it has a nobler destiny than juggling material pleasures. Since the underlying theme of this entire book is the Jew's battle with the juggler within him which would block him from fulfilling his true potential, the title of this story was judged most appropriate to be the title of the whole book.

A Word to the Reader

In writing this book one of my goals was to give its readers a view of the depth and scope of Aggadic wisdom. But the primary intention was to introduce the reader to the basic values of the Torah which lie in these stories and riddles. These are, among others, that human success is measured in terms of spiritual growth and refinement of character, not by the amassing of wealth and pleasures; that the Jewish nation exists to study Torah and to keep mitzvos; that its function in history is to remain steadfast to its values in the face of a Godless, selfish world. I am sure the reader will be able to clearly identify himself and the modern cultural heirs to ancient Rome in these chapters.

Although the book was written, as explained above, in a manner which will make it interesting and enjoyable, I will consider my efforts to have ended in failure if it offers no greater benefits to the reader than literary and intellectual enjoyment, or even the sensations of spiritual elevation. The concepts of the Torah are meant not merely to edify us but to create mindsets which are carried out into action. The true purpose of this book will therefore only be realized if the reader incorporates its ideas into his heart, mind and daily activities. It is my fervent prayer that this book will have such an effect and will thereby contribute to fulfilling the Jewish mission on earth: ridding ourselves and all of mankind of the juggler within us.

A.F.
Jerusalem
Erev Tish'a B'Av, 5750

Acknowledgments

I preface my acknowledgment of those who assisted me in this book with a brief and inadequate expression of gratitude to the one person who ultimately is most responsible for its writing, namely my honored father, Rabbi Joseph H. Feldman, formerly of Baltimore, Md., and now of Jerusalem. My father was the first to teach me to revere the words of the Sages, to discover the pure joy of plumbing their depths, and to inspire me to devote myself to Torah learning. May God grant him long life filled with health and accomplishment, and may he continue to serve for many years as a living example to his family and to his community of the nobility which Torah can confer upon a human being.

As for the actual writing of the book, my first debt of gratitude is to Yaakov Lavon of Yerucham, Israel, for his invaluable aid in editing this book. Yaakov is a master writer and critic who is as well a scholar well-versed in Jewish thought. Every chapter bears the imprint of his editing, and whatever level of eloquence which this book has attained is due in great measure to his skill. May the merit of his זכוי הרבים (contributing to the spiritual benefit of the public) bring him, together with his family, the blessings of physical well-being and the means to continue to contribute to the spreading of the Torah's wisdom.

As in everything else I have written in English, my brother, Rabbi Emanuel Feldman of Atlanta, Georgia, has lent his invaluable assistance in this work, as well. He took valuable time away from his scheduled studies on his sabbatical leave in Israel, which coincided with the finishing stages of the book, for a careful review of the final draft. His incisive criticisms and suggestions have all been incorporated into the final version. I extend my deepest gratitude to him for investing this book with his vast wisdom, experience and skill as a rabbi, an editor and a writer.

I extend my appreciation to the staff of Targum Press for the excellent and professional typesetting of the book.

My sincere thanks to Bernard Berniker for the devoted effort he invested into the internal graphic design and to Ben Gasner for gracing another book of mine with a cover expressive of his unmatched good taste and originality.

I extend my deep thanks to those who reviewed the manuscript in its various stages, some as much as five years ago: to Yonasan Rosenblum, whose painstaking review of, and critical comments on, an early draft of the book were important elements in its ultimate development; to Joseph Kaufman and Rafael Waldman for their important suggestions; and, especially, to my *mechuteness*, Mrs. Gerti Kornfeld, for her encouragement, corrections, and recommendations.

Finally, I acknowledge the contribution of my dear wife, Lea Feldman, as the first to recognize the wide impact which this book might have on the public. If not for her encouragement and assistance I would not have been able to complete its writing.

An Overview of Aggadata

1 THE TWO PARTS OF THE ORAL TORAH

When the Torah was given to the Jewish people, along with the written Torah (which we call תורה שבכתב or the Five Books of Moses) came teachings which were meant to interpret and apply the Torah's written words. These teachings, which were to be orally transmitted through the generations, are what we call תורה שבעל פה, or the Oral Torah. In later generations, the Talmud and the Midrashim were made the repository of this Oral Torah.

There are two distinct components of the Oral Torah: Halachah and Aggadata.[1] Halachah constitutes about ninety per cent of the Talmud and nearly all of the Halachic Midrashim, namely the *Mechilta, Sifra* and *Sifrei*. Aggadata makes up the other ten per cent of the Talmud — unevenly distributed among all its tractates[2] — and virtually the whole of the other Midrashic works.[3]

Halachah is the easier of these two categories to define. It consists of the definitions, the sources and the explanations of all laws that govern Jewish behavior. The purview of Aggadata, on the other hand, is the Jewish world of ideas. Primarily it deals with the principles of faith, the philosophy, and the ethical ideals of Judaism. In addition it includes all those interpretations of Biblical verses and stories which are unrelated to Halachah; expositions of the importance of the

1 This is the Aramaic term, which is more commonly used. In Hebrew it is "Aggadah."

2 With the exception of Tractate Avos, which deals exclusively with Aggadata.

3 Midrash Rabba, Midrash Tanchuma and the Zohar are the best-known.

mitzvos and the rewards and punishments which they entail; stories from the lives of the righteous; lessons in character training; and even, sometimes, what appears to be practical advice on worldly matters such as business and personal health.

Halachah and Aggadata are distinct from each other not only in their content but in their respective modes of expression. Halachic discussions usually begin with the sources of the laws in the Scriptures, and then elaborate on the laws through carefully reasoned questions and answers, comparisons and distinctions, proofs and refutations, until conclusions are reached.

Aggadata, on the other hand, conveys its teachings by other means. Most of the ideas in Aggadata are derived from Scriptural texts, just as Halachah is; but they rarely stem from the simple translation of the verses. In order to reveal the concepts of Aggadata, the verse is usually read at another level of meaning, the exegetical level known as *"derash."* Although the Sages' dictum states that the simple meaning of the text is always true ("אין מקרא יוצא מידי פשוטו"),[4] the Torah has many levels of meaning, which are alluded to by seemingly superfluous words, unusual usages, and the juxtaposition of verses. *"Derash"* is the exegetical method of interpreting the allusions lying beneath the surface of a verse.

A more important difference between the two domains of the Oral Torah is that whereas Halachic discussions are rigorously logical, Aggadata is often noticeably obscure. This obscurity is intentional: in Aggadata the message — often some of the most basic ideas of Judaism — is garbed in what appear to be parables, riddles or even practical advice without apparent religious content. In line with this, one great authority writes that the above-mentioned dictum, that a verse never departs its plain meaning, applies only to the Torah's verses and not to Aggadic statements; in fact, he writes, the plain meaning of Aggadata is usually not its true meaning.[5]

4 Shabbas 63a.

5 *Yad Eliahu,* Part I, Responsum 25, *s.v.* ואף, by R. Eliahu Ragoler, (5554-5610/1794-1850); Rabbi of Kalisch, a student of R. Chaim of Volozhin (the foremost student of the Vilna Gaon) and a world-renowned Torah scholar and Kabbalist.

2 THE LANGUAGE OF ESOTERIC WISDOM

What led the Sages to conceal some of the Torah's most essential teachings? The commentaries give several reasons for this:[6]

For about a millennium and a half, from the giving of the Torah at Sinai until the times of the Talmudic Sages, the wisdom of the Oral Torah was not written down but transmitted by word of mouth from teacher to student. Eventually, however, the Sages began to fear that their students' memories might no longer be counted upon to retain the vast wisdom of the Torah, as had been the rule in previous generations, and it might be lost. They decided to commit it to writing, a process which eventually led to the redaction of the entire Oral Torah.

The Sages' decision to commit the Oral Torah to writing created no problem with respect to the laws of Jewish behavior, i.e., the Halachah. But with respect to the more abstruse concepts of Judaism, the Sages found themselves in a dilemma. Unlike Halachah, these concepts cannot be readily understood by everyone; indeed up until then they had been taught only to the wisest of the students of each generation. If they were now committed to writing and so made available to all, they would be exposed to the misunderstandings and distortions of untutored readers. On the other hand, if they were not written down, they might — just as the Sages feared — be lost forever.

The problem was solved by writing these ideas down in, as it were, coded form: the obscure form of parable and hint. The keys to their true meaning would continue to be transmitted orally; they were relatively few and ran no great risk of being forgotten. In this manner the Torah's deepest wis-

6 Rambam, *Introduction to the Mishnah*, printed in the Vilna (Romm) edition of the Talmud, folio 55a after Berachos, *s.v.* אחר; Maharal of Prague, *Be'er HaGolah*, "The Fourth Well"; R. Moshe Chaim Luzzatto, *Ma'amar Al HaHaggados*. The following three paragraphs are based on Rambam and R. Luzzatto.

dom would be preserved, and at the same time it would still be protected from the ravages of misunderstanding. Wise students would be shown the way to divine the true meanings behind the parables, while the inept would take them for nothing more than charming tales or shrewd advice.

Thus, it proved necessary to transmit the most profound concepts in Torah by the least comprehensible means, for these are the very ideas that are most liable to be misunderstood.

As an example, let us consider the following passage:

> It is written, "And God made the two large luminaries"[7] [indicating that sun and moon were originally created the same size]; yet it is written, "The large luminary and the small luminary"[8] [indicating that later the moon became smaller].
>
> The moon complained before the Holy One, blessed be He: "Master of the world! Can two kings use the same crown?"
>
> "If so," God replied, "go and diminish yourself."[9]

This story contains, in cryptic form, the philosophical underpinnings of one of the deepest puzzles of Creation: why did God place man in a material setting where His presence is hidden?[10]

Similarly, the essential meaning of blessings such as are said in the daily prayers is explained by the puzzling account of a conversation between a High Priest and God in the Holy of Holies on Yom Kippur. God asks the priest to "bless" Him, and the priest replies, "May it be Your will that Your mercy overcome your anger."[11] This seemingly incredible account offers a crucial explanation of an important part of our daily activities.[12]

Now we can appreciate why the Zohar, the most esoteric

7 Bereishis 1:16.

8 *Ibid.*

9 Chullin 60b.

10 A full exposition of this Aggadata and its explanation are beyond the scope of this work. The interested reader is referred to R. Moshe Chaim Luzzatto, *Daas Tevunos,* Friedlander Ed., pp. 59 and 159.

11 Berachos 7a.

12 See R. Chaim of Volozhin, *Nefesh HaChayim,* Section Two, for an explanation.

of the Aggadic works, is so filled with parables of parents, children, kings and queens that no one who has not learned the keys to their underlying secrets from the mouth of a master could possibly understand them.

3 THE LANGUAGE OF THE WISE

Not all of Aggadata deals with esoteric wisdom. There are many examples of Aggadata where ideas which could be successfully conveyed in ordinary language are nonetheless delivered in an oblique manner.

For example, the Talmud advises a person whose father owns a supply of figs to sell them as soon as a market opens up for them and not wait for his father to sell them.[13] The Vilna Gaon explains that this is an admonishment to scholars to teach their wisdom to the public. Even one still in the learning stage himself (a "son") and dependent upon his teacher (his "father"), should teach whatever wisdom he knows (the supply of "figs") to anyone who desires to learn from him ("when the market opens up"); he should not relegate this obligation to his teacher.[14]

Similarly, many parables cited in the present volume do not seem so abstruse that they would be liable to misunderstanding if conveyed in a straightforward manner. Why did the Sages convey them in such obscure terms?

There are several reasons for this:

1) They sought by this means to teach their students that wisdom is acquired only by those willing to expend the necessary effort. In addition, they were able in this way to keep their wisdom from those who were not prepared to make the intellectual commitment necessary to acquire it. The purpose of gaining wisdom is to carry it out in action; people who will not exert themselves to understand wisdom do not appreciate its value and certainly will not trouble themselves to live by it. To

13 Berachos 62b.

14 Vilna Gaon, *Beiur HaGra La-Aggados,* Berachos, *ad loc.*

have learned wisdom and not to have applied it is worse than not to have learned it at all; better, then, that such people remain ignorant of it. The riddles, the parables, and the word-plays were all ways of separating the serious students from the dilettantes. As Rambam puts it, Aggadata was kept obscure

> to sharpen the students' minds and to inspire their hearts; and also to blind the eyes of those fools who do not restrain[15] [the desires of] their hearts, and who, if the full force of the truth were revealed to them, would reject it because of their character deficiencies.[16]

2) The Sages commonly had many intentions behind their sayings. The explanations given for the Sages' parables, even those given by the most expert commentaries, do not necessarily exhaust all the intended levels of meaning. A parable is the most economical way of conveying all these levels of meaning at once.

3) By using parables the Sages were able to add overtones of meaning to their ideas which could not be expressed by an ordinary statement. In the example mentioned above, using "figs" to represent wisdom suggests the verse, "He who guards the fig tree will eat its fruit."[17] Thus we are led to the Sages' insight on this verse, that Torah constantly provides its students with fresh insights, like a fig tree on which one can always find a freshly-ripened fig.[18] The image of a "market" for the acquisition of Torah wisdom suggests the Midrashic image of Torah learning as a "purchase";[19] it is acquired in exchange for physical and financial sacrifice. The use of "father" to symbolize a teacher refers to the dictum that one's students are like one's own children,[20] thus reminding us of the ideal relationship between teacher and student.

15 Lit., admonish.
16 Rambam, *loc. cit.*
17 Mishlei 27:18.
18 Eiruvin 54b. This is based on the fact that figs do not ripen all at once.
19 Midrash Rabba, Shemos 28:1.
20 Sifrei to Devarim 6:7.

Besides these, there are other shades of meaning implicit in this parable. A plain statement exhorting a novice to teach his wisdom to others even while he needs a teacher himself could not possibly be laden with such potency of suggestion.

4) The Sages often used the same metaphors to convey (relatively) comprehensible ideas as they used to convey their more esoteric teachings. By using these metaphors early on in a student's career, they introduced him to the meanings hidden therein and thus prepared him for the later time when he would be worthy of studying the hidden aspects of wisdom.

5) Often the Sages' words are not to be interpreted as parables but are to be taken at face value; their intent is simply to convey some fact about human nature or to give some practical advice. But even when they found it necessary to discuss such mundane information, they made certain that their sayings were imbued with other levels of meaning, which a diligent and understanding student would be able to discover. As true men of wisdom, the Sages wasted no words; they tried to fill even their ordinary conversation with as much wisdom as the occasion permitted.[21]

The reader will find that the Aggadata cited in this volume are of various sorts. Some of them convey esoteric ideas which, without careful elaboration and analysis, might easily be misunderstood and perverted. (Even the elaborations of these concepts given here only scratch the surface of the wealth of literature which appears on these subjects.) Others — this seems to characterize most of the Savvei DeVei Atuna riddles — are words of wisdom masked to separate the wise student from the ignorant. All of them emphatically demonstrate the unequalled profundity of the Sages' wisdom.

21 *Cf.* Sukkah 21b, "Even the Sages' secular conversation is Torah and requires study."

Part One
The Rabba bar Bar-Chanah Stories

שפיל ואזיל בר אווזא ועיניה מטייפי

"Humbly walks the duck, but its eyes are turned to heaven."

(*Bava Kama* 92b)

Do not malign the words of a sage even if they seem trivial, for they contain the loftiest wisdom.

(*Commentary by the Vilna Gaon,* ad loc.)

Introduction to Part One

These stories recount the experiences of a Talmudic sage, Rabba bar Bar-Chanah, while travelling at sea. They are bizarre tales of being swamped by gigantic waves, meeting fantastic animals, and other incredible and incomprehensible incidents.

The commentaries differ as to whether or not these accounts are to be taken literally. Some maintain that they are accounts of incidents which actually happened to Rabba; miraculous ones to be sure, but the occurrence of miracles for the saintly is hardly unusual in Jewish history.

However, several major commentators, such as Rashba, Ritva, Maharal, Maharsha, and the Vilna Gaon, are apparently of the opinion that the stories are not to be taken literally. Some understand them to have been visions seen by Rabba, probably in a dream; the Vilna Gaon refers to them simply as "stories" (*ma'asim*). However Rabba came by their imagery according to this view, the stories are parables offering various truths about the evil drives in man, about the study of Torah, and about Jewish destiny. This is the approach upon which this book is based.

The main subject around which these stories revolve is man's struggle with his *yetzer hara.* This term is translated as "the evil inclination" or "the inclination towards evil"; but it is necessary to define the concept more fully. What is evil and what is the human inclination towards it?

The Torah teaches us that mankind was created for a purpose: to arrive at a clear recognition of God's sovereignty and to live a life which reflects this recognition. "Good" is anything which moves us towards this end; conversely, "evil" is that which thwarts our progress towards it.

Man has an innate drive to seek out the meaning of his life

and, ultimately, to seek closeness to God. This drive, because it advances man toward his true goals, is called his *"yetzer tov,"* or his natural inclination towards what is his ultimate good.

But man's nature is such that he can be distracted from his true goals by excessive, purposeless indulgence in material pleasures and the pursuit of power and prestige. Once man becomes involved in his self, his drive to come close to God — his *yetzer tov* — weakens and eventually falls silent. The pulls and appetites which drive man to pursue false goals are collectively called *"yetzer hara,"* or the inclination to evil, for, as above, "evil" is that which keeps us from reaching our ultimate goa!.

These material drives are not inherently evil. Material pleasures can be used purposefully, to sustain life or to make life more joyous: pleasure, in this case, enables man to be a better servant of God. Prestige and power can be used to subdue the evil in the world: in this case it is advancing the true ends of humanity. When so used, these drives are "good." But when material drives are turned to the service of man's selfishness, when they are used indiscriminately and without purpose, when their goal is merely to supply sensations for the sake of sensations, then they are "evil."

But why, then, did God create a material world if it could be so misused? As explained in Chapter One, this very potential for misuse provides man with his greatest opportunity for Divine service. The recognition of God's sovereignty is attainable to the fullest only when it is possible to believe that there is some alternative truth. And so the physical world was created, so that within its realm evil could come into existence and provide an alternative to Divine service. By rejecting this evil, man can then come to a full recognition of God's dominion.

Each of the following stories reveals an aspect of man's *yetzer hara*; taken together they form a mosaic of its characteristics. Once we learn to recognize the various manifestations of the *yetzer hara* within us, we will be well on our way to freeing ourselves of its domination.

1
The Juggler and the King

Said Rabba bar Bar-Chanah: I saw Hormin the son of Lillith running along the battlements of the city wall of Mechuza. A cavalryman below, riding on an animal, could not keep up with him.

Once two mules were saddled for [Hormin] and stood on the two sides of the River Donag. He jumped from one mule to the other while holding two cups of wine in his hands, pouring from one to the other without a drop falling to the earth.

That was the day when things "rise to the heavens and descend to the depths" [Tehillim 107:26]; *finally the King's men heard of [Hormin's doings] and put him to death.*

(Bava Basra 73a-b)

1.1 HORMIN AND AHORMEZ

> A certain Persian wizard said to [the Jewish sage] Ameimar: "The upper half [of man] belongs to Ahormez [god of heaven]; the bottom half belongs to Hormin [god of earth]."
>
> "If it is so," countered Ameimar, "why does Ahormez permit Hormin to transport food and drink through his territory?"[1]

To all appearances, man is essentially similar to any other animal. He is an organism perfectly designed for survival, possessing intelligence, emotions, and a body equipped to

1 Sanhedrin 39a.

provide him with a constant supply of his vital needs. The human organism, viewed from this perspective, is nothing more than the sum total of all of the mechanisms by which it sustains itself.

But describing man in terms of his capacity for survival is inadequate. Man is clearly unique, meant for more than sustaining his existence.

Nothing demonstrates this more than man's intelligence: it has a capacity far beyond what would have been necessary in animal terms. The mind of the beaver or the rat, for example, is exactly matched to the requirements of the animal's survival. Man, however, has an intelligence which both in quality and in quantity far exceeds his physical needs. Even more significant is the fact that man's most passionate intellectual concerns are totally irrelevant to his material goals. He investigates galaxies millions of light-years away and the ramifications of abstruse mathematical formulae. He is peculiarly contemplative, unsatisfied with merely mastering the world around him. He must sit and wonder about the mysteries of his existence, what the natural laws are that govern it, and why he was put on this earth.

In the same fashion, many of man's emotional needs transcend the concerns of mere survival. His most treasured feeling is, strangely, that of altruism — "strangely," for it seemingly operates squarely against his survival. Certainly, sharing his food with the poor and the weak will not keep man's belly full; yet this is one of his most honored duties. Similarly, the human appreciation of beauty is a non-utilitarian trait, yet so vital to him that he will often forgo much physical gratification in order to create or possess a thing of beauty. Why would man be driven to do this if he were intended only to survive?

This alone would be enough of a puzzle: why an otherwise perfectly adapted organism should have so many needs and drives that are irrelevant and even antagonistic to its survival. But there is an even greater enigma than this, namely, that exactly those pursuits that are least useful for survival are those which grant man the greatest satisfaction, and which, when he is deprived of them, cause him the greatest anguish. For consider: a life that contains only physical gratification leaves man feeling empty and frustrated, without a sense of purpose and meaning in his life. Not only does this make him unhappy, but his mental health, and ultimately his survival, is threatened. Non-utilitarian pursuits, such as altruism, esthetics, and the contemplation of truth, are necessary to grant man a life of total satisfaction. This is so even though such pursuits are totally useless from the standpoint of material survival.

In short, man is composed of two contradictory natures, one that he shares with the animals and one that makes him disdain the physical world and reach out to grasp the world of the spirit. Which of these two represents man's true essence? This puzzle has occupied people's thoughts since ancient times.

The Persian opinion is summed up by the wizard's dictum at the head of this chapter. He explained the human dichotomy simply: two gods created man, and therefore two opposing forces are at play within him, one pulling him towards earthy pursuits and the other towards the heavenly spheres. Hormin (Ahriman), god of earth, darkness, and evil, designed man's physicality to function like that of any other natural being, for he wished man to be just another animal. On the other hand, man's outsized intelligence and sensitivity were created by Ahormez (Ahura-Mazda), god of heaven, light, and good. Ahormez, said the Persians, wanted man to recognize him and give him glory, and therefore he invested man with the capacity to reach heavenward and aspire to serve the god who made him (or at any rate that half of him). Since he was created by two opposing deities, it was understandable that man should have contradiction built into his nature.

The Persians believed that the diaphragm (located between the lungs and the stomach, approximately in the middle of the body) was the dividing line between the earth-god's domain within man and that of the heavenly god. The diaphragm separates between digestive and reproductive organs, which fulfil essentially animal functions, and the organs of speech, feeling, and thought, which raise man above the animals. Therefore the wizard said, "The upper half [above the diaphragm] belongs to Ahormez, and the bottom half belongs to Hormin."

Ameimar, the great Jewish sage, was unperturbed by the wizard's logic. "If it is so," he asked, "why does Ahormez allow Hormin to transport food and drink through his domain?" The food digested by the lower half of man (Hormin's domain) is brought into the system by the mouth and the esophagus (part of Ahormez' domain). The very same mouth, then, which extols heaven concerns itself as well with the mundane act of eating. If it had been created by a heavenly god opposed to his earthly counterpart, this could not be so. Certainly, only one God could have fashioned a being in which the mundane and the spiritual are so thoroughly mixed.

The Jewish explanation for man's apparent dichotomy, hinted at by Ameimar, is that there is no dichotomy at all. One God created the two apparently opposite natures in man in order that they should work together for a single purpose: to achieve man's destiny.

That destiny is to receive the greatest good that can be bestowed on any creature: the ability to draw close to God. The tools with which man prepares himself to acquire that ability are intelligence, sensitivity, and an innate yearning to seek out the reasons for his existence. All these drive him to discover his Creator and urge him on to recognize His supremacy; this is why he was invested with their relentless urgings. This, then, is the reason why man feels empty and unfulfilled when his life lacks a spiritual dimension: subconsciously he realizes that he is misusing a life that was meant for nobler pursuits. It also explains why a man who spends his life moving towards God is filled with lasting satisfaction. That is how one feels when he has fulfilled the true purpose of his creation.

Is man's physical nature contradictory to these goals? Certainly not; for it, too, is woven into the pattern of the Divine objective. For the body deepens man's knowledge of God by intensifying the experience of drawing close to Him.

The experience of drawing close to God is a thing of varying degrees. The most meaningful degree of experience exists when one draws close to Him in spite of the animal pulls of his body. His appreciation of God is then that much more meaningful to him. If not for darkness one does not know to appreciate light; if not for ignorance one cannot rejoice in wisdom; if not for the body's call to physical pleasure, one could never come to love God with full intensity.

The mitzvos were given to man to enable him to manifest his acceptance of God's sovereignty in his physical acts. By carrying out these commandments he transforms the organs of his body from tools of survival and gratification to vehicles for expressing devotion to God. When this state is reached, the sensation of closeness to God has reached its highest degree.

Physical existence thus advances man toward his ultimate goal by intensifying his appreciation of the Divine. In the Jewish view, then, the two sides of human nature complement rather than contradict each other. Both the physical and the spiritual sides of man were created with the same aim in mind: to enable man to reach the heavens, to know the one God who wants to reveal His goodness to him. Man's animal nature is a veil intentionally drawn between him and God, meant to be thrust aside in order to provide the full intensity of the religious experience.

1.2 HORMIN'S DOUBLE KINGDOM

I saw Hormin the son of Lillith. . .

As we have said, man was created to develop a close relationship with his Creator. But he has the free choice not to do so. He may, if he wishes, take the world at its face value and act as if no God beckons him to a higher purpose. He may designate pleasure for his body and the stimulation of its nerve-endings as the ultimate goals of his life, thus turning the means of his continued existence into its end.

He may even go so far as to pervert the prodigious intelligence with which he has been endowed. It was intended to aid him in discovering his true purpose, but he can make it a mere tool to devise ever-new ways of obtaining yet more physical gratification.

When this happens, then, in the terms used by the Persian wizard, Ahormez's domain has been conquered by Hormin: the intellectual and spiritual side of man has become the servant of his animal nature.

The runner in the story above is called "Hormin" because he is the complete hedonist, to whom the satisfaction of his senses and lusts is the ultimate and only goal of life. All men indeed are born with various pleasure drives; however, they possess concomitant spiritual tendencies which temper and balance these drives. Hormin is singular in that he has "succeeded" in utilizing even his spiritual abilities for the advancement of his goal of constant and total gratification. Even his upper half, in the Persian terminology, is in the hands of the god of earth and darkness.

More precisely, he is called "Hormin the son of Lillith." The Torah tells us of a female demon called Lillith who represents the enticements men undergo to engage in illicit pleasures.[2] Hormin, the totally earthbound man, is described as being born of Lillith. In the Sages' terminology, one who has shaped his entire personality around a particular decision is said to be "born of" that decision. Hormin has decided to make sensual pleasure his absolute goal. He is the son of Lillith.

2 Zohar Vayikra 19a. This demon is mentioned in Yeshayahu 34:14.

1.3 THE WALL OF TORAH

. . . running along the wall. . .

> *I am a wall, and my breasts are like its watchtowers.*[3]
> "I am a wall" — this refers to the Torah. "And my breasts are like its watchtowers" — these are the Torah scholars.[4]

If the Jews are a people dedicated solely to carrying out the will of God, then the Torah is what gives them the strength to remain steadfast to their purpose. It is the Torah which enables them to reject irrelevant goals and values that might usurp their true destiny. It is the Torah which elevates them and carries them forward to their goals. A city wall protects from dangers without while sheltering the life within; similarly, the teachings and practices of the Torah protect the Jewish nation from invasion by foreign values from without, while at the same time propagating the authentic Jewish life that flourishes within. "'I am a wall' — this refers to the Torah."

A city wall must, in order to fulfil its function, have watchtowers where the defenders of the city stand guard over it. The defenders on the wall of the Torah are its scholars. Unlike ordinary watchmen, they did not achieve their position by virtue of their physical skill and prowess but rather because they sustain the inhabitants within the wall. The Jewish people are able to resist foreign invasion only when they are involved in Torah learning; for when they sense the nobility of its wisdom and its way of life, they are not drawn to cheap alternatives. Thus, the scholars who acquire the Torah's wisdom and then transmit it to the nation sustain its existence. They, nurturers of the Jewish people, are like a mother's breasts, and this nurturing makes them at the same time the people's defenders. "'My breasts are like its watchtowers' — these are the Torah scholars."

3 Shir HaShirim 8:10.
4 Bava Basra 7b.

1.4 The Quarrelers With God

. . . running along the battlements of the city wall of Mechuza. . .

Those who quarrel with God shall be broken.[5]
Said Rava: these [quarrelers with God] are the flower of Mechuza's citizens; and they are called "destined for Gehinnom [Purgatory]."[6]

Why is Mechuza called a place of quarrels against God, and why are its finest citizens singled out for this censure?

Mechuza was a great commercial center of ancient Babylonia as well as a famous seat of Torah scholarship (Rava himself, the great Amora, taught there). The people of Mechuza honored the Torah, but for the wrong reason; for Mechuza was permeated with a spirit that subtly led its Jews astray until their best intentions were corrupted.

There was only one aim in Mechuza: to get all the prestige and glory that money could buy. That attitude so pervaded the town that eventually its people came to honor the Torah, not because it was the word of God, but because it could be used as a tool to get prestige for themselves. Raising up well-trained Torah scholars meant to them providing an ethically sound and enlightened leadership that would foster effective social institutions and harmonious communal life: a leadership, in fact, that would provide the right background for the citizens' personal advancement. Being part of that leadership oneself meant prestige, power, and fame. In short, the Torah became a means by which the people of Mechuza could better further their self-serving goals.

The purpose of man's life is to recognize God's glory and give honor to His commands; yet the transcending purpose of the people of Mechuza was to advance their own glory. If they had only realized it, they were pitting their own will

5 Shemuel I, 2:10.
6 Rosh HaShanah 17a.

against God's. This was their "quarrel with God": that they were only interested in having everyone recognize their own greatness, and had no time to consider their Creator's greatness. The leaders of Mechuza, the flower of its citizenry, the fosterers and paragons of its perverted values, were obviously "destined for Gehinnom."

Although Torah is a wall against Hormin — for it represents the antithesis of all that he stands for — still the wall of Mechuza seems to him a fine place for a run: Torah study that has been made the tool of glory-seeking intrigues him with its promise of a new way to achieve pleasure, his single and ultimate goal.

So Rabba bar Bar-Chanah looked and saw Hormin the son of Lillith running along the wall of Mechuza. In his search for total gratification, Hormin not only commandeered his intelligence; he even took on the role of Torah scholar in order to win universal respect for himself.

1.5 The Cavalryman's Race

A cavalryman below, riding on an animal, could not keep up with him.

The cavalryman represents the genuine Torah scholar. Just as a rider uses the power of the animal beneath him to reach his destination, so a Jew devoted to doing God's will uses his "animal" — his body with its physical strength and powers — to carry out his service of God. His body faithfully sustains his life, and it gladdens with the pleasures of the five senses so that he can serve God joyfully. It is a fine tool for Divine service.

The cavalryman, seeing the enormous effort which Hormin exerts to reach his goal, is inspired to work even harder to master the wisdom of the Torah. He thinks to himself, "If someone is expending so very much effort and energy for such a hollow achievement, how much more then should I exert myself in my noble calling." But the cavalryman should realize that he will never be able to out-perform Hormin. For Hormin's only motivation is the pull of his material desire; since he has strangled his spiritual desires, nothing stands in the way of his race. For the Torah scholar it is different. His chief motivation is his spirituality; but his physical aspect will never go away for it is part of God's gift to him. Its animalistic drives, as explained above, were given to him because when they are overcome they intensify his recognition of God. Because the cavalryman must continually struggle he cannot keep up with Hormin. But this is the way to his success: his goal is not to win a race but to deepen his commitment to the struggle.

1.6 Pouring Wine

Once two mules were saddled for [Hormin] and stood on the two sides of the River Donag. He jumped from one mule to the other while holding two cups of wine in his hands, pouring from one to the other without a drop falling to the earth.

The bestial, survival-oriented side of man has two aspects to its nature. The external aspect is the body with its nervous system; the inner aspect is man's primitive personality.[7] Each of these aspects of the self is concerned with feelings: the body with physical sensation, the personality with emotions. Each one has a particular motivating force: the body reacts to stimulation of its nerve endings by seeking physical pleasure, and the inner self reacts to emotional stimulation by seeking prestige and ego gratification. Because they arouse man to activity, the Sages compare these stimuli to two cups of wine. Like an aperitif which stimulates one's appetite for dining, they are stimulants of physical and mental activity.

Hormin's life could be described, then, as a constant switch

7 This concept is discussed more fully in Chapter 13, "The House in the Air."

from one cup of wine to another, from the cup of sensory excitement to the cup of ego gratification. Demanding constant pleasure as he does, the moment he has begun to derive pleasure from a sensory stimulus (the moment one cup of wine is full) he reminds himself of his ego needs and begins to set about fulfilling them (he pours the wine into the other cup). And then it is turnabout again: no sooner is his plan for securing prestige and glory complete than he begins thinking how to get more physical gratification. So passes the hedonist's life, pouring the wine from one cup to the other.

1.7 DEATH AND THE JUGGLER

. . . pouring from one to the other without a drop falling to the earth.

Hormin's skill in pouring the wine back and forth was not always perfect. There were thoughts which would steal into his mind and disturb his concentration, and with it his aim. He would sometimes ask himself if hedonistic pleasures were truly the whole purpose for his existence. He even would think of death, that must surely someday be his fate, and then his eyes would wander to the cold, damp earth beneath his feet. If the questioning mood was strong upon him, he would go on to picture the day when the body he worshipped so ardently would be placed in that earth to rot, and he would have to stand before his Creator and be judged for the life he had led. What would he say then? Would his life of pleasure be justifiable? When these thoughts passed through his mind, he would lose some of his enthusiasm for his way of life; symbolically speaking, he would not concentrate on his juggling, and some of the wine would miss the cup and spill to the earth.

Hormin began to fight these baleful thoughts, which after all were merely counterproductive, interfering as they did with his enjoyment of the true life as he conceived it. He learned to be more sure of himself; he grew more set in his ways. Eventually there came a day when he succeeded in banishing his morbid fantasies completely. He ceased to concern himself at all with what his end would be, and threw himself with all his energy into his lively prancing and juggling. On that day he was at last able to pour the wine from cup to cup without spilling a drop to the earth.

1.8 JUGGLING ON MULE-BACK

. . . two mules. . .

In the Sages' symbolism the two major impulses that motivate man — sensory stimulation and ego gratification — are compared to cups of wine. The activities and the ways of life which these impulses inspire are given a different symbol: they are compared to beasts of burden. Such animals carry out their masters' will, transporting them and their burdens to the appointed destination. Similarly, the life a man leads is the means which carries him to his goals.

Any animal could be a metaphor for human activity; but the activities of Hormin, inspired by his cups of wine, are compared to a mule. This is because mules are sterile, and Hormin's life, devoted as it is to providing an unending flow of pleasure for himself, is in the end also sterile; these activities cannot constitute a viable way of life.

The sensation of physical pleasure was intended by its Creator to help man sustain his life. Pleasure was meant to drive man to remember to perform those acts necessary for his survival (such as eating for his personal survival and reproduction for the survival of the species), and to serve as an occasional grace note that adds joy to life. It was never meant to become an end in itself. When pleasure is used in any way other than was originally intended, the senses become numbed by overuse; the expected thrill does not come, and instead of joy, it brings only emptiness. On this follows an even worse feeling of depression as the dim feeling creeps over man that his true fulfillment cannot lie this way.

If despite all this man continues in his abuse of pleasure, then as the senses become jaded new frontiers of stimulation must be constantly discovered. To fill the aching emptiness new stimuli must continually be devised, even at the risk of bodily harm: alcohol, drugs, sodomy, bestiality, and so on *ad nauseam*.

But just as only so many variations can be played on one theme, so there are only so many pleasures that can be devised, and only a finite number of nerve-endings to be excited. Eventually everything seems the same, and even the offer of "something new" only invokes a sickening sensation of *déjà vu*.

As the body's capacity for physical excitement wanes, either through the numbing of the senses or as old age relentlessly sets in, it could be said that this mule can no longer carry a rider. A substitute carrier, the "mule" of ego satisfaction is increasingly employed instead. But all mules are sterile, and nothing will come of this second one either.

This mule, in fact, is in a sense worse than the other: it is the cause of the breakdown of social life. Individuals who live for prestige, wealth, and recognition are bound for conflict with everyone around them. A society which trains its members to live for such goals sets their courses from the start to collide with one another. The seeking of prestige breeds jealousy, jealousy breeds anger, and anger breeds strife, enmity, and the destruction of family, community, and ultimately an entire society.

In a prestige-oriented life, success is just as fleeting for those few who reach the top of the heap as it was for those who remained near the bottom. "He who has a hundred dinars wants two hundred, he who has two hundred wants four hundred . . . . Man never dies with even half his heart's desires fulfilled."[8] The more wealth and fame one has, the more conscious he is of what he does not yet have. He be-

8 Koheles Rabba 1,34.

comes more and more jealous of the power that others possess and less and less satisfied with what he has already acquired. Success paradoxically breeds failure; no great surprise, for this way of life is itself fundamentally paradoxical: it expects lasting satisfaction from a pleasure which by its very nature is transient. And so each fleeting satisfaction leads to more unhappiness. This mule is just as sterile as the first.

Mules serve their masters while they live, but because they are sterile they are a species without continuity. A mule is the very paradigm of solid reliability, giving the appearance of rock-hard permanence; but when it is dead there is no colt to replace it. The image of two mules especially saddled for the performance perfectly suggests what Hormin's arena is; for the activities engendered by his cups of wine are sterile, offering nothing but the most transient benefit. If to the observer they appear viable, of lasting worth, then his perception is only superficial; for disintegration is inescapably woven into their very fabric.

1.9 THE RIVER OF WAX

. . . two mules [which] stood on the two sides of the River Donag. . .

If activities aimed at gratification of the pleasure drives are so clearly doomed to failure, how have they so successfully attracted most of mankind throughout history? The answer lies in man's power of fantasy. The imaginative faculty was created to enable man to picture situations which he cannot actually experience. It enables him to avoid pitfalls and to embark on paths of success — even to imagine the rewards that await the faithful servant of God. However, like every other human faculty it can be perverted if one allows the *yetzer hara* to gain the upper hand. Misused imagination becomes fantasy, the greatest enemy of man. Fantasy seduces man into believing that momentary pleasure is the solution to all his problems. It tells him that the glory he acquires will live forever, it persuades him to ignore the billions of humans throughout history who returned to dust and were forgotten.

Donag, in Hebrew, means "wax," a stuff that appears to have substance and strength enough to build upon, yet after a slight exposure to heat it melts, and anything built on it falls. So it is the perfect symbol for fantasy, which man in his delusion takes for firm reality but which collapses upon exposure to objective truth.

Thus Hormin saddles his mules for his dazzling acrobatic display on the banks of the River of Wax. For life is a river on which every elusive moment disappears as quickly as it comes into existence. If one wants to retain anything of the river one must reach out quickly and seize it to serve God before the river flows away forever.

Everything material is ephemeral; only those moments sanctified by Divine service are eternal. But Hormin, completely bemused with fantasy, fails to see the river for what it is. To him it appears static, solid, everlasting.

It is perfectly clear what will happen when the fierce, hot light of truth shines on Hormin's performance; but nothing is clear to a man sunk in fantasies. What more appropriate place, then, could be found for Hormin's mule-back juggling than the banks of the River of Wax?

1.10 THE KING'S DAY

That was the day when things "rise to the heavens and descend to the depths"; finally the King's men heard of [Hormin's doings] and put him to death.

The day referred to is the day when man is judged as to whether he deserves to remain alive. Since life was created for the sake of its potential to achieve closeness to God, when man can no longer live for that potential, life is taken from him.

"Until the day of his death You wait for him, and if he should return You will accept him immediately."[9] No matter how low man sinks in his sinful ways, God awaits his return. The gates of repentance are never closed as long as there is still hope: as long as man retains the potential to wonder what his life is for. But what happens when he becomes totally absorbed in his fantasy of success-by-continual-stimulation, when this pseudo-religion destroys his capacity to consider an alternative to his self-centeredness? When things have gone this far, hope is gone, and man has closed upon himself the gates of repentance.

When the King of Kings heard that Hormin had perfected his antics, having learned to banish completely any thought of anything beyond the moment's pleasure, He made that day the day "when things rise to the heavens" — when the soul rises to its heavenly abode, there to receive its reward, "and descend to the depths" — when the body is lowered down into its six feet of earth. That is the day when everything returns to its proper place, to its true affinity. And where will the soul of Hormin go? It cannot go up to Heaven, the ultimate spirituality; it has lost its affinity for such things. The only place left for it is with the body it so slavishly served, to join it in its complete and final ruin.

9 *Ne'ilah* prayer of Yom Kippur.

2

The Wave and the Club

Said Rabba bar Bar-Chana: Those who go down to the sea have told me that the wave which sinks a ship seems to have a fringe of white fire at its tip, but that when one strikes it with a club engraved with the Names of God "אהיה אשר אהיה יה ה' צבאות" and with "אמן אמן סלה" (Amen, Amen, Selah) it dies down.

(Bava Basra 73a)

2.1 The Sea Voyage

. . . the wave which sinks a ship. . .

Man's passage through this world is like a voyage across the sea to a distant land. The sea through which he travels is his physical existence on earth; the ship which transports him is his body; and his appointed destination is the reward of the world-to-come.

The ship of man has a difficult journey ahead of it. The sea that surrounds it — the physical world, roils with storms and turbulence — the hazards that face every living thing in the imperfect world of physicality. The frail craft of human life could capsize at any moment. The hazards are manifold, comprising threats of suffering, poverty, pain, and death. But the greatest danger of all that lurks in the sea is man's evil inclination, the *yetzer hara.*[1]

Physical suffering can be devastating, but it attacks only

1 The collective name for the drives and attitudes which interfere with man's search for spirituality and closeness to God; see the Introduction to Part One.

the body, leaving the soul unscathed. A meaningful life can be carried on somehow even when the body is disabled or racked with pain, for the soul that defines man's existence is still intact. The *yetzer hara*, however, attacks the very soul of man. Whereas the damage brought about by physical suffering extends only to one aspect of human existence, leaving other aspects open to expression, the *yetzer hara* has the potential to bring about total annihilation. For if it should succeed in its task, then the very reason for the creation of man no longer exists. As we saw in Chapter One, man was created and placed in this world in order to overcome evil and choose good. The *yetzer hara* with its temptations to materialism is a threat to this whole purpose. Of all the turbulent places in the sea of man's earthly existence, the *yetzer hara* is the most dangerous: it is "the wave which sinks the ship."[2]

. . . [the wave] seems to have a fringe of white fire at its tip.

In relation to the world, the evil inclination is like a wave disturbing the calm surface of the sea. Inside the human heart, it is like a fire whose flames are fanned by base passions. And so when the Talmudic sage Rav Amram reached such a high level of spirituality that his evil inclination left him, the Talmud tells us that it did so "like a pillar of fire."[3]

Like an uncontrolled fire which consumes and destroys whatever it touches, the *yetzer hara* attempts to destroy all human potential, both in this world and in the world-to-come. But the fire of the *yetzer hara* is not an ordinary fire; it has a "fringe of white at its tip."

2 Suffering is expressed by the metaphor of waves in Tehillim 42:8: "All Your breakers and waves have passed over me." The same metaphor is applied here to the *yetzer hara*, following the Sages' dictum (Bava Basra 16a), "The *yetzer hara* and the Angel of Death are one and the same." The significance is, as explained in the Introduction to Part One, that all evil has its root in the concealment of God's good from man in the physical world. Thus the evil inclination, which separates man from God, and suffering, the opposite of good, are both manifestations of the same phenomenon.

3 Kiddushin 81a.

Man's evil inclination rarely portrays sin as a forbidden act. Instead it seeks to convince man that the sinful act was never forbidden at all, and that in fact sin is actually a mitzvah, a positive act of devotion to God. The Scriptures offer a striking image for this concept, comparing the blandishments of the evil inclination to the temptations of a licentious woman:

> *. . . sweet drips the nectar of a strange woman; her palate is smoother than oil. But the end of her is more bitter than gall or wormwood, sharp as a double-edged sword. Her feet head down to death; her steps lead to the grave.*[4]

At its end sin is "more bitter than wormwood, as sharp as a double-edged sword." The sword of the Angel of Death, from which exudes the bitter drop of mortality, lies in waiting. Yet all the same, at its beginning sin was as attractive as sweet nectar.

That is how the serpent (man's original evil inclination when it existed in an externalized form) convinced Adam to eat from the Tree of Knowledge: if Adam and Eve should do so, the serpent argued, they would then be "like angels, who know good and evil."[5] Not only was the Tree of Knowledge not forbidden, ran his argument, it was actually God's will that they partake of it, for certainly God would be pleased if they became like angels.

The wave of the *yetzer hara* has fire at its tip: first it fans the flames of human passion, then it spreads throughout, destroying all of man. But in order to achieve its goal, the *yetzer hara* masquerades as an emissary of pure intentions: its fire is tipped with virtuous white.

2.2 Of Matza and Yeast

> Rabbi Alexandri would add at the end of his prayer: "Master of the world, it is clearly known to You that our

4 Mishlei 5:3-5.
5 Bereishis 3:5.

> wish is to do Your will. What, then, prevents us? The yeast in the dough and our enslavement by the nations."[6]

From another perspective, the evil inclination is comparable to the yeast in a dough. Controlled, the fermentation caused by yeast creates bread which supports life; uncontrolled, the dough turns sour and inedible. Similarly, if man's drives for pleasure and the control of his surroundings are properly harnessed, they give him the impetus to conquer nature and provide the means for human life to survive and prosper. If they are left unharnessed, then the result is that "jealousy, pleasure-seeking, and the lust for glory drive man out of his world":[7] human personality decays and disintegrates along with the entire social structure.

At the core of his being, a Jew is aware that the only thing that has significance for him is to fulfil his purpose in life and serve God. Because his innermost wish is therefore to do God's will, the "yeast" alone is not enough to deter him from carrying out his mission. Specious guarantees of sensual gratification do not have the power to overcome the heart's true longing for fulfillment. A Jew will recognize them for what they are and follow his proper road instead.

. . . and our enslavement by the nations.

But when the "yeast" is coupled with another impediment to spirituality, evil becomes nearly impossible to overcome. Foreign influences from the surrounding society can exert a tremendous pull on the Jews, drawing them away from spiritual endeavors.

These influences are of varied sorts. Sometimes they appear as forces physically antagonistic to Torah and Judaism: violence, pogroms, expulsions. At other times the threat is more insidiously aimed at the Jewish soul, attempting to pollute it with specious value systems, neological social and economic orders, or ideologies which either deny man's spir-

6 Berachos 17a.

7 Avos 4:21.

itual nature or give a false definition of the nature of his destiny. In all cases, the surrounding society poses a threat that evil may swamp man and the Jew may not carry out his mission on earth.

When the threatening forces of the surrounding society are subdued, the yeast can be controlled. This is the idea behind the absence of yeast in the dough that the Jews took with them out of Egypt.

> *They baked their dough into unleavened cakes [matzah] . . . because they had been driven from Egypt.*[8]

Their dough was baked unleavened, without the fermenting, souring influence of yeast, as a tangible symbol of their inner spirit, which was free at last of the corrupting and aggrandizing influence of the *yetzer hara*. That spiritual yeast had been banished from their mentality; for, once they were free from the domination of Pharaoh ("enslavement by the nations") they were able to overcome their evil inclination. Thus it was "*because* they had been driven from Egypt" that they "baked their dough into unleavened cakes." Yeast no longer exerted its influence in the making of their bread, just as the *yetzer hara* had ceased to exert its influence on their spirit.

This explains as well why the prophet, in describing the dispersion and exile of the Jewish people, says that evil will flourish "from the kneading of the dough until its fermentation."[9] As long as the Jewish people were able to function freely in their own Holy Land, the battle against evil could be won. But when they once again became "enslaved by the nations" (the essence of the Dispersion) the "yeast" began to burgeon almost uncontrollably. In the Exile, people find it nearly impossible to remain completely uninfluenced by self-serving or materialistic motives.

The picture, then, appears gloomy at best. Rabbi Alexandri seems to be saying that the "yeast in the dough" and

8 Shemos 12:39.
9 Hoshea 7:4.

enslavement by the nations together prevent us from carrying out God's will fully. In that case it is a foregone conclusion that our journey across the sea of life is doomed: the "wave tipped with white fire" is sure to sink our ship. Is there indeed no way to overcome this wave? If self-control alone is not sufficiently effective against the *yetzer hara,* what hope can there be for the Jewish people? What assurance is there that evil will not totally overcome and destroy the world?

2.3 A Promise Is a Club

. . . when one strikes [the wave] with a club engraved with the Names of God, אהיה אשר אהיה יה ה׳ צבאות, and with אמן אמן סלה (Amen, Amen, Selah) it dies down.

The wave can be beaten back with a club engraved with Names and words which signify God's promise that evil will not engulf the world and that His ultimate goal — to bestow good upon man — will surely be realized.

. . . engraved with the Names. . .

God has assured us that He will not permit His people ever to sink to an irredeemably low spiritual level. This was promised before the Exodus:

> *". . . when they ask me, 'What is His name?' what shall I tell them?" God said to Moshe, "אהיה אשר אהיה" [I shall be that I shall be].*[10]
>
> [With these words] God said to Moshe: "Tell the Jewish people that I shall be with them in this enslavement and I shall be with them in future enslavements."[11]

And it was expressed again later:

10 Shemos 3:14.
11 Berachos 9b.

Despite this, when they are in their enemies' land I will not despise them nor will I loathe them, neither destroying them nor abrogating My covenant with them, for I am the Lord their God.[12]

The first Name engraved on the club that beats back the wave is, therefore, אהיה אשר אהיה, which signifies that God accompanies His people even when they are enslaved by the nations and supplies them with the necessary spiritual nourishment to survive the Diaspora with soul intact.

2.4 THE INCOMPLETE NAME

[. . . the Name] יה . . .

There is a second assurance that God gave His people: His oath to redeem them ultimately from the Diaspora. This is expressed by the Name יה, particularly in the following verse of the Torah:

For God (יה) has sworn by His throne (כס) that there will be war between Him and Amalek throughout all generations.[13]

Three basic concepts lie behind this oath, and once they are understood the oath's significance becomes apparent:

- the Tetragrammaton (the complete four-letter Name of God) represents the total revelation of God's ways to mankind;
- the image of "God sitting on His throne" represents total recognition by mankind of God as Ruler of all;
- Amalek is the embodiment, in national form, of evil. It is the single nation which went to war against the Jewish people to keep them from receiving the Torah at Sinai[14] and which throughout history attempted to annihilate them.

In this verse both the Name of God, יה, and the word for

12 Vayikra 26:44.
13 Shemos 17:16.
14 Shemos 17:8; *cf.* Devarim 25:17.

"throne," כס, are given in an incomplete form: יה instead of י־ה־ו־ה, and כס instead of כסא. The four-letter Name represents total revelation of God to man; accordingly, the incomplete two-letter form represents unfinished revelation. By the same token, the incomplete spelling of "throne" (כס) represents an incomplete recognition by mankind of God's rulership.

As long as man is occupied with material pursuits and self-gratification, he is not free to recognize his Creator. Amalek, the nation that embodies evil, is the chief proponent of materialism and egotism and the main cause of mankind's preoccupation with such trivial pursuits. Amalek, then, is the immediate and tangible cause of the world's imperfection: as long as it reigns in the human mind clouds of darkness hide the glory of God from a benighted world.

Thus the meaning of the verse is: God's "capacity" to reveal Himself (the Name) and man's capacity to recognize Him (the Throne) are incomplete until evil (Amalek) is eradicated from the face of the earth.[15] God therefore has sworn by His Name — which must someday be totally recognized — that He will eradicate this evil from the face of the earth.

The missing letters in the incomplete Name of God can be recovered only through man's overthrow of evil; more precisely, through the Jewish nation's overthrow of evil, for the Jewish nation is the agency by which all of mankind will someday recognize God. Thus the Sages say that since the destruction of the Temple and the dispersion of the Jewish people (and their consequent inability to serve God fully) "God uses only two letters of His name."[16] Since universal recognition of God depends on the Jewish people, their exile is what has "made the Divine Name incomplete," and only when they have returned from the Dispersion and the Temple

15 Midrash Tanchuma *ad loc.*, cited in Rashi *ad loc.* In order to preserve the free will that He has given us, God chooses not to reveal Himself to us to any greater extent than we are ready to accept. The effect is as if He were limiting His capacity for revelation.

16 Eiruvin 18b. The literal translation is, "It is enough for the world to use two letters."

has been rebuilt can the other two letters be "used."

The missing letters of the Divine Name are therefore, in a sense, "a pledge," as it were, held by the Jewish people against God.[17] For when a lender holds a borrower's pledge he is assured that his loan will be repaid, for the borrower will certainly want to redeem his pledge. Since only the Jewish people can restore the two missing letters of God's Name, and this can be done only when they are redeemed from their exile, these two letters are like a pledge given by God to the Jews that He will indeed redeem them. Since the destiny of the world — to accept the total revelation of God — must inevitably be fulfilled, the Jewish people can be sure that God will retrieve His pledge and will not permit them to languish in exile forever.

Thus, engraved on the club is the Name יה, whose incomplete spelling represents one of the promises that beat the wave back.

2.5 THE ARMY REDEEMED

[. . . the Name] **ה' צבאות. . .**

Redemption is only half the story: with the Redemption will come complete revelation of God, and the Name will be complete. But for the Throne to be complete, evil must be overthrown, for until then mankind will not completely recognize God's kingship. The Name **ה' צבאות** represents the promise that the Jewish people will be given the spiritual strength to eradicate the evil of mankind by bringing it to the recognition that service of God is the ultimate purpose of human existence.

ה' צבאות means "God of the Armies." A king maintains his army for the purpose of repelling and overcoming his enemies. God suffers no rivals to his will, but metaphorically it can be said that whatever holds mankind back from accepting

17 Commentary of the Vilna Gaon here; ultimate source unknown.

His dominion in all aspects of life, such as the evils of selfishness and materialism, are His enemies. For whatever is bad, spiritually, for His world can be described as God's enemy.

Therefore it is His will that there be an army-people, whose only occupation is to do His will and to accept His kingship, who by their teachings and by their example of selfless devotion will carry on the war against God's "enemies" so that they can be beaten back. Therefore Scripture writes: "The God of the Armies is the King of Glory":[18] the God whose will it is to have an "army" is the God whose glorious kingship will be recognized by all of mankind when His army has succeeded in its mission.

As long as the nations of the world dominate the Jewish people in their exile, the Name ה׳ צבאות will never be clearly demonstrated to the world, for the Jews are not free to be an army and fight for holiness and repel evil. Accordingly, this Name too is a promise to redeem the Jewish nation from subservience to the Gentile nations. God is determined that His army shall defeat His "enemies," and they can only do so when they are redeemed; therefore that redemption is an inevitable event of history. And so we find it written in the Torah:

> *Our redeemer's name is "the God of Armies."*[19]

> *Their redeemer is mighty, His name is "God of the Armies."*[20]

2.6 THE POWER OF ACQUIESCENCE

[engraved on the club is]... Amen, Amen, Selah...

The Names of God describe aspects of His will. The aforementioned Names describe His will that He reveal Himself to mankind as God and Ruler. They further tell us that when the existence of the Jewish people is threatened, God will

18 Tehillim 24:10.
19 Yeshayahu 47:4.
20 Yirmiyahu 50:34.

manipulate the course of history to insure its survival. But before the Jews can fulfil the world's destiny by proclaiming God's Name to mankind, they must themselves accept His rulership. They do this by subordinating their own will to His and keeping His mitzvos.

The effort to accept and carry out God's commands is symbolized by the word "Amen." When said to another person, it signifies acquiescence in the other's will;[21] "Amen" in response to a blessing of God signifies acquiescence in God's will. In a larger sense, "Amen" is the symbol of all the mitzvos — the great pattern of accepting and fulfilling God's will. Thus the Jewish people is described as "the nation which responds with 'Amen'":

> *Open the gates and let the righteous nation enter,* שומר אמונים *(who keep faith).*[22]
> Do not read [this] as שומר אמונים (who keep faith), but as שאומר אמנים (who respond with Amen).[23]

The Jewish people in Exile is debarred from fulfilling its true purpose, for which it was created. What merit, then, can it offer to justify its continued existence? The fundamental merit of the Jewish people today is its constant affirmation that the fulfillment of God's commands is its primary goal. Thus the Sages say:

> From the day that the Temple was destroyed there is never a day that is not more execrable than the previous one. What, then, sustains the world? The saying of "Amen."[24]

21 Shevuos 36a.

22 Yeshayahu 26:2.

23 Shabbas 119b. The exegetic formula "do not read this but that" is intended to emphasize the congruence of two ideas by the means of pointing out their phonetic similarity when expressed in words. In this case, the point being made is that responding with *Amen*, i.e., perpetually acquiescing in God's will, makes a nation faithful *(emunim)* in the sight of God.

24 Sota 49a. The text reads in full: "What, then, sustains the world? The saying of *Kedusha deSidra* (the sanctification recited after the second Ashrey in the morning prayers) and of "*Amen, Yehei Shmei Rabba*" (in the Kaddish).

"Amen" is engraved on the club because responding to a blessing with Amen demonstrates the Jew's willingness to recognize fully that life is given him to carry out God's will. If this is so, then the Jewish nation deserves to be the agency of the total revelation of God's Names to mankind.

When the Names of God (with their implicit promises) and the Amens of the Jewish nation (expressive of readiness to live according to the Divine will) operate together, the wave with the white flame at its tip diminishes and recedes, vanquished forever.

3

The Price of Pride

Said Rabba bar Bar-Chanah: Those who go down to the sea have told me that there are three hundred parsas between one wave and another, and that each wave is three hundred parsas tall. [They said:] "One time we were walking along a path, and a wave lifted us so high that we could see the resting-place of the smallest star; it was as big as a field where one could sow forty bushels of mustard seed. Had we been lifted any higher we would have been burned by [the star's] heat.

"Then we heard one wave calling out to its neighbor, saying: 'My friend, have you spared anything from flooding for me to destroy?'

" 'See how powerful your Master is,' answered the other. 'I cannot even cross a hairsbreadth of sand.' As it is written [Yirmiyahu 5:22], 'Will you not fear Me, says God, will you not tremble before Me, who has made sand the boundary of the sea, an everlasting limit which cannot be trespassed?' "

(Bava Basra 73a)

Introduction

> Lust drives the chariot of the *yetzer hara;* the seat on which it sits is pride. (Vilna Gaon[1])

As we have seen, the great struggle of human life is in making the decision whether to follow the selfish inclination within oneself — the *yetzer hara* — or to follow the yearning of his *yetzer tov* to

1 Commentary to Megillas Esther, Chapter 1.

cleave to God. This is a war with no end to it, and is fought on many different fronts; but the chief battle is the ongoing one with *ta'avah* (the drive for pleasure gratification), which more than anything else tends to make man forget his true goals.

The pleasure drive can be overcome if one decides to make a true effort; if the battle is lost, that is because man refuses to fight it. The principle reason why man refuses is pride *(ga'avah)*. In his arrogance he believes that he himself, not God, is the purpose of creation. When self-advancement is accounted the greatest value, man will seek to fulfil his own wishes, not those of his Creator. Only when man is willing to shed his self-centeredness and learn to perceive himself as a servant of God can the powerful pull of materialism be conquered. So it is that pride is the indispensable foundation stone upon which lust can burgeon: *ga'avah* is the seat on which *ta'avah* sits in order to drive the deadly chariot.

Man's sea journey is threatened, as we have seen, by the fiery wave of the evil inclination. Accordingly, the wave is at its mightiest when it succeeds in raising man's heart up high, for human pride is such a potent force that once man succumbs to it, the odds against him become overwhelming.

This chapter deals with a particular danger of pride. Having succumbed to it, it is not enough now that man must contend with the *yetzer's* blandishments to indulge his material nature; from now on even spiritual endeavors become fraught with peril. In his relentless search for glory, a pride-motivated person sees even the performance of a mitzvah, his obligation towards his Creator, as a reason for self-praise. Having done a good deed, he will think, "No one is as righteous as I; no one has so completely mastered his evil inclination." Thus, each mitzva, instead of bringing him closer to God, further weakens his struggle against the evil that is enveloping him and carries him farther away into the darkness of materialism.

The struggle with this aspect of the *yetzer hara* of pride is the subject of this story of Rabba bar Bar-Chanah.

3.1 MEASURING THE WAVES

. . . there are three hundred parsas between one wave and the other. . .

We have seen in Chapter Two[2] that the image of waves in the sea represents the evil in the physical world that threatens to engulf man. Evil has twelve categories, each of which entices man in its unique manner for one month of the year.[3] Corresponding to these is the image of twelve waves in the "sea" of the physical world, the world of the *yetzer hara;* each wave holds sway over the sea for a month.

Why are there three hundred *parsas* between them? Let us make a simple calculation: the distance an average man can walk on an ordinary day is ten *parsas*[4] (approximately 28 miles, or 48 km.), making a total of three hundred *parsas* that he could walk in a month. In the course of each wave's dominion, then, if it is not stopped it will traverse a distance of three hundred *parsas;* and then the next wave begins its course.[5]

. . . and each wave is three hundred parsas tall.

Evil is not static, no more than is its converse, holiness. If it is not brought under control its power grows, as the Sages say: "Since the destruction of the Temple [when evil triumphed over holiness], there is never a day that is not more

2 See §2.1, and Note 2 thereto.

3 Vilna Gaon, in his commentary here. No source is cited. This concept might be related, however, to the Sages' dictum (Bava Basra 74a) that the punishment of Gehinnom is renewed every thirty days (for all forms of evil are synonymous, as mentioned in the source cited in the previous note.)

4 Pesachim 94a.

5 Waves in the sea travel faster than a man can walk; but those are physical waves, which need no aid from man to carry out their appointed duty in the creation. Not so the waves of the *yetzer hara*: their strength is only what is given them by men through their sins and their pride, and they can cover only as much distance as men do in their course of sin. Thus the *yetzer hara,* if not stopped in its tracks by repentance, will grow as much as man will let it, and travel as much ground as man does in his pursuit of pleasures. According to our metaphor, then, the wave will cover three hundred *parsas* in its month of dominion.

execrable than the previous one."[6]

When evil has been successful in its task of seducing man, it is said to have "ascended to the heights."[7] Following our metaphor, we can then say that for every *parsa* that the wave of the *yetzer hara* travels, it grows proportionately in height. At the end of its dominion of thirty days, its height would be three hundred *parsas,* equal to the distance it has travelled. The more the wave travels, the higher it grows: the power of the *yetzer hara* grows in proportion to man's submission to it.

3.2 THE WAY OF THE RIGHTEOUS

> *The path of the righteous is like a glow of light, shining more and more until day is established; but the road of the wicked is like darkness: they know not what they have stumbled over.*[8]

A man can travel on a narrow path, or he can travel on a broad, smooth road. How do the two paths differ? In the number of people who have been that way. The path that only few have gone remains narrow and bumpy, whereas the feet of the multitude tread out a broad and smooth roadway. The righteous (those who remain faithful to man's spiritual goals) travel on a "path"; the wicked (who have self-indulgently allowed themselves to stray after material goals) travel on a "road." The road of the wicked is well-trodden: many others have travelled it before. *Tzaddikim,* on the other hand, walk a way that only a select few have passed.[9]

Why are *tzaddikim* "like a glow of light that shines more and more until day is established"? *Tzaddikim* do not reach

6 Sotah 49a.

7 The image is from Ovadiah 1:3-4: "The arrogance of your heart has led you astray, you who dwell in the craggy rocks, the lofty dwelling; who say in your heart, 'Who can lower me to the earth?' If you fly as high as the eagle, if you make your nest among the stars, even from there I will pull you down, says God."

8 Mishlei 4:18-19.

9 Zohar; quoted in the Vilna Gaon's commentary here.

the high levels of righteousness at a stroke; rather, they work patiently and steadily to nurture their righteousness, making it grow little by little, like the dawn light which brightens by imperceptible degrees until at noon it is fully established in its glorious splendor.

3.3 THE STARRY PATH

"Once we were walking along a path, and a wave lifted us up. . ."

Evil will always try first and foremost to overcome man by making him prideful, for nothing is more fundamentally destructive of man's spiritual life than pride.[10] This is part of what King Solomon meant when he said, "Pride comes before the fall":[11] a man's pride is what precipitates the fall of the soul into the dark prison of materialism.

The moment that one begins to "walk along a path" — the little-trodden path of the *tzaddikim* — a "wave" is likely to come along and lift one up in pridefulness. For it is precisely when one has done a good deed that he is most vulnerable to the *yetzer hara*. When one has done something that he can feel legitimately satisfied about, pride becomes a serious temptation. After a few mitzvos one might well begin to believe that he is in fact a *tzaddik* and indulge in vainglorious fantasies.

". . . we could see the resting-place of the smallest star. . ."

The Torah calls the *tzaddikim* of the Jewish people, "stars."[12] Stars seem minute to the naked eye, but in reality each of them is far greater than Earth. So are the *tzaddikim*: they

10 See Introduction to this chapter.

11 Mishlei 16:18.

12 Megillah 16a: "The Jews have been compared to dust, and also to stars. [Why is this so? Because] when they fall, they fall down to the dust; but when they rise, they rise to the stars." The same metaphor is found in Daniel 12:3: "Those who teach the people to be righteous will be like the stars [that shine] for all eternity."

appear insignificant in the superficial view of their fellow men, yet in reality they are spiritual giants.[13]

The moment one has done a good deed, the temptation to self-glorification becomes so intense that one can easily imagine himself to be a member of that most elite of groups, the *tzaddikim* of the generation, the "small stars" whose true levels of holiness are never appreciated by their fellow men.

3.4 Of Stars and Mustard Seed

". . . as big as a field . . . of forty bushels of mustard seed."

> *The yetzer of man's heart is evil from his youth onwards.*[14] [Man asked God:] "If You say that it is evil, who then can make it good?"
>
> Answered the Holy One Blessed be He: "You [not I] make it evil. . . . There are worse things in the world than the *yetzer hara,* even bitterer than it, and yet you can sweeten them. Nothing is more bitter than mustard. . . . If you can sweeten what I created bitter when you so desire, all the more can you sweeten the *yetzer hara,* which is in your power."[15]

Mustard seed in its natural state is too bitter to be eaten. It must first be processed by being pounded to powder; then not only is it edible itself, it also enhances the taste of other foods. The same is true of man's drives for physical gratification. They are not only detrimental to his spiritual goals; they threaten his very existence. Life, even on a merely physical level, cannot flourish without self-control, for unbridled fulfillment of one's appetites will eventually ruin all life, as the Sages pointed out: "Jealousy, pleasure-seeking, and the lust for glory drive man out of his world."[16]

13 *Cf.* Avodah Zarah 10b: "the least among you [the Sages] has the capacity to revive the dead."

14 Bereishis 8:21.

15 Midrash Tanchuma, *Parashas Bereishis* 7.

16 Avos 4:21.

The process of learning to control and channel these drives is comparable to the pounding that makes the mustard seed edible: only by refining one's drives and training them to submit to the will can life be made livable. In Rabba bar Bar-Chanah's story, life with the *yetzer hara* under control is symbolized by the image of pounded mustard, a pleasant and tasty delicacy instead of a bitter, inedible muck.

Someone who has totally conquered his *yetzer hara,* subduing all of his primitive drives to his will, can be said to have carried out "the pounding of the mustard seed" on his entire physical being. This is represented by the figure of forty *se'ah* (bushels) in Rabba's story. Forty *se'ah* is the amount of space taken up by the average human body — for this reason it is the required volume of a *mikveh*[17] — and represents the totality of human physicality. Thus, a *tzaddik,* whose every aspect of *yetzer hara* has been pounded into an "edible" (i.e., viable) form, can be said to have forty *se'ah* of mustard at his disposal.

The beginning traveller who was lifted high by the wave imagined that he had attained the level of the absolute *tzaddik;* symbolically stated, he thought that he had acquired, at one leap, a field of forty bushels of mustard seed.

3.5 THE MIKVEH OF TORAH

There is an additional significance in the image of forty *se'ah* employed here. The Sages promise us that anyone who studies the Torah will derive spiritual purification from his studies.[18] However, this will only hold true if one's studies conform to the laws of the *mikveh.* If one immerses his whole body in the *mikveh's* water except for the tip of one strand of hair, then the immersion is of no significance and does not purify. In the same way, if one wants to purify his soul through Torah study, he must be totally involved in it, with all of his being.

The prophet Yeshayahu says "Fortunate are you who

17 Pesachim 109a.
18 Berachos 16a.

sow by all the water."[19] The Sages explain that he was referring to people who busy themselves with Torah study instead of worldly occupations. They are considered to be doing useful work ("sowing" — an activity that produces fruitful results) by studying the Torah ("water" — symbol of the Torah as the source of spiritual life for the world).[20] But, as the prophet points out, this is true only of those who sow by *all* the water: the purifying effect of Torah is not achieved by mere dabbling, but by submerging oneself in all forty *se'ah* of its waters, i.e., by total involvement in the study of its precepts.

3.6 ANGER AND PRIDE

"Had we been lifted any higher we would have been burned by the heat."

This heat referred to here, according to the Torah's regular metaphor, is anger.[21]

Anger is in fact suppressed violence (if given free rein, the emotions of an angry person develop into actual violence); it is a reaction to the frustration of one's desires. When someone feels that another person threatens the fulfillment of his desires, he experiences an urge to destroy that threat. But in most cases, one's training or beliefs make it impossible for him to express this urge, or even to acknowledge its existence. As a result, the desire to destroy the "offending" person is suppressed and anger is the compromise solution. But subconsciously every angry person still wants to destroy the object of his anger.

Pridefulness and anger go hand in hand. The anger response is based on one's assumption that fulfilling his desires is the ultimate good, the prime imperative of the universe. Within every angry person's mind lies the illusion, created

19 Yeshayahu 32:20, a literal translation.

20 Bava Kama 17a.

21 Referring to one who has killed for revenge when possessed by anger, the Torah (Devarim 19:6) calls this כי יחם לבבו — "when his heart becomes hot."

by his pridefulness, that everything and everyone surrounding him were created to serve his needs. Were it not for this fantasy, the fulfillment of one's neighbor's wishes would be as important to him as his own, and there would never be an occasion for anger.

Because anger is the ultimate expression of pride, anger and a feeling of closeness to God are mutually exclusive. One cannot subordinate himself simultaneously to God and to his own idolized self. Thus the Sages say: "Whoever becomes angry, [even if he is a prophet] the Divine Presence leaves him."[22] The Divine Presence cannot abide arrogance and self-aggrandizement, and so it cannot have contact with that person. Since cleaving to the Divine Presence is the source of prophecy, even if the angry person has previously attained the level of a prophet, he now loses it. Conversely, anyone who wants to achieve closeness to God must exercise the opposite of pride: humility and self-effacement.

Rabba bar Bar-Chanah points out that once one allows himself to be carried away by a wave of pride, it is inevitable that he will be driven to become upset and angry with any obstacle to the fulfillment of his desires.

3.7 SAND AGAINST THE WAVES

"Then we heard one wave calling out to its neighbor, saying: 'My friend, have you spared anything from flooding for me to destroy?'"

Once the evil inclination has succeeded in raising a man's heart high in arrogance, there is no end to how much of his personality it can destroy. Pride is a poison which spreads throughout the human personality until every aspect of life becomes invested with its influence. Unopposed and left to its own devices, the "wave" of *yetzer hara* that succeeds in

22 Pesachim 66b. The Hebrew text gives Nedarim 22b as the source, which is a similar saying.

making man proud is so destructive that there is little left for the next "wave" to destroy.

"See how powerful your Master is. . . I cannot even cross a hairsbreadth of sand."

How could anyone hope to overcome such all-pervasive power? Indeed, no one could; it can only be done because God is there to lend His assistance.

> Man's evil inclination grows stronger every day; and if it were not that the Holy One, blessed be He, aids man, it would overcome him.[23]

God will assist those who are ready to attempt to control the *yetzer hara* on their own. If they control it to the best of their ability when it is still in its beginning stages, God will not permit it to grow beyond control.

If one wants to control the *yetzer hara,* the primary requirement is a firm commitment not to give way to it in the slightest. In token of their having made such a commitment, the Torah compares *tzaddikim* to the sand at the edge of the sea.[24] A wave rushes in with all its power as if it were about to engulf the earth; water and sand whirl together; and the wave, having dissipated its power against the sand, withdraws defeated. The shoreline is still exactly where it was before; and so, in a sense, it can be said that the outermost edge of the sand holds back the sea in all its power. That hair-thin line of the shore withstands the sea's onslaught by refusing to budge in the slightest.

A *tzaddik* does not permit himself to be swayed even minimally by the *yetzer hara.* He knows that if he makes even a seemingly insignificant compromise with it ("a hairsbreadth"),

23 Sukkah 52b.

24 Bava Basra 7b: "*Tzaddikim* do not need [a city wall for their] protection, for the Torah says 'Can I count [the good deeds of the *tzaddikim*?] They outnumber the sand' [Tehillim 139:18]. If sand, which is a little thing, protects the world against the sea [by holding it back] then still more so the deeds of the *tzaddikim,* which are more numerous, protect them."

ultimately he will be forced to become its slave. Conventional morality tells a man to behave as he pleases and then, if any improper urges arise, to fight to overcome them. But the Torah teaches that this is absurd. To overcome desires which have already been aroused is a bitter and dreadful struggle which very few people are likely to win. Once one has let the sea wash away his shoreline it is bound to inundate his whole world. The Torah shows us the realistic way to behave, and commands us to obviate such difficulties from the start. For example, one avoids even innocuous contact or innocent seclusion with a woman who is forbidden to him, no matter how noble his intentions may be. A righteous man, scrupulously obedient to his Creator's will, does not let the sea encroach at all upon his shore, and so is safe from all its raging. By refusing to give up even a hairsbreadth of his integrity to his *yetzer hara,* he holds the entire sea of material desire at bay.

3.8 The Mountain Made of Spiderwebs

> The evil inclination is at first like a spiderweb, but at the end it becomes like a wagon's harness.[25]

As we have seen, mastery over the *yetzer hara* is achieved not by forcibly controlling pleasure drives after one has allowed them to grow powerful, but by refusing to permit the drives to gain power right at the start. At first, before habit has made a place for them in one's life and before the soul has been corrupted by the influence of evil, all temptations to do evil are easily controlled. If one is willing to exert himself a bit and control them, then God keeps them from growing any stronger, and in fact guards one from accidental wrongdoing. However, if one fails to respond properly at the beginning, the temptations grow stronger until they become nearly insurmountable. The Sages offer a

25 Sukkah 52a.

graphic description of these two states of human behavior:

> In the time to come, God will bring the evil inclination and slaughter it before all men. To the righteous it will appear like a tall mountain; to the wicked it will appear like a strand of hair. Both will weep: The righteous will weep and wonder, "How were we able to overcome so tall a mountain? "The wicked will weep and wonder, "How were we not able to overcome this strand of hair?"[26]

A *tzaddik* begins controlling the *yetzer hara* while its temptations are still manageable. Knowing his limitations and weaknesses, he keeps himself away from situations which are likely to develop into temptation. Thus he keeps the *yetzer hara* from developing into a mountain. When the time for reward comes, he will weep for joy: for, even though he never had to deal with overpowering situations, he receives the reward of one who has overcome a tall mountain — which in effect he has done.

Wicked people, on the other hand, are punished for not having controlled their *yetzer hara* when it was still manageable. The excuse that their drives were overpoweringly strong is not accepted. For while their temptations were still small they could easily have controlled themselves, and then God would have helped them by keeping their temptations from becoming so powerful. Therefore they weep with regret that they must now suffer so much for having neglected so easy a task. If only they had overpowered a single strand of spiderweb, all would have been well.

"Will you not fear Me?" says God. "Will you not tremble before Me, who has made sand the boundary of the sea, an everlasting limit which cannot be trespassed?"[27]

Why do you not fear Me? asks God. Is it because of the *yetzer hara?* But I have made sand the boundary of the sea. By

26 *Ibid.*
27 Yirmiyahu 5:22.

withstanding the simple temptations that you first knew, you too would have been able, like the *tzaddikim,* to withstand the *yetzer hara* easily.

Afterword

If the *yetzer hara* is so powerful that it can enlist our most urgent drives — even mitzvos — to entangle us in its service, is there still hope? Fortunately, we are assured that no matter how strong the *yetzer hara* is, God will come to our aid and vanquish it.

> *You return man even from extreme suffering, and You call out to him, "Return, you sons of man."*[28]
> [Man can repent] even if his soul is crushed [with sin].[29]

Man was created to do God's commandments, and God will not suffer a situation where man is entirely prevented from achieving his purpose. However, Divine assistance is conditional on man's first making an effort to overcome the evil inclination on his own; if our own strength is insufficient God promises to come to our aid.

Even if one has succumbed so often to the *yetzer* that he is already bound by its harness ropes, he can still extricate himself. For the process is reversible. Let man make the slightest effort to overcome the *yetzer hara* and God will assist him. Once he makes the smallest inroad into the power of evil which controls him, the process will begin to be reversed. God will aid him in returning the harness rope to the spiderweb which it originally was.

28 Tehillim 90:3.

29 Yerushalmi Chagigah 2:1.

4

The Mountain Goat

Said Rabba bar Bar-Chana: I saw a day-old mountain goat the size of Mt. Tabor. And how big is Mt. Tabor? Forty parsas. Its neck was three parsas long, and to rest its head it needed one and a half parsas. Then it emptied itself and dammed the River Jordan. *(Bava Basra 73b)*

Introduction

We have seen[1] that the primary motivating power behind man's natural drives towards evil, the *yetzer hara* which threatens to destroy life, is the drive for glory and prestige, which supports and feeds the other drives. But we have also seen that it is not ordinary adulation which the prestige-hungry person seeks; he feels a need to be recognized as a Torah scholar or a similar spiritually oriented being. Hormin the son of Lillith raced "along the wall of Mechuza" because it was a city where he believed he could find gratification for his desires.[2] The wave of pride lifts one up until he "can see the resting place of forty *se'ah* of mustard" — the Torah scholar completely immersed in his study.[3] It is as if the glory-hungry man is subconsciously aware of what really matters. He knows that man deserves honor only because he is a non-materialistic being,[4] and therefore directs his efforts towards portraying himself as deserving honor because of his selflessness — his idealism, humanism or philanthropy — while at the same time looking over his shoulder to see that everyone notices his outstanding qualities.

1 See Introduction to Chapter Three.

2 In §1.4.

3 In Chapter Three.

4 See §16:3.

This story of Rabba bar Bar-Chanah deals with the approach of the prestige-driven man to Torah study. Because of his conceit, he cannot bow to another's wisdom and sit at the feet of a teacher. No sooner does he begin studying than he immediately imagines himself to have reached the heights of scholarship. In the process of maintaining his imagined status, he attempts to destroy the reputation of all other scholars.

By describing the shortcomings of the glory-seeking student, Rabba teaches us what the proper attitude of a Torah student should be towards Torah and its teachers, and what is the best way to develop into a true Torah scholar.

4.1 FROM DONKEY TO GOAT

> One should always apply himself [to Torah study] as a bull submits to the yoke, or as a donkey submits to its load.[5]

> *His beauty is that of a first-born bull; his horns are those of a mountain goat* (ראם).[6]

A Torah scholar is compared in these passages to three animals: a bull, a donkey and a mountain goat. Each of these images represents a stage in his development into an accomplished *talmid chacham*. In his early stages he is comparable either to a bull (שור) or to a donkey (חמור). The bull and the donkey are man's principal animal servants, and each has his particular sphere marked out: the bull plows the fields, and the donkey carries burdens from place to place. Both these animals direct their enormous strength towards carrying out the wishes of their masters, but each one does it in his uniquely characteristic way.

In a similar manner, the Torah student directs all his efforts towards mastering the wisdom of his teachers, and this he can do in two different ways: one, by delving into the depths of their wisdom ("plowing"), and two, by toiling to

5 Avodah Zarah 5b.
6 Devarim 33:17.

memorize and retain all the voluminous material they have taught him ("carrying the load").

Thus King Solomon said, "Grain in plenty [is produced] by the bull's strength."[7] Wisdom is compared by the Torah to grain, for grain is the "staff of life" for the body, and wisdom is the basis of the spiritual life which provides meaning for human existence. A student acquires wisdom by being willing to apply himself to understanding its depths with all the strength and dedication of a domestic bull.

When he has matured, the Torah scholar is compared to a mountain goat. Both donkey and bull are domesticated animals, depending on a master for survival, but the mountain goat is a wild animal, independent of any master but its Creator. It runs sure-footedly among the mountain heights, just as the fully-developed Torah scholar deals deftly with the lofty heights of wisdom. Besides being free, the goat has an impressive set of horns that provide it with the capacity for self-defense, as well as for imposing its will on others. A *talmid chacham* who has matured into complete independence is the same: he can both offer his own opinions in matters of Torah, and forcefully defend those opinions against attack.

In the above-mentioned verse which alludes to the beauty of a bull and the horns of a goat, the Torah is referring to the qualities of an ideal Torah scholar. His perfect beauty is the product of his early willingness to efface himself before a teacher, into whose wisdom he diligently delves until he has achieved true understanding. After long years of study, he has developed wisdom of his own: now he has the horns of a mountain goat to defend his own opinions forcefully.

4.2 THE HORNED DONKEY

I saw a day-old mountain goat . . .

There once was a donkey who went to look for horns [to

7 Mishlei 14:4.

fight with]. He ended up losing his own ears.[8]

A donkey once went and got himself a pair of horns. He tied them to his head and, fancying himself now as powerful as a mountain goat, began engaging other animals in combat. His adventure was not successful: not only did he lose the fight, but the other animals' real horns tore off his ears.

This Talmudic parable tells us something about the right and the wrong way to begin one's studies. A young Torah scholar should concentrate all his efforts on absorbing and understanding his teacher's wisdom, just as a donkey faithfully carries its master's loads. The Sages advised the beginning student, "One must always absorb first, and later develop his own opinions."[9] First must come the amassing of information and organizing it into meaningful structures; after that comes the analysis of the wisdom, the struggle to descend to its depths, and the development of one's own insights.

Every Torah student is expected to argue, for only so can he come to understand his teacher's lesson. He will often present his tentative ideas in the course of his arguing, though he knows they are as likely as not mistaken. This is both good and necessary. But what happens when a student prematurely presumes himself to be an accomplished scholar, and instead of sitting at his teachers' feet he considers presenting his own insights more important than absorbing those of his teachers? He is jeopardizing his own development in two ways. First, he wastes precious time that he could have been using to learn true wisdom. Second and worse, by concentrating on impressing others he loses his capacity to accept, even from his own teacher. In the terms of the Talmudic parable, not only does he make himself ridiculous by pitting his fake horns against the real horns of the mountain goat; he ends up "losing his ears" — he becomes incapable of listening. Without ears ready to bend to the teacher's words, Torah can never be acquired.

8 Sanhedrin 106a. The Gaon reads "חמרא" (donkey) for "גמלא" (camel).

9 Avodah Zarah 19a.

The proverb quoted above offers the image of a horned donkey. To express his particular lesson, Rabba bar Bar-Chanah offers us the image of a day-old mountain goat: a student who has barely begun his studies ("one day old") yet who nevertheless fancies himself a mature Torah scholar (a "mountain goat"), qualified to air his opinions on every subject.

4.3 THE PROUD MOUNTAIN

. . . the size of Mt. Tabor.

> When Mt. Tabor and Mt. Carmel heard that the Torah was about to be given to mankind, they came from across the seas to volunteer themselves as the sites where it would be given. [Because of their impressive size they imagined themselves more eligible candidates than Mt. Sinai, a modest-sized mountain.]
>
> Bar Kappara taught: [When these two mountains presented themselves] a Heavenly voice went forth saying: "Why do you compete with Sinai? Both of you are blemished compared to Sinai; for the Torah calls both of you "hunchbacks."[10] Said Rav Ashi: we can learn from this that a prideful man is a blemished man.[11]

The very quality which led Mt. Tabor and Mt. Carmel to believe themselves worthy of being the site for the giving of the Torah — their loftiness — was the cause of their disqualification. Their loftiness led them into pride, and pride rendered them unfit to be associated with Torah study. The Torah was given on a mountain and not on a plain to symbolize that its wisdom stems from a loftier plane than that of ordinary existence. At the same time, to teach mankind the evil of pride, it was given on Mt. Sinai, the humblest of mountains.

The new-born student not only sees himself as a mountain goat, he thinks he is a goat as big as Mt. Tabor. His

10 *Cf.* Tehillim 68:16.

11 Megillah 29a.

vanity as well is as great as that of Mt. Tabor — and with less cause: at least Mt. Tabor was indeed a tall mountain, only that it sinned by being proud of its advantage. The fledgling student has no erudition, no stored-up wisdom to give him true worth; only his vaunting pride makes him imagine himself a great scholar. He is similar to Mt. Tabor in only one way: that his pridefulness disbars him from success in the study of Torah.

4.4 THE SEVEN "DAYS" OF LIFE

And how big is Mt. Tabor? Forty parsas.

The seventy years of a person's life follow the pattern of the seven days of the week: each ten years is the equivalent of one day. When he begins his seventh decade, man comes to the "day of rest," his journey's goal. He is an elder, eligible to become the leader of the community: "the elder who sits in the Yeshivah."[12]

The Kabbalists say that from Wednesday onward one should begin preparing himself for the holiness of Shabbos. This refers not only to the days of the week, but to the decades of one's life. Accordingly, from the beginning of "the fourth day of the week," i.e., after one's thirtieth birthday, one should begin preparing himself for "Shabbos," the last decade of his life. It is time to begin living in increased sanctity and acquiring the necessary wisdom to be a leader of the community.

"Thirty years old for strength," say the Sages,[13] meaning that a person is then at the peak of his powers of retention. The wisdom that he has received from his teachers up to that age can now be retained perfectly; and so he begins the decade during which he will put in order all his master's teachings.

12 Yoma 28b. The reference is to the status a community leader achieves.

13 Avos 5:21.

Once he has memorized and sorted all that he has learned, it is time to begin delving yet more deeply into the wisdom buried therein, and eventually to develop his own insights: "Forty years old for understanding."[14] Growth of understanding continues until sixty years of age, when man enters his last decade and becomes worthy of leading the community for the rest of his life.

Rabba bar Bar-Chanah presents this "seven-day" image of the human life-span in the form of distance travelled. The average distance a man can walk in a day is ten *parsas,*[15] so that each ten *parsas* of Rabba's story represents a day of the week, or for our purposes a decade of man's life. All forty *parsas,* then, signify the distance covered from Wednesday until the end of Shabbos, or in our case, the wisdom and sanctity achieved from age thirty, when one begins to organize his stored-up learning, until the end of one's life, the ultimate perfection attainable.

But these forty *parsas* measure the size of Mt. Tabor, the haughty mountain. The "day-old" student of Rabba's story has achieved no spiritual maturity at all; he is motivated by pride, and its concomitant, the lust for praise and glory. The spiritual accomplishment of study is not enough for him; he demands adulation. If he does not get what he wants, his only response (since he has nothing real to take pride in) is to shore up his flagging ego by imagining himself ever greater and greater. So now it is no longer enough for him to see himself as a "mountain goat"; he must be the greatest scholar imaginable. So he fantasizes that he has already travelled the full route to maturity, through the final four decades of life to the highest level of perfection attainable by mankind. "How big is Mt. Tabor? Forty *parsas.*"

14 *Ibid.*

15 Pesachim 94a; app. 28 miles or 48 km.

4.5 THE LONG NECK OF PRIDE

Its neck was three parsas long...

> When Rav saw a crowd of people following in his wake, [to prevent himself from vainglorious thoughts] he would recite the verse: "Even if one rises to the sky, his head touching the clouds, [in the end] like dung he will forever be lost; those who knew him will ask, 'Where is he?'"[16]

The clouds, say the Sages, ride an average of three *parsas* above the ground.[17] So, to suggest a pride so great that one feels his head reaching the clouds, Rabba says that the goat's neck is three *parsas* long.

The prideful student still has not obtained the adulation that he so desperately longs for, and his ego is in danger of drooping. Once again, his only response is to imagine himself still greater than before.

4.6 VANITY'S REACH

...and to rest its head it needed one and a half parsas.

If our prideful student had been living at the time that the Children of Israel were wandering in the desert, he would not have been permitted to live within the Israelite encampment. The Divine Presence accompanied the Jews in their travels through the desert, as the Torah says, "For the Lord your God walks about in the midst of your camp."[18] And of a prideful person the *Shechinah* says, "I cannot live in the same world as he does."[19] So there would have been no place for such a person in the camp, and he would have been told to take his tent and pitch it outside the camp. This was where

16 Iyov 20:6-7; Sanhedrin 7b.
17 Bava Basra 75b. This is about 14 km.
18 Devarim 23:14.
19 Sotah 5a.

the *erev rav* (the "mixed multitude"), who personified haughtiness,[20] were obliged to pitch their tents.

The Camp of the Israelites (מחנה ישראל) was three *parsas* in diameter.[21] In the center of the circle, surrounded by the Levites (מחנה לויה), was the Camp of the Divine Presence (מחנה השכינה), where the Mishkan (Tabernacle) stood. Moshe Rabbenu's tent was right next to the Mishkan. The day-old goat, coerced by the merciless logic of his lust for adulation, and frustrated by the inexplicable (to him) refusal of others to offer it, is reduced once again to imagining himself ever greater. Now he has gone all the way towards ultimate pride: he perceives himself as the natural colleague of the very greatest among the people of Israel, even Moshe Rabbenu himself, whose tent he pictures as his rightful place of rest. The truth is that he would not even have been allowed into the Camp of the Israelites; so if he had wanted to speak with Moshe Rabbenu, he would have had to stretch his neck out a distance of one and a half *parsas* to reach Moshe's tent.

4.7 The Last Resort

Then it emptied itself and dammed the River Jordan.

From the start the principal object of this student has been to gain praise and admiration from others around him. He is quite blind to his own essential absurdity; so when he perceives that he has utterly failed in getting the adulation that he feels he must have, his only thought is, What can he do to force others to praise him? His problem all along has been that there is nothing in him worth praising: he has no real insight or wisdom to offer that deserves acclaim, and he is too lazy to work to achieve something real.

Having nothing positive to offer, the only direction he

20 Zohar, Bereishis 25a.

21 Sanhedrin 5b.

can move in is a negative one. Realizing that he has not succeeded in earning on his own merits the glory for which he so desperately lusts, he thinks that at least he will get it by default, through eliminating all other candidates for glory. He therefore sets out to destroy the reputation of everyone around him. He imagines that when he has besmirched everyone else's reputation sufficiently, then the people's inexplicable blindness will at last be lifted, and, the field now being clear, they will be able to recognize his splendid qualities. That this will not work is obvious at first glance; but then, nothing is obvious to someone so intoxicated with dreams of glory.

Rabba expresses this final effort by imaging the Torah scholar as the River Jordan[22] and the day-old goat's attempt to denigrate others as fouling that river and damming its flow. The goat hopes that by creating a foul odor around the *talmid chacham* he will prevent his Torah teachings from influencing the community. But of course, a river is not easily dammed for very long, and eventually the foul-smelling blockage is dissolved and carried away,[23] and the pure water flows forth again.

22 Vilna Gaon's commentary here; ultimate source unknown.

23 Rashbam's commentary *ad loc.*

5
The Three Serpents[1]

On that day, God with His hard, great, and mighty sword will judge Leviathan the outstretched snake and Leviathan the coiled snake, and He will slay the serpent in the sea.

(Yeshayahu 27:1)

5.1 THE SNAKES AND THE SERPENT

Like the primeval serpent that enticed Adam and Chavah to turn away from God, the snakes in this verse represent man's inclination towards evil, i.e., the drives which keep him from carrying out God's will. The "snake" no longer exists today in the physical manifestation it had in the Garden of Eden, so it cannot tempt us directly. Today it exerts its influence indirectly, through internal promptings and external forces brought to bear in the attempt to tear man away from God's will. All the same, it is no less powerful today than then.

In the above verse the prophet was referring to the End of Days, when the temptations which draw man toward evil will be banished from the face of the earth. There are two classes of temptation: one is referred to as *nachash,* "snake," and the other as *tanin,* "serpent."

Nachash is a tendency in man to refuse to carry out God's will. Since this refusal can take two forms, the prophet refers

1 In the original Hebrew text the ideas discussed in this chapter are part of the next chapter, "The Frog and the Tree." However, because the interpretation of the three serpents is only incidental to the main message there, it is presented here as a separate chapter.

to two snakes. On the one hand, there is the tendency to rebel against God's will: this is man refusing to subordinate himself to any will but his own. On the other, there is the tendency to ignore God's will: this is when man becomes involved in satisfying his own pleasures to the point where he has no time to think about fulfilling the commands of his Creator.

In the prophet's vision, one snake is stretched out straight (נחש בריח) and the other coiled (נחש עקלתון).[2] The willful rejection of God's plan for the world is an "outstretched snake" which attacks its enemy frontally. On the other hand, man's permitting himself to be seduced into the pursuit of pleasure-fulfillment to the neglect of his true goals is a "coiled snake." It does not attack its enemy head-on but instead squeezes it to death with an embrace so powerful that its vital organs cease to function. The "outstretched snake" of rebellion is pictured as male, since that is generally the more aggressive sex, and similarly the "coiled snake" of seduction is pictured as a female.

These are the two kinds of *nachash* that attack man.

Tanin is another sort of antagonist: it attacks the study of Torah. As we have seen, all evil was created by God to block out spirituality from the world, so that man would be forced to struggle for it and therefore appreciate it more deeply.[3] But God also gave power to a special sort of evil whose purpose is to test man's commitment to spirituality by interfering with his quest for the knowledge of Torah.

When an individual sets out in pursuit of the knowledge of God's word, impediments immediately arise which keep him from his goal. This is the *tanin* operating. It sets in motion obstacles to Torah learning. Financial hardship, failing health, and an antagonistic social climate suddenly arise; other occupations are made to appear more vital and worthwhile; the search for spirituality seems a chimera; mastering

2 Lit., "the rod-[shaped] snake" and "the crooked snake."

3 See §1.1.

the huge expanse of Torah looms as an impractical and unattainable endeavor.

The two "snakes" which cause man to exchange God's will for the pursuit of gratification, wealth, and power feed on man's physical nature, and so, like man himself, are pictured as land-based (terrestrial) creatures. The *tanin,* on the other hand, which sets impediments in the way of man's search for Torah, is called a sea-serpent. Man's journey towards the spiritual perfection of Torah knowledge entails his forgoing his attachment to his natural earthiness. This is a situation like that of an explorer setting out to discover a new continent, who must leave his natural terrestrial habitat and set out to sea. In this context, then, the "sea" represents man's quest for spiritual development within the confines of the physical world. The *tanin* which rises up to threaten that journey is therefore "the serpent in the sea."

The day when God will judge these snakes is the End of Days when God will reveal Himself to mankind and demonstrate once and for all that there is no other purpose for existence than His service. When this happens, the evil which appeared throughout history as an alternative purpose will no longer exercise its pull on humanity. The revelation of this truth is a mighty sword which will forever destroy the evil which kept man from his destiny. For then the world will be full of God's wisdom, and never again will man believe that human success can be achieved by following the temptations of the three serpents. This is how God will "judge the outstretched snake and the coiled snake, and slay the serpent in the sea."

5.2 The Snake That Hates Wisdom

> **The hatred which boorish people harbor towards Torah scholars is greater than the hatred of the Gentiles towards the Jewish people; and their wives have even greater hatred than they themselves. A Baraisa teaches: One**

> who once studied Torah and then left it has the greatest hatred of them all.[4]

This Talmudic statement is a parable conveying, in somewhat different symbolism, a further discussion about the three serpents. Its simple meaning is an explanation of why the boor, his wife and the one who has rejected Torah study hate the Torah scholar. They hate him because he is a threat to their very existence. They know that he considers their life goals, materialistic as they are, to be completely meaningless. Their sense of being threatened metamorphoses into hatred for those who embody the wisdom which challenges their way of life.

The male boor devotes his life to success in a struggle for power and ego satisfaction; he therefore hates the Torah scholar who rejects these pursuits.

His wife, on the other hand, hates the Torah scholar for other reasons. Ego and power struggles generally are more a male concern than a female one; she has a more immediate fear of the Torah scholar. She is concerned that his way of life, which is geared towards spiritual achievement, might endanger the physical well-being of her family. Her fear for the well-being of her young coupled with her inability to fend entirely for herself cause her to feel more threatened than her husband by the Torah scholar. This greater sense of threat engenders a greater hatred in her for the Torah scholar than that of her husband.

Finally, the one who studied Torah and left it hates the Torah scholar more than all. His antagonism to Torah is not due, as in the case of the male and female boor, to a preference for emotional or materialistic satisfaction. He willfully left Torah because of a deliberate decision that the word of God is unimportant; he therefore bears an intrinsic dislike for the word of God. The hatred of the boor and his wife depends on external factors, and it will diminish if they per-

4 Pesachim 49b.

ceive themselves as achieving their goals. But the one who has left Torah bears an ideological antagonism towards the Torah scholar. His hatred is independent of the achievement of any goals. It is therefore a more permanent hatred than the boor and his wife.

Although this passage is true on a simple level, its principal meaning lies on the deeper symbolic level. The male boor, *am ha-aretz* ("man of the earth") in Hebrew, represents the land-based male snake of rebellion, the "outstretched snake" which militates against accepting God's dominion. He "hates" the Torah scholar: that is, this tendency in man holds him back from growth in Torah.

"Their wives hate [scholars] more than they themselves do" — this refers to the coiled snake of seductive pleasure which, like the wife of the boor, is the female of the outstretched snake. It "hates" Torah more than the male snake does: whoever submits to its enticements is even more removed from spiritual growth than one who submits to the male snake.

But there is a greater antagonism to spirituality within man than his physical nature (the land-based snakes). This is the *tanin* or sea-serpent, represented by "the one who once studied Torah and then left it." Like that person, the antagonism of the *tanin* is directed towards the study of Torah itself. Therefore it "hates" the study of Torah more than the two land-based snakes.

On the deeper level, then, man can teach himself to submit to God's will (in spite of the first snake); he can train himself to forgo his desires (in spite of the second snake); but the antagonism inherent in the natural world to Torah learning (the *tanin*) never weakens. It "hates" the Torah most of all.

5.3 The Knees of the Scholars

In his unrelenting war against Torah study, the *tanin* raises up all sorts of obstacles. All can be coped with one way or another by the young scholar himself; but one problem is seemingly insurmountable.

Regarding the obstacles which the *tanin* sets against Torah study, the Sages said: "The knees of young rabbis ache and become tired because of them."[5] "Them" refers to the forces inherent in the world which are antagonistic to spirituality — the arsenal of "the serpent in the sea." The Zohar[6] explains that "the knees of the young rabbis" refers to the financial supporters of the Torah world. As the knees support the upright body, so those who are blessed with wealth maintain the Torah study of the world.

When the *tanin* attacks the Torah, its most vicious attack is on the means of its financial support. So the Sages teach us about Yaakov Avinu's struggle with the angel of Eisav:

> *He saw that he could not overcome him [Yaakov], so he touched the inside of his thigh; and the inside of Yaakov's thigh was dislocated as he struggled with him.*[7]

The Sages, examining this verse in its universally symbolic sense, explain that "Yaakov's thigh" refers to the financial supporters of Torah study.[8]

Yaakov bequeathed to his descendants, the Jewish people, the ability to survive as a nation until the end of days. Inherent in this bequest is their capacity to accept the Torah and to study and keep its laws for all times, for only through Torah can Yaakov's children reach their ultimate destiny.

The forces of evil struggle mightily with Yaakov to keep him from his appointed goal. When Yaakov's offspring weaken in their resolve to study and keep the Torah, these forces undermine that commitment in other ways. The forces of evil attack those who give their wealth to support Torah study, and convince them to cease their support. "The knees

5 Berachos 6a.
6 II, 111b.
7 Bereishis 32:25.
8 Zohar I, 171a.

of the young rabbis" — their financial supporters — "ache and become tired" — they no longer manage to control their lust for wealth, and cease to share with the young scholars. Although they will always offer an ostensibly impeccable reason for ceasing their support, it is really "because of them" — because of the "serpent's" persuasions.

For example, they might offer the excuse that government taxation is too high and leaves them no extra funds to contribute. This is no excuse at all, for the Sages teach us, "Whoever accepts upon himself the yoke of Torah will have the yoke of the government removed from him."[9] On the contrary, taxes have grown heavy because these men did not wholeheartedly accept their part of the yoke of the Torah, namely supporting it. The truth is that "whoever throws off the yoke of Torah from himself has the yoke of government come down upon him."[10] The real reason, then, is that the *yetzer hara* has succeeded in disaffecting these men, simultaneously blinding them both to the importance of their support of Torah and to the consequences of ceasing it.

When the *tanin* brings such trials upon a young scholar, how will he succeed in overcoming them? That is the theme of the next story of Rabba bar Bar-Chanah.

9 Avos 3:6.
10 *Ibid.*

6

The Frog and the Tree

Said Rabba bar Bar-Chanah: Once I saw a frog that was as big as the city of Hegronia. And how big is the city of Hegronia? Sixty houses. A serpent came and swallowed [the frog], and then a raven came and swallowed the serpent. It flew up and sat on a tree. Consider how strong that tree was! Said Rav Pappa bar Shemuel: "Had I not been there myself, I would never have believed it." *(Bava Basra 73b)*

6.1 THE TIRELESS VOICE

The only animal in the world that gives forth its voice constantly, day and night without stopping, is the frog. Just as the frog tirelessly serves its Creator with its voice, so the Torah scholar tirelessly gives forth his voice in the song of Torah study, day and night. Thus, the voice of the frog is used by the Sages as a symbol of the Torah scholar, the *talmid chacham* who is constantly occupied with the study of Torah.[1]

This story describes the trials which stand in the way of a Torah scholar's growth.

1 The following passage (Zohar Shemos 30a; the Vilna Gaon in his commentary gives the source as Midrash Rabba) is an example: "Why did the Egyptians deserve the Plague of Frogs? Because they kept the Jewish people from studying the Torah, [for when they study Torah they are] comparable to the frogs which are never silent, by day nor by night."

6.2 MASTERY OF TORAH

. . . a frog the size of the city of Hegronia. . . Sixty houses.

The "houses" of Hegronia represent the tractates of the Talmud, each of which "houses" a discrete part of the wisdom of the Torah. Together the sixty tractates comprise the structure of the Oral Torah. If one wants to be a true *talmid chacham,* it is not enough to know some, or even most, of the Torah's wisdom; one must be expert in every one of its areas — a "frog" which occupies the area of "sixty houses." For every word of the Torah bears on every other word, so that only when all is known is the significance of anything fully understood.

6.3 THE STOREHOUSE OF THE SOUL

. . . as big as the city of Hegronia. And how big is the city of Hegronia? Sixty houses.

Now Rabba bar Bar-Chanah did not say, as he might have, that the frog was the size of sixty houses, but rather that it was the size of a *city which contained* sixty houses. This phrasing was chosen to teach us an important principle regarding the study of Torah.

For what is a city? Sixty houses cannot exist securely, much less prosper, if they stubbornly retain their individual identities and go each of them its own way. To flourish they must be part of a larger whole, subordinating themselves to the supreme authority of a city government. Similarly, Torah must be studied within the framework of a particular and essential attitude which governs its study. This attitude is the fear of God.

> *Your faithful times shall bring [you] strength, salvation, wisdom, and insight. . .*[2]

2 Yeshayahu 33:6.

"Faithful" — that is the Order Zeraim.
"Times" — that is the Order Mo'ed.
"Strength" — that is the Order Nashim.
"Salvation" — that is the Order Nezikin.
"Wisdom" — that is the Order Kodashim.
"Insight" — that is the Order Tohoros.
Nevertheless. . .the fear of God is his storehouse.[3]

The Sages teach that on an exegetical level of meaning the six terms in this verse refer to the Six Orders of the Mishnah which comprise the entire corpus of the Oral Law.[4] God has promised manifold blessing for one who learns the Six Orders, and one might think that this is all he need worry about: are not strength, salvation, wisdom, and insight enough for anyone? The last words of the verse teach us otherwise: "the fear of God is his [the scholar's] storehouse."

It is not enough to reap and gather the Torah's wisdom. Just as the produce of the fields needs a suitable storage place or else it cannot be preserved from rotting, so the words of the Torah must have a proper storehouse. The only place where the Torah can be preserved is a heart full of the fear of God.

"Fear of God" has a twofold meaning with respect to Torah learning: an appreciation of the awesomeness and importance of Torah, and a readiness to carry out into practice the Torah one has learned. Unless these attitudes prevail, even if one has labored to harvest the entire wisdom of the Torah he will not be able to keep his harvest from wasting away. For Torah cannot be studied in the same way as any other body of knowledge; that is, by merely mastering its subject matter. Other disciplines affect only the mind: one studies them, and gains information of which he was previously ignorant. But the Torah is not merely matter for mental consideration; there is a spiritual aspect of the Torah's wisdom which is part and parcel of it. This spiritual aspect at once affects heart and soul, elevating and purifying them.

3 Shabbas 31a.

4 *V.* Rashi *ad loc.* for how the Six Orders are derived from this verse.

The spiritual aspect of Torah requires that its student approach it with the proper attitude, one that carves out the proper storehouse for the words of Torah in man's heart. The Torah's words will be understood and remembered, and affect man's spirit, only when they are studied with the fear of Heaven; for that is their storehouse.

6.4 THE UNIQUE LOVE

> *Sixty are the queens, eighty concubines, and maidens innumerable; my dove, my perfect one is unique. . . .*[5]

Not only is the fear of God the prerequisite of success in Torah study; there is nothing that makes a man more beloved of God. The "sixty queens" in this verse are the sixty tractates of the Mishnah, the "eighty concubines" are the eighty chapters of the Midrash, and the "innumerable maidens" are the endless statements of the individual Sages.[6] Each of the realms of God's Torah is as close to Him as a queen, a concubine, or a handmaiden is to an earthly king. Nevertheless, God's special love, His "unique and perfect dove," is man's fear and reverence for Him.[7]

The Torah uses human terms to help us understand the various aspects of God's relationship to man. No such parable can be perfect, of course. Certainly God does not love in the same manner that humans love. Usually humans love that which is good for them; God loves that which is good for man. What, then, is the Divine equivalent of human love?

A human loves that which guarantees his ability to carry out his plans. Similarly, we describe that which is instrumental in carrying out God's will as "beloved" by Him. As stated previously, His plan calls for man to recognize Him and to carry out His will. The means through which this plan is realized is the Torah: its wisdom and its commandments

5 Shir HaShirim 6:8.

6 Midrash Rabba *ad loc.* (*Parashah 6*).

7 Commentary of the Vilna Gaon here; ultimate source is unknown.

bring man to this recognition. Thus God "loves" each of the realms of His Torah. But none of this wisdom can be assimilated by man unless he approaches it with the correct attitude: the fear and reverence of Heaven. This fear is the most basic ingredient for the fulfillment of God's desire for us and for His world, and is therefore the most beloved of all things to Him.

The various topics of the Torah are each discrete units, each a separate body of knowledge, each understood in its individual way. But the fear of God remains a constant; it is the same no matter which topic of Torah is being studied. There are sixty tractates ("queens"), eighty chapters of Midrash ("concubines"), and innumerable discussions by the Sages ("maidens"), but there is only one body of knowledge which is critical for the success of all of these studies: the knowledge of the fear of God. It is, then, the object of a singular, changeless love by God.

6.5 THE SERPENT AND THE RAVEN

A serpent came and swallowed the frog . . .

As explained in the previous chapter,[8] there is a force which God built into the natural world whose function is to test the Torah scholar by making it difficult for him to achieve success in his learning. This force the Torah calls "the serpent in the sea."[9] One of the methods used by the serpent is to create financial hardship, thereby making it seem impossible for the scholar to continue his studies.

This is the problem of "the frog as big as Hegronia," the diligent and expert scholar in this story. The serpent made it seemingly impossible for him to continue his studies and support himself at the same time; in the symbolism of Rabba's story, "the serpent swallowed the frog."

8 "The Three Serpents," §5.1.

9 Yeshayahu 27:1, as explained in §5.1.

6.6 Overcoming the Serpent

. . . and then a raven came and swallowed the serpent.

The female raven is different from all other birds: while female birds of all species tirelessly feed their young until they can fend for themselves, the raven ignores its young and does nothing for them. How do the young ravens, abandoned by their mother, survive? The answer is that God Himself feeds them. In His mercy He sends insects to fly into their mouths, and so they grow even without their mother's help.[10]

The raven's unlovable child-rearing practices were made the symbol of absolute trust in God as opposed to reliance on the aid of mortals. For God taught the raven to abandon its young in order that we should learn from it that anyone who relies on Him completely will not be disappointed.[11]

The raven can be an excellent teacher for the Torah student before whom the "sea-serpent" has placed the formidable difficulty of supporting himself while he studies. When man trusts God totally to sustain him, He will supply him with all his needs; "the raven swallows the serpent."

Thus, interpreting the Torah's description, "black as a raven,"[12] the Sages teach:

> Where can one find [success in the study of] Torah? With one who, like a raven, leaves his children to God's care.[13]

10 Rashi, Eiruvin 22a, s.v. *oreiv.*

11 *Cf.* Iyov 38:41: "Who is it that provides food for the raven when its young cry out to God?" Also Tehillim 147:9: "He gives food to the animals, to the raven's young who call [to Him]."

12 Shir HaShirim 5:11.

13 Eiruvin 22a; lit., "someone who is cruel to his children like the raven." Cruelty is certainly a negative trait not recommended for anyone, certainly not for Torah scholars. The comparison between the two is that the scholar's absolute trust in God, which appears *superficially* like the cruelty of the raven, results in the same mercy shown the young ravens.

And similarly on the verse, "You, God, save both man and beast,"[14] they teach:

> Rav Yehudah said in the name of Rav: This [refers to] men who despite their great intelligence do as animals do.[15]

An animal has no intelligence with which to plot and scheme about obtaining its sustenance; it relies entirely on God to provide for it and God answers its wordless plea. Man needs to learn when to "do as animals do": he must avoid reliance on his own cunning and trust God completely, and then He will save him.

6.7 THE MIGHTY TREE

[The raven] flew up and sat on a tree.

> *They came then to Marah, but they could not drink the water at Marah, for it was bitter; therefore [that place] was called Marah. . . . God showed him a tree; he threw it into the water, and the water turned sweet. There He made a law and an ordinance for him, and there He tested him.*[16]

On the surface level, this is a lesson in the kind of trust we have been examining: when the Children of Israel could not drink the bitter water, God prepared a tree to sweeten it for them.

But this incident also has a deeper significance: Torah is likened to water[17] and its supporters are likened to trees.[18] When one cannot drink the living water of Torah because of the bitterness of poverty, God prepares a "tree" to sweeten

14 Tehillim 36:7.
15 Chullin 5b.
16 Shemos 15:23-25.
17 Ta'anis 7a.
18 Mishlei 3:18: "[The Torah] is a tree of life for them that support it." On the exegetical level this is taken to mean that Torah confers the quality of a tree of life to those that support it. This verse does not say, "for them that study it," but "for them that support it." (Vilna Gaon here, apparently a paraphrase of Talmud Yerushalmi, Sotah 7:4 [see Peney Moshe] and Midrash Rabba Vayikra 25:1)

that bitterness and make the water potable once again.

The young student withstands the trials of society's inherent antagonism to Torah and goes on to strengthen his faith that God will care for him in his poverty. He has become a "raven," one who "swallows the serpent": the "serpent's" obstacles cease to interfere with his goals. God will prepare him a "tree" to support him, the tree of life which sweetens the water of Torah that had become bitter.

6.8 THE TREE OF LIFE

Consider how strong that tree was!

The great reward that awaits those who support the Torah is stated explicitly in the Scriptures.[19] They are honored more than the Torah scholar himself. Zevulun, the son of Yaakov Avinu, who supported the Torah study of his brother Yissachar,[20] is always mentioned by God Himself in the Torah before his brother.[21] For in certain respects he who supports Torah has reached a higher level than the scholar himself. Why is this so?

In explaining the verse, "[God wants you] to love the Lord your God, to follow His ways and to draw close to Him,"[22] the Sages comment:

> How is it possible to draw close to God, when He is likened to a burning fire? [The answer is that] one must draw close to the Torah scholars [who embody God's wisdom] by supporting them and giving them a means of livelihood.[23]

Thus he who supports a Torah scholar has achieved the coveted level of being close to God Himself.

The most important factor in the acquisition by the supporter of Torah of such an exalted spiritual level is the ex-

19 Devarim 33:18, Midrash Tanchuma and Rashi *ad loc.*

20 *Ibid.*

21 *Ibid.*; also, for example, Bereishis 49:13-14.

22 Devarim 11:22.

23 Kesubos 111b.

traordinary strength his mitzvah requires. True strength is to be measured not in physical but spiritual terms: it is the ability to overcome one's natural urges. As the Sages put it: "Who is strong? One who controls his worldly desires."[24]

The strongest of all are those who have learned to overcome one of man's most powerful urges: the drive to amass wealth. These heroes are called by the Torah "strong and valiant ones who obey His word"[25] and men and women "of strength."[26] What enormous strength, then, is there in the "tree," one who liberally shares his wealth with a Torah scholar.

6.9 THE WEALTHY OF BABYLONIA

Said Rav Pappa bar Shemuel, "Had I not been there myself, I would never have believed it."

It is not surprising that Rav Pappa should be amazed at the "tree's" heroic strength of character. He was a Babylonian scholar, and in Babylonia the wealthy did not adequately support the Torah scholars of their land. Because of their neglect of this sacred duty the Sages say, "The wealthy men of Babylonia are destined to Gehinnom [purgatory]."[27]

"Here in Babylonia," says Rav Pappa, "I have never seen anything similar to the 'trees' of Eretz Yisrael. Had I not been there myself and seen how its wealthy men willingly distribute their funds for the support of Torah, I would never have believed it. How fortunate I am to have seen human valor at its highest pitch!"

24 Avos 4:1.

25 Tehillim 103:20. In Midrash Rabba (Vayikra 1:1) the Sages apply this verse to land-owners who leave their fields fallow according to the law during the entire Shemittah year, controlling their urge to profit by raising crops.

26 Boaz, in Ruth 2:1, is called איש חיל, "a man of strength" (also translated "a man of wealth)" not because of any physical strength he may have possessed (for he was more than a hundred years old at the time) but in recognition of his outstanding control over his natural urges. Similarly, Mishlei 31:10 refers to a woman who "stretches out her hand to the poor" as אשת חיל, a "woman of strength" (also translated "a woman of valor").

27 Beitzah 32b and Rashi *ad loc.*

7
The Basket in the Sky

Said Rabba bar Bar-Chanah: A certain merchant said to me, "Come, I will show you where earth and heaven kiss." I followed him, and saw that [heaven] was made all of windows. I took my basket and placed it in one of the windows of heaven.

After I had prayed, I [came back and] looked for it, but I could not find it.

"There are thieves here!" I said [to a man there].

"It is only the heavenly sphere turning," he told me. "Wait until tomorrow, and you will find it here." (Bava Basra 74a)[1]

7.1 THE MERCHANT

A certain merchant said to me. . .

> The *yetzer hara* is called "a merchant," for it peddles all kinds of evil for the body.[2]

The cleverest peddler in the world is the *yetzer hara.* It is totally unscrupulous and utterly indefatigable; not too surprising, since it has been saddled with the tawdriest merchandise in the world. Since nothing in its stock has the slightest chance of providing satisfaction, the *yetzer hara* must rely entirely on flim-flam, fast talk, and false promises to unload as much of its goods as it can on unwary customers.

In this story Rabba bar Bar-Chanah tells of his experiences

1 The reading follows that of *Ein Yaakov.*

2 Zohar, Bereishis 80a.

with the *yetzer hara's* sales tactics, how he finally realized that the *yetzer hara* was deceiving him, and of the truths he then perceived about how God provides sustenance to the world.

7.2 THE PROMISE OF TWO TABLES

A certain merchant said to me, "Come, I will show you where earth and heaven kiss."

The *yetzer hara* has a special interest in peddling its wares to Torah scholars, so as to tear them away from the study of Torah.[3] How can he persuade such people to buy his wares? By portraying in glowing colors the material and spiritual pleasures of wealth and power which will infallibly accrue to the scholar if he will only exchange his Torah learning for the activity of the marketplace. "You have no idea how delightful worldly pleasures are, and what a mitzvah they can be," he says. "In fact, satisfaction is guaranteed!"

At first the scholar looks at the matter objectively, and gives no credence whatever to the suggestion. He remembers what the Sages said about worldly pleasures: "One moment of satisfaction in the world-to-come is better than all of the pleasures of this world."[4]

The "merchant," however, is undaunted. He continues his smooth-tongued sales pitch with a spiel much like the following:

"How true! There's nothing better than the world-to-come. But you don't have to wait for your pleasures! I'm offering you a chance to have your cake and eat it. I'm here to show you how to have the best of both worlds.

"Now, you're a learned man. Didn't the Sages say that there are two 'tables'?[5] Some people only enjoy this world, and lose out on the world-to-come — poor fellows. And

3 See "The Three Serpents," §5.1.

4 Avos 4:17.

5 Berachos 5b.

some, like you, only enjoy the world-to-come, and lose all the wonderful, marvelous pleasures of this world. But there are those lucky few that get to feast at both tables. The Sages said it, after all,[6] and we all believe what they said! Why shouldn't you be one of those lucky ones?

"Naturally, everything worthwhile takes a bit of sacrifice. So, of course, you might have to give up some of your studies for a while. But you'll be successful in the end, I guarantee that absolutely; and then you'll get back to Torah — better than ever and happy as a lark — with all the good things of the world at your fingertips. Now, isn't that worth a bit of sacrifice?

"Of course, I wouldn't want to take you away from mitzvos, not for one moment. But if you follow my advice you'll be doing the most important mitzvah there is, every second you're working. A learned man like you will know that the Sages said, 'A man who profits only from his own labor is greater than one who fears God.'[7] What could be as important as the fear of God? Yet by working for your living you will be doing something even greater than that!

"Quickly, now, come along with me. I'll show you how you can have both heaven and earth. I can show you where they kiss."

7.3 Windows in the Sky

I followed him, and found that [heaven] was made all of windows.

The scholar, his wits muddled by the "merchant's" incessant blandishments, follows his advice. He leaves his studies and goes into business; he works hard at achieving financial success — but to no avail. Recalling with anguish the specious "guarantees of success," he begins to come to his senses, and realizes what was evident all along to anyone who troubled

6 *Ibid.*
7 Berachos 8a.

to look: that human endeavor is not competent to obtain success and wealth. As the wisest of men said, "Bread is not the possession of the wise, nor wealth the possession of the astute."[8] No one can be sure that his efforts will succeed; as the Torah says many times over, it is God who decides who will be rich and who will be poor:

> *He commanded the sky above and opened the doors of Heaven.*[9]
>
> *God will open His goodly storehouse, the Heavens, to you, granting rain for your land in its time, and blessing all your endeavors.*[10]

The hoodwinked scholar sees clearly now why it is that he prays on Rosh HaShanah, "Open the gates of Heaven, Your goodly storehouse fling wide." Heaven is made all of windows, and all the wealth in the world comes through them. It is God who opens His gates according to His will and showers plenty on His world, not man who gets wealth through his business acumen. The peddler's fast talk was only flim-flam; he had nothing to sell at all.

7.4 THE FLOW FROM THE WINDOW

I took my basket and placed it in one of the windows. . . After I had prayed. . .

When the Torah scholar has come to his senses, he understands that everything comes from God and everything depends on prayer. God waits for man to draw near to Him through prayer before He sends the flow of good to the world. God stands at His windows to accept man's prayer, and in response causes His blessings to flow through the windows down to the world.

So the scholar "puts his basket in the window of heaven":

8 Koheles 9:11.
9 Tehillim 78:23.
10 Devarim 28:12.

he recognizes that all his needs will be fulfilled through God's mercy, and he goes to pray. Only when this is done is it time for him to go and do business, with a heart full of hope that God will send success to his endeavors.

7.5 The Prayer Thief

. . . but I could not find [my basket.]
"There are thieves here!" I said.

> The wise men of Alexandria asked Rabbi Yehoshua, "What should a man do to become wealthy?"
>
> "He should do plenty of business and deal honestly."
>
> "But many have done so unsuccessfully!"
>
> "Let them pray to the One to whom all wealth belongs."
>
> . . . [If everything depends on prayer, then] why is it necessary to teach us [the first thing]?
>
> To tell us that one without the other is no good.[11]

For the flow of blessing to descend to man from Heaven, man must first be worthy of receiving the Divine beneficence. If he deceives or steals from his neighbor, he ceases to be worthy of receiving the flow of good from Heaven, and his prayer is useless. As King Solomon warns: "This the way of every one who steals property: it takes the life of its [new] possessor."[12] If "the basket was not filled at the window" — if his prayers were not answered and his business did not go successfully — then, thinks the scholar, "there must be thieves here" — his dealings must not be sufficiently honest. Perhaps if he becomes even more scrupulous in his transactions, then a flow of wealth will cascade down to him? "Not necessarily so," is the answer he is given.

11 Niddah 70b; *cf.* Vilna Gaon's commentary *ad loc.*

12 Mishlei 1:19.

7.6 THE TURNING WHEEL

"It is only the heavenly sphere turning. . ."

Although God in His justice rewards the righteous for their devotion to Him and punishes the wicked so that they will mend their ways, His ultimate plan, as we have seen, is not merely to reward man but for all mankind to recognize Him as Creator and King. In order for him to arrive at this ultimate destination, man must have a vehicle to lead him to it. This is the function of the myriad aspects of this world. Thus, Providence prepared a world of wealth and poverty; of happiness and sorrow; of health and suffering; of discoveries and inventions; of wars and conquests; of plagues and cures. All these vicissitudes, so that man may confront the problems of existence and ultimately realize that only devotion to spirituality and self-effacement before God can solve his problems. Human history is nothing more than God manipulating His world and guiding it to its ultimate destiny, the recognition by man of His sovereignty.

There are, then, two aspects to God's Providence. One is that man is rewarded for good and punished for evil. But there is another, overriding aspect of Providence: the relentless push towards the goal of man's total acceptance of God and God's revelation to him. The fate of people, in this latter aspect, is not determined by their deeds but by what sort of cog they are meant to serve as in the wheel of destiny.

This "wheel" might require, for instance, that there be certain circumstances — e.g., wealth, poverty, well-being or sickness — in the lives of certain nations or individuals, even though according to their deeds they do not deserve to be in these situations. By serving God in these situations they contribute — in a way often known only to God — to the ultimate denouement of history.

But, then, "Shall not the Judge of all the world do justice?"[13]

13 Bereishis 18:25.

Does not man receive his just reward? He does, of course, but not always immediately; this is the function of the world-to-come. Should a conflict arise between the reward a person deserves for his deeds, whether good or bad, and the role that Providence demands that he play in advancing the wheels of history, then in this world the latter takes precedence, and all differences — whether for reward or punishment — are settled in the world-to-come.

This is the meaning of the Sage's statement, "Health, children, and sustenance are determined not by merit but by *mazal.*"[14] The aspect of Providence that leads the world to its destiny is called *mazal,* "fortune," in token of the fact that most of the time man does not understand its seemingly random disposition of human affairs. But the plan is there all the same, and the state of one's health, children and sustenance is often not determined by the merits of one's deeds but by how one fits into the ultimate design of history.[15]

When a person's role has been determined by this aspect of Providence, even prayer, though it be accompanied by the most scrupulous honesty, might not immediately bring him material success (unless it is accompanied with acts of great merit which have the capacity of changing one's *mazal*). Thus it is not necessarily dishonesty that prevented the scholar's prayers from being answered: "It is only the heavenly sphere turning."[16]

7.7 TOMORROW AWAITS

"Wait until tomorrow, and you will find it here."

14 Mo'ed Katan 28a.

15 This concept is more fully explained in R. Moshe Chaim Luzzatto's דעת תבונות (Friedlander Ed., Bnei Brak, 5733, pp. 192-194; English translation, *The Knowing Heart,* Feldheim Publ.). *Cf. Tiferes Yisrael* on the last Mishnah of Kiddushin, and *Derashos HaRan,* Chapter Eight.

16 *Cf.* Maharsha in his commentary to this parable, Bava Basra *ad loc.* For a fuller explanation of how prayer can affect the Providence of *mazal* see *Tiferes Yisrael* and *Derashos HaRan ad loc.*

> *These things that I command you today. . .*[17]
> "Today" is for doing them; "tomorrow" is for receiving the reward.[18]

Justice is always done in its own time. One must know that "today," the present world, is for doing the mitzvos that we were commanded. This is not the world of reward, for this world must be pushed into line and goaded towards its final destiny. "Wait until tomorrow" — until the world-to-come — "and you will find it there" — one's reward awaits him there, in full, with nothing lacking.

All that remains, then, is for the scholar to realize that the most effective way to arrive at that reward is to return to his Torah and study the word of God.

17 Devarim 11:13.
18 Eiruvin 22a.

Part Two
The Savvei DeVei Atuna Riddles

רצונך שתכיר מי שאמר והיה העולם,
למוד אגדה שמתוך כך אתה מכיר אותו

Is it your desire to recognize the One who spoke and created the world? Study Aggadah, for thereby you shall recognize Him.

(*Sifrei Parashas Eikev*)

Introduction to Part Two

The riddles of the Elders of Athens ("Savvei DeVei Atuna") are a series of debates between the Sage Rabbi Yehoshua ben Chananyah and an academy of wise men, debates which were conducted in the form of riddles.

The Talmud relates that Rabbi Yehoshua ben Chananyah, having been ordered by a Roman ruler to demonstrate the superior wisdom of the Jews by debating sages of this Academy, sailed to "The Academy [lit., the house] of Athens" to meet its Elders.[1] After ingeniously gaining admittance to the Academy, Rabbi Yehoshua introduced himself to the Elders as a wise man of the Jews. They immediately challenged him to a debate. The Elders posed question after question to Rabbi Yehoshua, but he deftly parried and answered them all until, at the end, he was recognized as their superior.[2]

The Talmudic account of these debates presents them in the form of tersely worded riddles which the Elders and Rabbi Yehoshua hurled back and forth at each other. (Whether they actually debated in riddles, or whether this is merely the concise medium by which the Sages chose to record them, is not clear.)

According to the interpretation given them by the Vilna Gaon, these debates were not mere exercises in intellectual one-upmanship. The riddles which the Elders of Athens presented to Rabbi Yehoshua had a central theme: refuting the Jewish people's claim to being the Chosen People. The debates were over the essential value

1 This was most probably one of the famous academies of Athens, founded in the days of Plato and Aristotle hundreds of years earlier. Even after Rome conquered Greece, these academies maintained uninterrupted activity until their closure by the edicts of the Emperor Justinian in 529 C.E. (J. B. Bury, *The History of the Later Roman Empire*, Dover Publications, 1958, *Vol. II*, p. 369 ff.)

2 Bechoros 8b.

of Roman and Jewish cultures, and, most of all, over which of them deserves to be followed by mankind. The Elders attempted to demonstrate that Roman culture was superior to the Jewish Torah, and that the Roman obsession with personal advancement in wealth and position was the best answer to the needs of the human condition.[3] For the Jews the question of which culture is superior meant which culture best answers God's expectations of man.

The debates are clearly founded on an assumption shared by Rabbi Yehoshua and the Romans: that they were the descendants respectively of Yaakov and Eisav. Their argument only continued the ancient quarrel of the twin sons of Yitzhak, the founders of two antithetical cultures. Yaakov believed that life was given man to serve God and recognize His glory; Eisav believed that life's purpose was for man to serve himself and further his own glory.

For the Jews this matter had been settled hundreds of years earlier, when Yaakov, not Eisav, received the Divinely inspired blessings from his father Yitzhak. The Romans, however, believed that the matter was not ended there. They saw their military triumph over the Jewish people and the destruction of the Holy Temple as the last round of the argument and the final proof of their cultural superiority. In their view the Jewish people had been shown to be an impostor on the world scene and did not deserve to exist.

No two world-views could be more diametrically opposed; and because the argument was over the meaning of life itself, no greater antagonism could ever exist between proponents of differing world-views.

Each time the Elders attempted to show the inferiority of the Jews, Rabbi Yehoshua refuted their proofs; often he countered by demonstrating Roman culture to be non-viable, sterile, and unable by its very nature to offer man any relief from the troubles he is born to.

3 As to why Athenian wise men would be espousing Roman world-views a scholar of Greek history explains as follows: "It is well-known that the Athenians displayed obsequiousness towards their Roman masters and their values (*cf. The Annals of Tacitus* [in Latin], ed. Furneaux, Oxford, 2nd ed. 1896, Book II, 53, 4, and Furneaux's note thereto). The natural and expected result of this is the unqualified support which the Elders of Athens should have given to the Roman claim to world dominion."

In the course of Rabbi Yehoshua's rebuttals we are introduced to many of the basic concepts of Jewish philosophy. Why were the Jews given the Torah? Why must they suffer? What is the essential difference between Jewish and non-Jewish culture? What is the destiny of the Jewish people? How will the End of Days come about? Why do righteous people suffer? The Vilna Gaon's interpretations of the debates bring life to all of these ideas and integrate them into our perspective of Jewish history and of existence itself.

8
The Match

The Elders of the House of Athens asked Rabbi Yehoshua ben Chananyah: "If someone sought a woman's hand in marriage and was refused, why would he go on to seek a woman of higher lineage?"

Rabbi Yehoshua took a peg and thrust it into the bottom of the wall; it would not go in. He tried farther up, and it went in. "It too has found its match," he said.[1] *(Bechoros 8b)*

8.1 LOOKING FOR A WIFE

"If someone sought a woman's hand in marriage..."

Granted that the Jewish people had received the Torah; the Elders argued that this had nothing to do with their intrinsic worth. Eisav's descendants, the Romans, they explained, were more worthy than the Jews in God's estimation. Their supposed proof for this came from the Torah's own teachings; for when God was about to give the Torah to the Jewish people, the Torah tells us that

> *He shone forth to [the Jewish people] from Sei'ir, and appeared from the mountains of Paran.*[2]

The Sages comment on this verse:

1 The precise term for "match" in the original is בת מזליה, "the one that fits his destiny." It is translated here as "match" according to the Vilna Gaon's commentary.

2 Devarim 33:2.

> What was God doing in Sei'ir [the capital of Eisav]? And what was He doing in Paran [the capital of Yishmael]? This [verse] teaches us that God first brought the Torah to all the nations of the world, but they would not accept it; only the Jewish people accepted it.[3]
>
> Eisav asked, "What is written in it?"
>
> "You shall not murder," was the answer.
>
> "Master of the world!" said Eisav, "murder is our ancestral heritage."
>
> Amon and Moav asked, "What is written in it?"
>
> "You shall not commit adultery," was the answer.
>
> "Master of the world!" said they, "immorality is our way of life."
>
> Yishmael asked, "What is written in it?"
>
> "You shall not steal," was the answer.
>
> "Master of the world!" said Yishmael, "robbery is our livelihood."[4]

Only after all the nations had refused to accept the Torah did God bring it to the Jewish people. The Elders of Athens argued that if God had come first of all to Eisav, then that nation must have more intrinsic worth in God's estimation than any other; and if He came last to the Jewish people, then they must have the least worth in His view of any nation on earth. The Elders demonstrated their point by comparing God's choosing a nation to the process of a man choosing a bride, a metaphor employed by the Torah itself.[5]

Let us imagine a man attempting to get himself a wife of the noblest possible lineage. If he was disappointed in his first try because the prospective bride's family considered him unsuitable, would he try for someone of an even nobler lineage? Obviously not: if the first family refused him, there would be no point in going to someone yet more highborn. Certainly the suitor will compromise and seek a woman of humbler origin.

It is reasonable, then, to assume that when looking for a

3 Avodah Zarah 2b.

4 Sifrei *ad* Devarim *loc. cit.*

5 *Cf.* Yirmiyahu 3:1, 31:32; Yeshayahu 50:1; Hoshea 2:8-9,18,21, and 3:1.

nation to receive the Torah, God would first have tried to get the acceptance of the nation most apt to understand His wisdom. Only if they refused would He have gone on to seek out some other nation — one less suitable, of course. Each refusal entails the seeking of a less suitable bride. Therefore, if God came to the Jews only *after* He asked Eisav, Amon, Moav and Yishmael, then the Jewish people must occupy the bottom rung of the ladder of importance. By the same token, the first nation approached, Eisav-Edom, the Elders' patrons' ancestors, must surely be the most suitable of all the nations for receiving Divine wisdom.

It did not matter, argued the Elders, whether Edom did or did not accept the Torah — although it could be conceded that they erred in refusing to accept it. Still, it mattered only that they were intrinsically the most apt of all peoples for wisdom. They, and not the Jews, must be the true Chosen People. That being so, their wisdom and philosophies were bound to be superior to anything the Jews could offer.

8.2 THE GOAD AND THE PEG

[He] took a peg and thrust it into the bottom of the wall; it would not go in. He tried farther up, and it went in.

Rabbi Yehoshua answered the Elders with a simple demonstration from the physical world: a demonstration that hides within it a multi-faceted philosophy of the nature of worth and wisdom.

His first step in refuting the Elders' reasoning was to explain what qualifications a nation must have to be worthy of receiving the Torah.

Torah is no less than the wisdom of God Himself, and only a nation which approaches Torah with an awareness of its supernal significance is worthy to receive it. The primary requisite is that the nation which accepts the Torah should do so irrevocably. There can be no conditions, such as "The Torah must not interfere with our life-style; if it does, then we will ignore it." As King Solomon, the wisest of men, tells us:

> *The words of [God's Torah] are like goads and like firmly-planted pegs. . .*[6]

And the Sages explain:

> Just as the goad makes the ox plow straight, thus bringing life to the world, so the Torah's teaching makes its students leave the paths of death for the paths of life. But then, as a goad is a portable instrument, perhaps [one might think that] the Torah too can be picked up and put down? Therefore the Scripture says, "like firmly-planted pegs."[7]

Koheles compared the Torah to two things: an ox-goad and a firmly-planted peg. A goad keeps the ox from wandering to the side as it plows. By insuring that the furrows are made straight, the goad stimulates a process which brings forth abundant grain to sustain the world. The Torah is comparable to an ox-goad in that it too brings spiritual sustenance to the world if people permit themselves to be guided by it.

But in order for the Torah to work its full effect on man, it must also be like a wooden peg,[8] which when driven into a wall is meant to stay there permanently. A peg is not a "portable instrument," picked up for use one day and thrown down the next. Similarly, Torah once learned must become a "permanent installation" in a person's life. It cannot be a passing fancy; one must agree to live by it totally and unconditionally. One's acceptance of its teachings must be final, irrevocable and immutable. A conditional acceptance of the Torah is really no acceptance at all.

Why is this so? To understand this we must return to an idea that we have mentioned previously, the ultimate plan

6 Koheles 12:11.
7 Chagigah 3b.
8 Or nail.

for Creation. This was that mankind should recognize God and accept His sovereignty. It was to enable this to happen that the Torah was revealed to man, for by accepting the Torah and its commandments one accepts God's sovereignty. But if one's acceptance is conditional — if he is willing to experiment with the Torah, but intends to reject it if he finds it too demanding — then he is recognizing only the sovereignty of his own comforts and desires.

What, then, would happen if the Torah were given to a nation that was ready only for conditional acceptance? Far from showing mankind an example of self-subordination to God, the opposite might very well be shown. If God's imperative could be rejected after a trial period, the Torah might end up as a demonstration before all of mankind that man's desires, not God's, are to be considered supreme. The giving of the Torah under such conditions would be self-defeating. Consequently, only a nation for whom the Torah will be both a goad *and* a peg can be trusted with it.

How did the Jews demonstrate that they were ready to accept the Torah irrevocably? When they were approached about receiving the Torah, they did not ask, as the other nations did, "What is written in it?" Instead they responded, "We shall do, and we shall listen."[9]

8.3 THE ANGELS' SECRET[10]

> Said Rabbi Elazar: When the Jews put "We shall do" before "We shall listen," an echo went forth from Heaven saying, "Who revealed to My children the secret of the angels?" As Scripture says, "Bless God, His angels of mighty strength, who do His word, listening to the word He utters"[11] — first they do, then they listen.[12]

9 Shemos 23:7.
10 This chapter does not appear in the Hebrew text.
11 Tehillim 111:10.
12 Shabbas 88a.

> A heretic once saw Rava so absorbed in a topic of the Torah that [he did not notice that] his fingers, upon which he was sitting, were being crushed and were dripping blood. [The heretic] said to him: "You impetuous nation, that put your mouths before your ears! You are just as impetuous today [as your hand will witness]. You should first have heard what was in the Torah, and then, if you felt able to do it, accepted it, and if not, refused it."[13]

If Reuven asks Shimon to travel somewhere with him, Shimon will as a matter of course ask, "What for?" But if Reuven holds a pistol to Shimon's head while making his request, Shimon will not ask any questions. For when one's life depends on it, he acts without asking any questions.

The angels are created for one purpose alone: to carry out God's bidding. They have no other reason for existing; therefore they "do" (carry out) God's will before they "listen" (inquire as to the reason for the command and its purpose). They cannot act otherwise, for their entire existence hinges upon this one purpose.

It was the same for the Jews at Sinai: they were aware that their very existence depended upon accepting the Torah. Inherited from the Fathers of the Jewish people was the deep-seated belief that life was meant for one purpose only: to serve God and to carry out His will. Avraham permitted himself to be thrown into a flaming pit for the sake of the One God he believed in;[14] Yitzhak offered himself as a sacrifice to God on the altar of the Akeidah;[15] Yaakov lived a life of suffering in order to bring forth children who would carry his values forward.[16] This is the heritage which the Forefathers bequeathed to their descendants. When the Jews were offered the Torah, as the bearers of this belief they recog-

13 *Ibid.*

14 The Sages teach us that this is what happened at "Ur Kasdim" (Bereishis 11:32 and Midrash Rabba *ad loc.*).

15 Bereishis Chap. 22. The Sages teach us that Yitzhak went willingly to what he and his father Avraham mistakenly assumed was to be his sacrifice.

16 Bereishis Chaps. 29-35.

nized that there was no alternative for them but to accept it. Like the angels, they said, "We will do," before "We will listen."

This, too, is why Rava could become so absorbed in his studies that he would not notice his bleeding fingers. Someone whose life depends upon the Torah will not be concerned with his personal comfort. His hand may drip with blood, but he will not stop concentrating on his effort to understand the vital will of God. Rava, then, was doing no more than what one might expect from a scion of the nation that had said, "We will do," before "We will listen."

The heretic who taunted Rava believed in only one reason for life: obtaining as many pleasurable sensations as possible. Since this was his sole yardstick, anyone who acted without considering his personal comfort was "impetuous." Had the heretic been offered the Torah, he, too, like the nations of the world, would first have asked, "What is written in it?"

8.4 Wisdom for the Rich

What was true at the time of the giving of the Torah applies in all generations. Unlike any other wisdom, Torah cannot be mastered by study alone. It must be "given" to man by God; without Divine assistance a Jew will not be able to retain his Torah wisdom.[17] God "gives" Torah only to those who realize its awesome worth. Only those who recognize Torah as the vital word of God merit possessing its wisdom.

> A Roman noblewoman asked Rabbi Yose bar Chalafta: "Why does the Torah say, '[God] gives wisdom to the wise'?[18] He ought to give wisdom to the foolish [who need it more]."
>
> He answered her, "If two men come to you to borrow money, one rich and the other poor, to which will you give the loan, the rich one or the poor one?"
>
> "The rich one," she said.

17 Megillah 6b.
18 Daniel 2:21.

> "Why?" he asked. [Doesn't the poor man need it more?]
>
> "The rich man has the wherewithal to repay; but how would the poor man repay?"
>
> "Do not your ears hear what your mouth has said?" said Rabbi Yose. "If God gave His wisdom to fools, they would sit and study it in outhouses, theaters and bathhouses. Therefore He gave it to the wise, who only study it in synagogues and study-halls."[19]

The wise man's choice of a holy place — a synagogue or a Beis Midrash[20] — in which to study the Torah is indicative of his attitude towards it. He recognizes the Torah as the word of God and treats it with reverence. Because he has the proper attitude, Torah for him is "like a peg": he will live by it unconditionally and irrevocably, even if this causes him difficulties. The wise man merits the gift of wisdom, for like the promise of a borrower which is kept when he repays his loan, he will keep the promise of his ancestors, "We shall do, and we shall listen."

On the other hand, the fool lacks the prerequisite of the Torah's wisdom. By studying it in outhouses, theaters and bathhouses he gives evidence of his lack of awe for Torah. (It is, in fact, this lack of recognition that makes him a fool.) Like the poor man who will not repay his loan, he will never keep the promise of those who accepted the Torah; he does not deserve to acquire its wisdom.

8.5 Of Pegs and Nations

He took a peg and thrust it into the bottom of the wall; it would not go in. He tried farther up, and it went in. "It too has found its match," he said.

The prophets tell us explicitly that at the End of Days every human — both Jew and non-Jew — will recognize that

19 Koheles Rabba 1, *ad vers.* כל הנחלים.

20 A house of Torah learning.

there is a God, and that man was created to serve Him by fulfilling His word. This is the end purpose of Creation, a purpose which will not be accomplished until every single human on the face of earth arrives at this recognition. The path to the world's fulfillment is the Torah, which teaches man what God wishes of us and how He is to be served. It was only natural, then, that God should wish to give the Torah to all the nations, in particular to nations of no great moral status.

Eisav, Amon, Moav, and Yishmael personified the various aspects of human evil. They based their lives on those perverted values — violence, lust and greed — which close man off from the recognition of God. Thus from the point of view of the world's destiny they needed the Torah more than the Jews. So God, who in His infinite goodness desires only the benefit of mankind, offered the Torah to these nations first. Like the fools in the Roman noblewoman's question they needed the Torah more, but like those fools they showed themselves to be bad risks for receiving it. For if they had understood the secret of "we will do and we will listen" — the secret of immutable acceptance — then that would have been a sign that they are good risks. But their self-centered inquiries made it all too clear that the Torah could not be entrusted to them. Thus the nations were not ready for the Torah, and God was, as it were, obliged to take another route to bring them to the desired goal. They will ultimately arrive there, but only after mankind has made a long and arduous trek through history.

Rabbi Yehoshua's parable of the pegs and the wall was intended to express this idea. Let us suppose, he says, that to serve his purposes a householder wants to drive a peg into his wall at the lowest possible point, but he finds that the very bottom of the wall is too thick and dense to be penetrated. He has no choice, then, but to look for a more receptive spot for his peg: higher up, where the wall is not so thick and dense. When he finds a suitable new spot, he drives his peg in, for then the peg "has found its match."

Similarly, God's ultimate aim is to permeate even the lowliest elements of the world — those that are most distant from Him — with His wisdom. So, at the time of the giving of the Torah He attempted to make His will known even to the most depraved nations. But these elements were too steeped in materialism to want to receive it: the wall was too thick. He therefore gave the Torah only to that nation which was "its match": the Jews, who were prepared to accept it.

Though God was not able to reveal His will to all of mankind as He had originally desired, nevertheless His plan will ultimately be fulfilled. Through the agency of the nation which did accept the Torah, all of mankind will someday be brought to the recognition of God. At that time all men — including Eisav, Amon, Moav, and Yishmael — will understand that they must efface themselves before God's will.

8.6 THE CHOSEN PEOPLE

The Elders liked to think that God had approached them first with the Torah because they were superior to the Jews; this was their proof that they were the true Chosen People. But the Elders could never understand what the purpose of the Torah is. It is not a collection of wise proverbs meant for one's edification. It is the instrument with which to overcome all the evil of the world and bring the revelation of God to mankind. God first asked the other nations to receive the Torah not because they were wiser but because they needed it more, being so thoroughly immersed in evil.

As we have said, God in His infinite goodness desires the welfare of all His creations; from this perspective, that of the ultimate goal of creation, there is no "chosenness." The only "chosenness" that exists refers to the nation that was ready to be the "match" for God's "peg," prepared to devote its entire existence to carrying out God's plans for His world. The Jews were elected for this mission because they responded to God's call to receive the Torah with "We shall do and we shall listen," unlike the other nations who refused to accept it lest it interfere with their material desires. They alone — unlike the forebears of the Romans and their fellows — saw the Torah as their very "lives and their length of days"[21] and accepted God's will totally and unconditionally. For this reason they alone are the Chosen People.

21 Second blessing of Maariv prayers, based on Devarim 30:20.

9
The Reed-Cutter

[The Elders asked Rabbi Yehoshua:] "If someone loaned money and then had to seize the borrower's property [when he defaulted], why would he give [him] a further loan?"

He answered them: "A man once went to the pond and cut a bundle of reeds. It was too heavy for him to lift, so he cut more and laid [the new bundles] on top [of the first one] until someone came along and helped him to lift [them all]." (Bechoros 8b)

9.1 THE LOAN OF TORAH

"If someone loaned money and then had to seize the borrower's property [when he defaulted], why would he give [him] a further loan?"

God's granting of the Torah to the Jewish people was analogous to a loan, as we have seen in the previous chapter.[1] Just as a borrower obligates himself to pay the loan back in accordance with the lender's original wishes, so the Torah must be "paid back" — the original wishes of the Giver of the Torah must be fulfilled. The Jews who received the Torah must work towards carrying out God's plan: to sanctify the world through the study of Torah and the performance of mitzvos so that God will ultimately be able to reveal Himself to mankind.

Immediately after the destruction of the First Temple and

1 See §8.4.

the Exile to Babylon, the Sages tell us that the leaders of the Jewish people enacted numerous Rabbinic decrees designed to obviate the possibility of transgressing Torah law. Understanding that their Exile was a punishment for not having kept the Torah properly, they set about making reparation for their sins. One of the elements of repentance is the determination never to repeat the sin. The enactment of safeguards to serve as "fences" around the Torah would, they felt, demonstrate their resolve never to return to their evil ways.

> Why must you keep two days of Yom Tov in Syria? Because you refused to keep one day in Eretz Yisrael.
>
> Why must you take *challah* twice in Syria? Because you refused to take it once in Eretz Yisrael.[2]

But, protested the Elders, what sense was there in this? Rabbinic decrees are meaningful only if God acquiesces in them — otherwise what obligation is there to observe them? Certainly God does not concur with these new enactments, argued the Elders. The Jews had forfeited Temple and Land because they were unwilling to keep the original laws. God, in effect, had called in His original loan of Torah; why would He give another by endorsing new laws? What hope is there that a people who defaulted on one loan would repay a new one?

9.2 An Orchard and a Heavy Bundle

The answer to the Elder's criticism is that they had not really understood the reason for the Rabbinic decrees.

2 Talmud Yerushalmi, Eiruvin 3:9. By Torah law, festivals (Yom Tov when work is forbidden) are each only one day long. The Rabbis, however, decreed that outside of Eretz Yisrael Yom Tov must be kept for two consecutive days.

Torah law decrees that a portion of *challah* must be separated from dough and given to a *kohen*. After the Destruction, the Rabbis decreed that in lands near Eretz Yisrael two portions of *challah* must be separated. (This decree is not in force in other lands.)

> *You shall guard My guarding.*[3]
> [The Sages explain:] Make a guard for My guarding. [If the Torah guards the Jewish people from sin, then the Sages must make decrees and enactments to guard the Torah from being violated.]
>
> Said Rav Ashi: What is the principle behind [Rabbinic enactments]? It is like someone who watches his orchard from within the orchard: he can guard the part right in front of him but not what is behind him. But if he watches from outside, he can guard it all.
>
> [The other Sages comment:] Rav Ashi's example is inaccurate. Someone who watches his orchard from within is at least guarding what is in front of him. But without the Rabbinic measures, none of the Torah at all would be kept.[4]

It is easy to keep a commandment when one's attention is directed towards it, but it is not so easy to avoid transgressing a commandment unwittingly. For example, if one handles a tool on Shabbos he might forget that it is Shabbos and, out of habit, perform a forbidden labor with it; to avoid this the Rabbis forbade handling the tool. The unwitting violation of Shabbos is part of the "orchard" which is "behind him," i.e., out of immediate sight. The Rabbinic decrees create a buffer zone around the Torah's commandments, insuring that even the parts "out of sight" remain guarded. In other words, the Rabbinic enactments ensure that one will not unwittingly transgress the laws of the Torah.

Rav Ashi's colleagues hold that he is underestimating man's capacity for sin, and with it the need for Rabbinic enactments. If the Rabbis did not provide a "fence" around the Torah, then even the commandments "before him," i.e., those of which one is directly aware, would not be kept.

For example, one might be aware that it is Shabbos and yet decide to willfully transgress it because of an overriding desire to earn money or to protect one's property. The Rabbinic

3 Vayikra 18:30.

4 Yevamos 21a.

decrees reduce this possibility. For example, when one may not even handle a tool which might be used to violate Shabbos, the temptation actually to use the tool is further removed, since to do so one would have to decide to transgress two prohibitions — a less likely occurrence. Similarly in regard to all commandments, the buffer zone of Rabbinic decrees keeps temptation at a distance. Without them even the part of the orchard "in front of him," i.e, the commandments of which one is conscious, would not be guarded.

This is the meaning of Rabbi Yehoshua's parable:

A man once went to the pond and cut a bundle of reeds. It was too heavy for him to lift, so he cut more and laid [the new bundles] on top [of the first one] until someone came along and helped him to lift [them all].

The reed-cutter saw right away that he would need help to carry his load. But he wisely saw that one bundle was not enough to attract the attention of passersby: they might not perceive that it was too big to lift unaided. If there were enough bundles lying there, he thought, then surely people would see for themselves and offer their help. And so it was. He not only had help to lift his original bundle, but also was able to bring several more that he never could have managed on his own.

It is the same with loans: if one cannot repay the first one, it may sometimes be worthwhile to borrow some more. The first loan might not have been enough to generate a proper income, but when the second loan is added enough earning power will be generated to repay both loans.

Rabbi Yehoshua's answer, then, is that the Jews never willfully rejected the Torah; they had sinned only because there were too many temptations enticing them to violate its laws. Deep in their hearts they loved Torah as much as when God originally asked them if they agreed to receive it, when in their recognition of its vital worth they responded with

"We shall do and we shall listen."[5] The Rabbinic enactments are a demonstration of this love, of how much the Jews truly desire to carry out God's word. They are an expression of a fervent hope: that by adding these restrictions they will be kept away from their temptations and fulfil their original obligations faithfully.

The destruction of the Temple and the Dispersion were not God "calling in his loan" to the Jewish people. They were merely God's way of admonishing them to make greater efforts to keep the Torah. The Rabbinic enactments represent one form of these efforts. When the nation repents fully and again begins observing the Torah properly, the Temple and Land will be returned to them.

Why would the lender want to add another loan? To give the borrower a chance to pay both of them back.

9.3 ANOTHER INSIGHT: THE WOODCHOPPER AND THE STONE-MASON[6]

Rabbi Yehoshua's parable has yet another meaning, one which concerns the right way to study the Torah and master it. It is based on a saying of the wisest of men:

> *A stone-mason is wearied by his stones; a wood-cutter is warmed by his wood.*[7]

The Sages explained its deeper meaning:

> The "stone-mason" is the student of Gemara, and the "wood-cutter" is the student of Mishnah.[8]

The Mishnah is that part of the Oral Torah which contains, in brief form, the corpus of Jewish law. The Gemara is the lengthy analysis of the theory and reasoning behind these

5 Shemos 23:7; see §8.3.

6 In the original text, this insight serves as the basis for the previous interpretation of the parable.

7 Koheles 10:9.

8 Bava Basra 145b. The Mishnah and the Gemara together make up the Talmud.

laws. In the light of this distinction, the Midrash quoted above seems contrary to common sense: if Gemara "fatigues" and Mishnah "warms," the implication is that studying the plain laws is preferable to, and more satisfying than, studying their depths and philosophy. This is not reasonable, and in fact the Sages say elsewhere:

> Studying the Mishnah is conducive to spiritual growth, and one receives Heavenly reward for it. But nothing is more conducive to spiritual growth than studying Gemara.[9]

And elsewhere again they actually express criticism of Mishnah study:

> Those who study [only] Mishnah wear the world to a ravelling.[10]

The first passage praises Mishnah above all; the second puts it in second place; the third denigrates it. How can these conflicting statements be reconciled?

Let us consider what would happen to a person who studies *only* Gemara, without having studied the Mishnah first. Just as a laborer quarrying rocks becomes fatigued by the immense strain of his labor, so one who attempts to master the underlying theory of the Torah without first finding out its basic content will be worn out by this impossible task. And so the Sages tell us,

> If you see a student who is having great difficulty with his study of Gemara, [you may know that] it is because he does not know the Mishnah well enough.[11]

The only way to achieve true understanding of the Torah is to study Gemara *after* having first studied all of the Mishnah.[12]

9 Bava Metzia 33a.

10 Sotah 22a.

11 Taanis 8a.

12 This is not the method generally employed in Yeshivot today because, as the Chasam Sofer and other great authorities explain, it is necessary to train students first in the proper way of reasoning, or else their understanding of even the rudiments will be faulty.

First comes breadth, then depth, and the two together bring wisdom. Success in one's studies is in fact impossible without breadth, for "the Torah is poor in one place and rich in another":[13] when the answer to one's question is not to be found in one part of the Torah, then it can be found in another part. Only the study of Mishnah will provide this necessary breadth. Once the necessary background in Mishnah has been acquired, Gemara study will be both fruitful and personally satisfying, like the warmth of the wood-chopper's fire.

The first passage, then, describes the fate of one who studies Gemara without a background in Mishnah. The other two passages, in the same way, instead of contradicting each other describe other methods of study and their results. "There is nothing more conducive to spiritual growth" than studying Gemara *after* having studied the Mishnah. Since true understanding of the Torah, including its correct application in daily life, can only come from the Gemara, Mishnah study with nothing further following it is inadequate. It is, of course, a mitzvah to study Mishnah and therefore meritorious, but this is provided one understands that without the underlying methodology one's study is only superficial. However, someone whose only study is Mishnah could potentially become a plague, "wearing the world to a ravelling," if he imagines that his grasp of the Torah is deep and methodical and that he is equipped to apply it to real-life situations. Such a person "wears the world to a ravelling" by diverting it from its true destiny, which is carrying out the laws of the Torah. By deciding questions of law on the basis of Mishnah alone, without understanding the underlying theory, one will necessarily follow incorrect syllogisms and draw untenable conclusions. Thus one's actions will not be in accordance with God's desired destiny for His world, and the world, instead of progressing, is "worn out."

This principle is the basis of the second meaning of Rabbi Yehoshua's parable.

13 Yerushalmi Rosh Hashanah 3, 5.

9.4 THE VIEW FROM THE REED-POND

"A man once went to the pond and cut a bundle of reeds"

A reed-cutter, in the Talmudic symbolism, is someone whose understanding of the Torah is superficial. For example, when Rav Nachman bar Gurya, on being quizzed about the Shabbos laws, displayed ignorance of their theory, the scholars of Nehard'a rebuked him: "Your teacher must have been a reed-cutter in the pond"[14] — meaning that he did not give a competent explanation of this part of the Torah.[15]

This image is based on an obvious fact of life. If a person wants to warm himself, he goes and cuts down trees and then chops them up for a fire. But what if he has no axe? In that case, the only available fuel is reeds from the pond, which need only a knife to cut them. On the other hand, their fire is meager and smoky.

The wood-chopper is the man who, having studied Mishnah, has gone on to master the Gemara. His sharp, strong axe cuts abundant wood with which to warm himself. The reed-cutter is someone unable to study Gemara, because he has not developed the capacity for studying in depth; he must make do with the poor, smoky fire of reeds that are all he can cut.

"It was too heavy for him to lift, so he cut more and laid [the new bundles] on top [of the first one] until someone came along and helped him to lift [them all]."

The most common cause of lack of depth in learning is not having enough information at one's disposal, as the Sages say (in a passage quoted partially above):

14 Shabbas 95a.
15 Rashi *ad loc.*

> If you see a student who is having great difficulty with his study of Gemara, [you may know that] it is because he does not know the Mishnah well enough. If he wishes to succeed, he should study [his Mishnah] diligently.[16]

This student simply must resist the temptation to engage in the study of Gemara until he has mastered the Mishnah. If he continues his impossible labor, it will exhaust him as if he were quarrying rocks, and he will be left with no fire at all to warm himself by. The only way that he can succeed is to continue his Mishnah studies and not be discouraged by his lack of deep understanding. He must remember that even if at first he does not grasp the deeper meaning of things, once he has gained enough knowledge, then (even though his knowledge is still superficial) he will be ready to be taught the Gemara, well prepared at last to master its depths and intricacies.

The "reed-cutter" found his bundle of Mishnah too heavy to lift. Undaunted, he continued "cutting" and making new "bundles," piling them up more and more. When his time was ripe, someone came along to teach him the deeper meanings of the Mishnah and helped him to "lift them" and carry them all home.

16 Taanis 9a.

10

The Roman Parade[1]

Once every seventy years the Romans take an able-bodied man and put him on a lame man's back. They dress him in the clothes [that God made for] Adam, and place Rabbi Yishmael's embalmed face over his head . . . and proclaim before him:

"The chief's reckoning is a counterfeit,
The brother of our master, the fraud.
What did the deceiver gain by his deceit,
The fraud by his fraudulence?"

Said Rav Ashi: Their tongues tripped them up. Had they said, "the fraud, our master's brother," it would have meant what they intended. But "the brother of our master, the fraud" means that "our master" is himself "the fraud."

(Avodah Zarah 11b)

10.1 A Pageant of Victory

Even after the Destruction of the Temple by the Romans and the subsequent Exile, the Jewish people held fast to their belief in the prophetic promise that they would never cease to be God's chosen people and that ultimately He would redeem them. The Romans saw in this tenacious belief nothing more than defiance, a stubborn refusal to submit to their domination. Determined on stamping out such last sparks of

1 In the original text the story of the Roman Parade is part of the next chapter. Unlike the rest of this book, many of the interpretations in this chapter stem from the Maharal of Prague's commentaries to Avodah Zarah, *ad loc.*, and not from the Vilna Gaon.

rebellious spirit, they established the custom described above: a parade whose pomp and splendor was designed to demonstrate that their victory over the Jews was final and that any hope of redemption was vain.

. . . the Romans take an able-bodied man and put him on a lame man's back.

Rome was the heir of Eisav,[2] and the struggle for ascendancy between Rome and Jerusalem was the next round of the ancient struggle between Eisav and Yaakov. Theirs was a dispute not over land or possessions, but over the meaning of existence. To Yaakov, man's purpose is to serve God; to Eisav, it is to serve man. To Yaakov, life is the means for spiritual growth; to Eisav, it is the means for personal advancement.

The previous round of this struggle had taken place between Yaakov and the patron angel of Eisav:

> *Yaakov was left alone; and a man wrestled with him until daybreak.*[3]

This "man" was Eisav's angel.[4] Even though he was successful in dislocating Yaakov's thigh muscle (the גיד הנשה), thus causing him to limp for a while, the angel was nevertheless vanquished at the end of the combat.[5] In consequence of his victory, God granted Yaakov his other name, Yisrael, signifying that his beliefs would ultimately triumph over those of his brother.[6]

The Romans saw in their victory over the Jews a repudiation of Yaakov's victory over the angel, and evidence of the triumph of their self-serving philosophy. In celebration of

2 According to the tradition preserved by the Sages (e.g., Avodah Zarah 11a and Rashi *s.v. Antoninus*). A Biblical source is Bereishis 36:43 (*cf.* Rashi *ad loc.*).

3 Bereishis 32:25.

4 Midrash Rabba on Bereishis, *loc. cit.*; quoted in Rashi *ad loc.*

5 Bereishis *ibid.*, v. 26-32.

6 The Torah (Bereishis 32:28) explains that this name means, "You have wrestled with an angel and with men and won."

their conquest they would take an able-bodied man, representing Eisav, and mount him on the back of a lame man, representing Yaakov, to indicate their nation's total and final victory over the descendants of Yisrael. In effect they were saying, "The limping Yaakov is now a slave, carrying his master Eisav."

10.2 THE BEAUTY OF ADAM

They dress him in the clothes that [God made for] Adam. . .

When Adam sinned, he failed in the mission for which he had been created: to carry out his Creator's will. The result was that he was driven from God's grace and from the Garden of Eden. Twenty generations went by before the world was ready for the next try, when Avraham took a spiritual leap on behalf of humanity and began the process of rebuilding man in order to restore him eventually to his original stature. The key to that process was Avraham's belief, upheld in the face of an idolatrous world, in one God.

Avraham's ideas took hold. They were spread and expounded by his son Yitzhak, and reached their fruition with his grandson, Yaakov-Yisrael, who completed the forming of the Jewish nation. By investing his descendants with an everlasting spiritual orientation, Yaakov insured that the Jewish nation would ultimately carry out man's mission on earth: to recognize that cleaving to God is his true reason for existence.

It is no wonder, then, that the Sages tell us that "the beauty of Yaakov Avinu was like that of Adam."[7] The "beauty" of Yaakov refers to the spiritual perfection which he achieved in his lifetime. It was similar to the perfection which Adam possessed when he was originally created, but which he lost when he sinned. Yaakov made it possible for man to regain his lost image. His descendants would now be worthy of

7 Bava Metzia 84a.

standing at Sinai to receive the Torah with which they could accomplish all that Adam had failed to do.

To the Romans, nothing was beautiful but power, wealth, and glory. They lived by the creed of their forbear Eisav, that man was created not for any spiritual destiny but for his own aggrandizement. The Roman Empire, because it excelled in building roads and aqueducts, mustering armies, conquering lands, and dominating nations, was to the Romans the finest flower of human achievement. What more could mankind possibly aspire to? Surely not Yaakov but Eisav, claimed the Romans, echoed the beauty of Adam. So they took the clothes that God had made for Adam and dressed the able-bodied man in those garments. The beauty of Adam, they said, is Eisav's inheritance!

10.3 THE VALUE OF PLEASURE

... and place Rabbi Yishmael's embalmed face over his head...

> [When Rabbi Yishmael the High Priest was about to be put to death for teaching Torah,] Caesar's daughter looked out the window and saw his astonishing beauty. She asked her father to spare him, but he answered, "I have sworn to kill him."
>
> "In that case," she said, "have his face skinned so that I may gaze upon it."
>
> Caesar ordered his face skinned while he was alive.[8] His daughter had the face embalmed so that its beauty would last, and it became one of the national treasures of Rome.[9]

When one senses in an object a dimension which transcends the physical, he experiences a sense of beauty. That was the sensation felt by anyone who beheld the face of

8 Midrash Eileh Ezkerah.

9 Rashi to Avodah Zarah 11b.

Rabbi Yishmael the *Kohen Gadol* (High Priest), which reflected an aspect of life not accessible to other people.

The *Kohen Gadol* was permitted to draw closer than all other men to the Divine Presence. Of all the people in the world, only he was permitted to enter the innermost chamber of the *Beis HaMikdash* on Yom Kippur. As the holiest of men in the holiest of places on the holiest day of the year, the *Kohen Gadol* was able to put man in contact with a reality far beyond that of the physical world. That transcendent reality which only he experienced directly shone forth from Rabbi Yishmael's face, giving it a beauty that astonished all who beheld it.

Beauty inspired the Romans as it inspires all humans; but its value to them was not that it brought man into contact with loftier levels of existence, but simply that it afforded them pleasure. Most people would doubtless consider it an abhorrent contradiction to destroy a noble life amidst excruciating pain for the sake of possessing a thing of beauty: how can beauty be consonant with the obscenity of murder? But according to the Roman values by which Caesar's daughter lived it was no contradiction at all. Another's life must fall by the wayside if it conflicts with the ultimate value of one's own pleasure.

As the Jewish nation had been vanquished, so, the Romans believed, was their culture. The Jewish belief that man was created for transcendent experience had been proven wrong; rather, transcendent experience was created for man. What, therefore, could be more fitting than to celebrate this by taking the embalmed face of the High Priest and placing it over the able-bodied man's face? Let everyone see how holy splendor befits Eisav!

10.4 A BROTHER'S VINDICATION

". . . the chief's reckoning is a counterfeit. . ."

All through the streets of Rome the procession went, proclaiming that the blessings Yaakov had gotten from Yitzhak were worthless, and that the prophecy that his descendants would be redeemed at the end of days was only chauvinistic propaganda.

"What did the deceiver gain by his deceit? . . ."

Yaakov dressed himself in his brother Eisav's clothing, and thus deceived Yitzhak into blessing him.[10] The blessings were to be the source of Yaakov's material survival; but, say the triumphant Romans, the deceiver gained nothing by his deceit; his fraudulence got him nowhere. Eisav has been vindicated; and the blessings which Yitzhak gave Yaakov have at last come back to their rightful owner.

* * *

At first it would seem that the Romans have a good point. The Temple is burnt; Jerusalem is destroyed; Yaakov is enslaved.

What, then, of Yaakov's blessings? What is the answer to the jeers of the Romans? Also, what is the meaning of Rav Ashi's cryptic comment on their taunt, that "their tongues tripped them up?" What significance lies in the fact that another meaning — which they obviously did not intend — can be read into their words?

The following exchange between the Elders and Rabbi Yehoshua, regarding "the mule which gave birth," will answer these questions.

10 Bereishis 27:28-29.

11
The Promissory Note

[The Elders of the House of Athens asked Rabbi Yehoshua:] "Show us a lie."

He told them: "We had a mule which gave birth; it had a note hanging from its neck which read, 'My father's estate owes a thousand zuz.'"

They protested, "But can a mule give birth?"

"That is why it is a lie." *(Bechoros 8b)*

11.1 The Defeated

"Show us a lie."

Following the perspective expressed by the Roman parade,[1] the Elders demanded of Rabbi Yehoshua that he demonstrate why the Romans were lying when they said that they, not the Jews, were the truly blessed nation. "Show us how you can reasonably claim that Yitzhak's blessings, 'Nations will serve you . . . You shall be lord over your brothers'[2] can apply to you Jews, who have been completely subjugated and driven from your land by us, Eisav's heirs."

Rabbi Yehoshua's riddling response explores in depth the concepts of bereavement and return.

1 Described in the previous chapter.

2 Bereishis 27:29.

11.2 THE BARREN MOTHER

"We had a mule which gave birth. . ."

The Prophets use the image of a mother to represent the idea of the Jewish nation, and the image of children to represent the individual Jews who are its members. Thus, the loss and recovery of children are the images through which the Prophet Yeshayah speaks of Exile and Return.

> *Your children are hurrying. . . . Cast your eyes about you and see; they have all gathered together and come back to you.*[3]

> *The children you had lost will yet say in your hearing, "I have no room; move over so I may sit." You will say to yourself, "Who bore me all these children, I, bereaved and lonely? Exiled and wandering — who raised these? For I was left alone; whence came they?"*[4]

Another similar image used by the Prophets for the Jewish nation in Exile is the barren woman who will finally be blessed with motherhood when her children all return to her at the end of days:

> *The barren woman shall rejoice exultantly when her children are happily gathered in to her.*[5]

> *He settles the barren woman as a happy mother of children.*[6]

The Jewish view of its national barrenness is that this is only a temporary condition, and that some day it will again be a happy mother of children. The Romans thought differently; they dismissed the Jewish nation as a "mule" — an animal which is by nature sterile. They argued that the Jewish nation, having suffered military defeat and dispersion, was

3 Yeshayahu 49:18.

4 *Ibid.*, 49:20-21.

5 The fifth blessing recited at weddings, which looks forward to the return of the Jewish people to its land.

6 Tehillim 109:9.

permanently bereft both of its "children" and of its destiny. The proof of this was the Exile, the final and complete dashing of the Jews' foolish dream of a great future that awaited them.

Rabbi Yehoshua countered that if the Jewish nation is a mule, then this mule gives birth. For Exile, he says, may lend the Jewish nation the superficial appearance of a mule, but all the same, beneath the surface this nation is not sterile. It has gone into exile to atone for its sins, and to rebuild itself towards that day when it will return to its original glory. Exile rectifies the faults of the Jewish people, the very faults and sins that permitted the Romans to overcome them. When the time is ripe and reparation has been made for these sins, then "the children will return"; the Jews will return to their land and their Temple and their values will prevail over Eisav's.

All the same, Exile seems like a revocation, however temporary, of God's promises to the Jews. Rabbi Yehoshua now goes on to demonstrate that beneath the apparent sterility of Exile a process is in operation designed to reassert Jewish destiny.

11.3 The Debt of Redemption

". . . [The mule] had a note hanging from its neck which read, 'My father's estate owes a thousand zuz.' "

God asked Avraham: "Which do you prefer [for your children if they must be punished some day]: that they pass through Gehinnom or go into Exile?"

All that day Avraham sat and pondered which one to choose. God advised him to choose Exile.

That is why Scripture says [that the Jews could not have gone into Exile] "unless their Rock had sold them, and God had handed them over."[7] "Their Rock" (צור) is

7 Devarim 32:30.

> Avraham[8] (as the Scripture says, "Look to the rock [צור] whence you were hewn . . . look to Avraham your father"[9]); "and God had handed them over": God counselled Avraham to prefer Exile.[10]

God told Avraham that his children would someday sin so greatly that they would of necessity be punished. Which would he choose for them, Gehinnom or Exile? Would their punishment be annihilation from the face of earth and their souls being given over the castigation of Gehinnom? Or would they remain a nation, and atone their sins by being spread to the four corners of the earth and suffering the torment of hostile nations?

Within the framework of achieving God's purposes for His world, Exile was the better choice (which is the meaning of "God advised him to choose Exile"). God created this world so that mankind might come to recognize Him here and now, on this earth. If the Jewish people could atone for its sins and rebuild itself in this world, God's plan would be realized. But if the Jews were annihilated, even if they were punished in Gehinnom for their deeds God's plan would nevertheless have failed.

The crucial question was, could the Jews survive Exile? For if Exile would cause them to lose their faith, how could Avraham submit them to it? Could his descendants, then, maintain their faith no matter how long the Exile lasted, no matter what tortures the nations submitted them to?

The decision depended on the level of faith which Avraham could bequeath to his descendants — which, in turn, was a function of his own depth of faith, for he could not bequeath more than he himself possessed.

All that day Avraham sat and pondered the question. He struggled with himself to reach a devotion to God so tran-

8 The word "rock" (צור) is applied here, on the *derash* level of meaning (see above, "An Overview of Aggadata," §1), to Avraham.

9 Yeshayahu 51:1-2; adduced in Midrash Shocher Tov.

10 Midrash Rabba Bereishis, Par. 44, 21.

scendentally absolute that faith would forever be a permanent feature of the Jewish people.

Avraham was finally successful in attaining the necessary level of faith, and so he was able to "choose" Exile for his children. The Jews would be an eternal people, never to lose their faith in God, and never to be wiped off the face of the earth no matter how much they sinned. They would atone their sins; they would survive any test and would be redeemed; they would sanctify God's Name on earth.

It was Avraham, then, who "sold" his children into exile. He afforded them the alternative of Exile and its atonement. If not for Avraham's unshakable devotion to God, the consequence of their sins would have been annihilation; because of him they merit Exile. When they finally return to the Land at the end of days, it will be by the merit of their Father Avraham and the surety of redemption which he bequeathed to them.

11.4 A THOUSAND FOR THE VINE

'. . . my father's estate owes a thousand zuz.'

Shelomoh had a vineyard in the plain of Hamon. He gave the vineyard over to watchmen; each one must bring a thousand silver coins for its fruit.

"My vineyard is before Me."

"The thousand is Yours, Shelomoh, and two hundred for those who watched over its fruit."[11]

Every "Shelomoh" in Shir HaShirim refers to God.[12]

The Scriptures liken the Jewish people to a vineyard whose fruit is worth a thousand silver *zuz* (dinars). The King from whom all peace comes[13] gave His vineyard into the care of rapacious watchmen: the Jewish people when it is in Exile

11 Shir HaShirim 8:11-12.

12 Tractate Soferim 5:17.

13 The deeper meaning behind the name "Shelomoh."

must suffer the "care" of the rapacious Gentiles. Nevertheless, the King reminds the watchmen that the vineyard is His, and His eye is on it — "My vineyard is before Me." The watchmen may take their fee of "two hundred,"[14] but the precious fruit of the holy vineyard — the "thousand" — belongs to the King, and the "watchmen" will have to deliver it when He calls for it at the End of Days.

This is the last link in understanding Rabbi Yehoshua's "lie." Avraham has promised — and God has agreed — that his children must be ultimately redeemed, that the Jewish people, symbolized by the vineyard worth a thousand silver coins, must be returned by those nations among whom they were exiled. The Jewish nation therefore has a "claim" on Father Avraham that he keep his promise that her children be redeemed. For it was the faith in God with which he invested his descendants which initiated the process of Exile; that same faith guarantees their ultimate return.

The mule-that-gives-birth has a promissory note hanging from its neck which gives proof of its claim. It is a note for a thousand *zuz* against Avraham, their Father: he is obligated to return the Jewish children, the fruit of a thousand coins' worth, to their mother, the Jewish nation.

She who was once a mother of children appears now to be as sterile as a mule. But when her children return to her, it will become apparent that she was never actually a mule in the first place. She is like a mule on the surface, but really she can give birth.

11.5 THE PROOF OF THE LIE

They protested, "But can a mule give birth?"

The Roman Elders reiterate what they, with their superfi-

14 God expects the Exile to take its toll on a certain proportion of the nation, a reference to the fact that the Gentile oppression is part of the Divine plan of atonement. *Cf.* Rashi *ad loc.*

cial vision, saw as the only pertinent facts. Jewish independence is ended, the Temple is ashes. How can you claim that your people will ever regain its eminence? It is as sterile as a mule. Rabbi Yehoshua calmly answers:

"That is why it is a lie."

He answers that the Exile itself is his proof. If the Jewish people were a "mule," without hope or future, it would have been annihilated as other nations are when their sins grow too great. Yet God did not allow this to happen; He has preserved them by sending them into exile, and continues to maintain them in all their far-flung dwellings. If the Elders are right, why should He have bothered keeping them alive? The Jewish survival in Exile, then, is evidence of God's will that the Jews should remain forever in existence, and that they should eventually be redeemed.

This mule is no ordinary mule at all; it may look like one to the careless observer, but anyone who examines beneath the surface will find that it is fertile, burgeoning with the power of birth.

11.6 A Song of Return

> A certain heretic once asked Beruryah:[15] "It is written, 'Sing, you barren woman who has not given birth.'[16] If she has not given birth, what has she to sing about?"
>
> She answered, "Fool! Look at the end of the verse. It says, '. . . for the children of the desolate woman will be more than the children of the married woman'[17] [in which case she has given birth].
>
> "What then is the meaning of 'barren woman who has not given birth'? — 'Sing, O Jewish nation, even when you are like a barren woman; for you have not

15 The wife of Rabbi Meir, famous for her brilliance and erudition.

16 Yeshayahu 54:1.

17 *Ibid.*

> borne children destined for Gehinnom' — like you, you heretic!"[18]

Beruryah's answer seems to be no answer at all. A barren woman obviously has no children; if the Jewish nation has indeed given birth, then why is it called "barren"? And, which was the question from the start: what *is* the "barren mother" singing about?

Like Rabbi Yehoshua, Beruryah was saying that the barren woman in the verse merely appears to be barren, and this is because all of her children have gone into exile. Although this is a great sorrow for her, she still has something to sing about, for of all the children she has borne, none is destined to wither away in Gehinnom. Her children will exist forever. Even though they are lost to her today, she knows that they will be back; and when they return they will be "more than the children of the married woman [the Gentiles]." They must first pass through a terrible Dispersion to atone for their sins, but that very Dispersion is the road that leads homeward, to her. She sings, knowing that her seeming barrenness insures that some day her children will return in triumph.

11.7 POSTSCRIPT: THE TRIPPED-UP TONGUE

Said Rav Ashi: Their tongues tripped them up. Had they said, "the fraud, our master's brother," it would have meant what they intended. But "the brother of our master, the fraud" means that "our master" [Eisav] is himself "the fraud."[19]

At last we are ready to understand Rav Ashi's retort to the Roman parade. What did it matter if they spoke ambiguously? And what does ambiguity count for when measured

18 Berachos 10a.

19 Avodah Zarah 11b. This is the end of the passage cited at the beginning of Chapter Ten.

against the armed might of a victorious empire? These questions have the same answers as the riddle of the fertile mule.

Rav Ashi's comment refers to the two levels of reality which were at play at the time of the Exile. Superficially the Romans had trampled the Jews to the dust, but beneath the surface lay the reality that the Jewish people was eternal, and that they would ultimately return to their land and Temple. Superficially Roman culture had emerged victorious, but beneath the surface lay the reality that by their very conquest they had initiated a process which would ultimately cause the values of Yaakov to prevail over their own.

Corresponding to these two realities were the two meanings inherent in the ambiguous syntax of the Romans' sneering taunt. "The brother of our master, the fraud," could be understood to mean that Yaakov is the fraud or that the master, Eisav, himself is the fraud. "Their tongues had tripped them up": they had not intended this second meaning, but Providence put these words in their mouths to indicate that just as beneath the surface of their words lay another meaning, so beneath the surface of their domination existed another reality.

The triumph of Rome was the beginning of a process which would have the opposite effect of what seemed on the surface to be taking place. Despite Eisav's present successes, this process would ultimately expose him as an impostor who had tricked mankind into believing that he had a real solution for its problems.[20] When Exile has worked its atonement on the children of Yaakov, the Jewish Torah will prevail, and Eisav's performance on the stage of world history will be shown to have been a tragic masquerade.

Although from a superficial aspect the Romans might conclude from their current history that "the brother of our master [Yaakov] is the fraud," in the long run the truth will become evident: that "our master [Eisav] is the fraud."

20 See "The Midpoint of the World," §14.6, where this is discussed more fully.

12
Salt and the Mule

[The Elders of Athens asked Rabbi Yehoshua ben Chananyah:] "When salt spoils, what can one salt it with?"

[Rabbi Yehoshua answered:] "With the afterbirth of a mule."

"But does a mule have an afterbirth?"

"But can salt spoil?" *(Bechoros 8b)*

12.1 A COVENANT OF SALT

"When salt spoils, what can one salt it with?"

When the Jews accepted the Torah, they thereby entered into a covenant with God. This covenant was repeated three times, at Sinai, in the Plains of Moav, and after entering the land of Israel.[1] A covenant between God and the Jewish people is categorized as a ברית מלח — "a covenant of salt."[2] The significance of this phrase is that a Divinely-made covenant partakes of the quality of salt. Just as salt preserves food and keeps it from spoiling, so will these covenants endure forever, eternally preserved from abrogation.

Like any covenant, the covenant of the Torah entails mutual obligations. For God's part, it is an oath that He will

1 Sotah 37b.

2 Divrei HaYamim II, 13:5, with respect to the covenant of kingship: "God, the Lord of Israel, has given kingship over Israel to David forever, [which is] for him and his sons a covenant of salt." Also, Bemidbar 18:19, with respect to the covenant with the *kohanim* (the priests): "It is a covenant of salt forever before God for you and your children with you." This expression is taken to apply to all covenants with God, including, in this case, the covenant over the Torah.

cause His Divine Presence to dwell among His people, and that even if they are sent into exile they will eventually be redeemed from it. For the Jewish people's part, it is an undertaking that they will never leave off their commitment to the study of Torah and the observance of the mitzvos.

The Jewish people bases its hope for future redemption on God's oath as expressed in this covenant. But the Elders of Athens questioned this assumption. The Jews had violated their side of the covenant, as the Prophet Yirmiyahu clearly states:

> *. . . not like the covenant which I made with their fathers on the day I took them by their hand to bring them out of Egypt, for they violated My covenant. . . .*[3]

If the covenant was violated, is it not absurd for the Jews to believe that God's oath to redeem them is still binding? A covenant is mutual; if the Jewish people did not keep their part of it, then surely God need no longer keep His promise.

Phrased in symbolic language, the Elders argued that when salt spoils there is nothing left to salt it with. "Your covenant," they said, "may be a ברית מלח, 'a covenant of salt,' but you have made the 'salt' in it spoil. Since there is nothing in the world that can preserve spoiled salt, what hope is there that your covenant will be preserved? In other words, the element which makes the covenant permanent — its mutual observance — no longer exists. Your misdeeds have clearly abrogated the covenant with God: no greater evidence of this could be asked than your expulsion and exile from your land. The covenant is no longer viable and there is no hope that redemption will ever come."

[Rabbi Yehoshua answered:] "With the afterbirth of a mule."

"You are claiming, in effect," replied Rabbi Yehoshua, "that we are nothing but a nation of 'mules.' Just as mules

3 Yirmiyahu 31:31-2.

are sterile animals unable to continue their species into the next generation, so, you say, we too have become bereft of our ability to survive into the future and reach our destiny.

"What if a 'mule' were to produce an afterbirth? Would that not prove that it is really not a mule? We too give forth an 'afterbirth' which gives the lie to our external appearance, and which shows that we are really fertile beings.[4] That is our children. We may have not kept our personal obligation to occupy ourselves with Torah, but we still continue teaching Torah to our children. As long as we do so, God will not forsake us and the covenant will be kept."

12.2 WHENCE CHILDREN?

"But does a mule have an afterbirth?"

"Your answer begs the question," countered the Elders. "You say that your covenant is alive because you continue to teach Torah to your children. But what guarantee is there that in your future there will be children to teach? What reason is there to believe that you will continue to exist as a nation? Existence is only guaranteed to a Jewish people which keeps the covenant, and your Scriptures say that you have violated it. Without a covenant, then, what hope do you have of God's redemption?"

12.3 A COVENANT IS FOREVER

"But can salt spoil?"

Rabbi Yehoshua explained himself. The Elders' premise that the covenant has been abrogated, though it is based on Scriptures, is incorrect. A covenant between God and His people by its very definition can never lapse, any more than salt can become spoiled. God and the Jewish people have

4 See "The Promissory Note," §§11.4-5, for an exposition of the Jewish people's superficial resemblance to a "mule."

forged a mutual relationship which can never be discontinued.

What about the prophecy of Yirmiyahu which indicates otherwise? The prophet says explicitly that the Jews have violated the covenant; but a covenant has two aspects to it. First, it defines the relationship between its two parties. As stated above, this is a relationship which can never end. Second, and what Yirmiyahu is referring to, is the implementation of the covenant, which entails certain obligations. In this case God has obligated Himself that He will dwell among His nation and fill them with His knowledge. It is this aspect, the aspect of the implementation, which Yirmiyahu says we have violated.

There is a prerequisite for the realization of God's covenant with Israel. The Torah says,

> *They will make me a sanctuary and I will dwell among them.*[5]

If God is to dwell among the Jewish people, they must first make Him a sanctuary. The present situation is that their sins do not permit God to exercise His promise to dwell among mankind; the Jews have refused to make Him a sanctuary, and God, therefore, cannot implement His covenant.

Yirmiyahu, then, did not mean that the covenantal relationship had lapsed, but that the conditions for its implementation had been violated. Because the relationship itself is never-ending, God will never cease to manipulate history in order to bring about the covenant's fulfillment. The Jewish people will be taught to reject their spurious attitudes towards life, to end their reliance on might and wealth. They will repent their ways and they will requite their sins. Ultimately the sanctuary will be made for God to dwell in, and the covenant will express itself.

Once again Rabbi Yehoshua has demonstrated that the Jewish exile is not a sign that the covenant has been broken; paradoxically, it indicates the opposite. For it shows that God does not reject His nation no matter how far they stray, that

5 Shemos 25:8.

He seeks to direct them to their ultimate destiny. Had the relationship of the covenant been abrogated, then upon ceasing to keep Torah the Jewish nation would have been destroyed, as thousands of other nations were destroyed before it. The fact that this did not happen proves that the covenant is viable, still the active force behind the development of Jewish history.

This, then, is the basis for Jewish hope. God has not forsaken His people, nor will He ever. When Exile has worked its desired effect upon the nation, they will surely be redeemed.

12.4 Reviving the Covenant

Why did Rabbi Yehoshua say that the afterbirth of the mule ensures that the covenant will be kept? If the covenant is still viable, then God will redeem the Jews whether or not they teach Torah to their children. What role does children's Torah study play in implementing the covenant?

A branch which has been cut off can regrow, but only if a bud remains. A fire can be rekindled if a small spark remains. The covenant can be re-invoked, but only if a residual devotion to Torah exists. The covenant needs a world to exist in, and only a world with the sound of Torah study in it can respond to God's call. A world without Torah study has no hope, for it is too far removed from anything spiritual for God to revive it. If the world were to remain one moment without the study of Torah, it would thereby become so completely incapable of destiny that God would return it to its primordial state of תהו ובהו (chaos). As Scripture says:

> *If not for my covenant [requiring the study of Torah] day and night, I would not have laid down the laws of heaven and earth.*[6]

The bare minimum which God requires to keep His world in existence is that there be young children studying Torah.

6 Yirmiyahu 33:25, according to Pesachim 68b.

The "afterbirth of the mule" prevents the return of the world to a state of chaos and makes it possible for the covenant still to be implemented when the redemption comes. As long as Torah is taught to Jewish children, there is hope for redemption.

12.5 THE STILLBORN FUTURE

If the children's devotion to spirituality is our promise of future redemption, then why does Mashiach not come when the children grow up? Generation after generation has passed childhood into manhood and grown old and died, and still he has not come. What sort of promise is this, that never comes true?

Rabbi Yehoshua thought of this question too, and answered it with his choice of the symbol of the afterbirth.

The Rabbis tell us that the Mashiach is called "the stillborn child,"[7] for again and again God tries to bring him forth, but never does the world reach such a state of development as will admit of his coming. Never has the world finished its "pregnancy"; always the coming of Mashiach miscarries and his mission is stillborn. The afterbirth slips out uselessly, with no child in it: the world is full of the uproar and turmoil that attend Mashiach's coming, but no redemption arrives.

The coming of Mashiach depends on one thing more than all: complete devotion to Torah. "Make your Torah your main business, and your work occasional," say the Rabbis.[8] For children this is so, but children grow up to have families and jobs, and Torah all too often is pushed off to the sidelines, forgotten in the rush for prestige and wealth.

The world cannot complete its development if its inhabitants do not. It is not surprising, then, that the world enters again and again on its "pregnancy" of Mashiach: each time that children begin to learn Torah, hope springs afresh. Nor

7 Sanhedrin 96b. The first of the Savvei DeVei Atuna riddles (omitted in this volume, as explained above in "About this Book," sub-heading "This English Rendition") deals with this idea at length.

8 Avos 1:15.

can it be surprising that the world "miscarries" again and again: each time that those children, now grown up, stifle their souls in the marketplace, hope dies again, and Mashiach with it. The bloody mess of Mashiach's placenta slips out, and no redemption comes.

As long as children learn Torah, the mule is no true mule: it is fertile and can conceive. But its pregnancy will never be finished, the long-awaited "child" will never be "born," until their youthful devotion to spirituality is carried all through their lives to its destined fruition.

13

The House in the Air

[The Elders demanded of Rabbi Yehoshua:] "Build us a house in the air." He pronounced a Name of God [by whose influence] he suspended himself between heaven and earth, and told them, "Send me up bricks and mortar from down there."

"But who could lift them all the way up there?" they asked.

"Then who could build a house between heaven and earth?"

(Bechoros 8b)

13.1 Journey Through Night

> There are three watches in the night. At the first watch, a donkey brays. At the second, the dogs bark. At the third, an infant sucks from its mother's breast and a woman converses with her husband.[1]

The world of physical existence is "compared to night,"[2] say the Sages. Just as night blocks the light of day, so does the temporal world block out the light of the Divine Presence. When the Sages spoke of three watches in the course of a night, they were, besides the plain meaning of their words, referring to the three stages of man's physical existence in the world, each lasting for about a third of a lifetime. Besides his body, man is composed of three elements called נפש, רוח ונשמה (*nefesh, ruach,* and *neshamah*). The *nefesh,* or life force, is the externally oriented part of man, the senses and

1 Berachos 3a.
2 Bava Metzia 83b.

drives which connect him with the world about him. The survival drives for food, sex, shelter, and the like, which sustain the human race, have their origin in the *nefesh.*

The *ruach,* or spirit, is the internally oriented part of man, which enables him to think and feel, and gives rise to his sense of self. It is the origin of all intellectual, emotional, and social activity.

The *neshamah,* or supernal soul,[3] is man's link with the trans-physical realms of the Creation, with the spiritual world and with God; it is the source of man's craving for a relationship with God. Everyone is cognizant of his *nefesh* and his *ruach,* but not everyone is cognizant in the same natural way of his *neshamah.* One's awareness of his *neshamah* depends upon how great is his sensitivity to spiritual matters; and this sensitivity is a reflection of how much one has sanctified his life by removing materialistic strivings from it.

Man's free choice can be used to direct his *ruach* and *nefesh* either towards the service of God or egotistically, towards supplying himself with gratification. In the first case his *ruach* and *nefesh* will serve to express the yearnings of his *neshamah.* In the latter case the *ruach* will be reduced to satisfying the demands of self-worship — power, possession, and prestige — and the *nefesh* will be directed to supplying pleasureful neural stimulations, such as food, sex, and warmth.

In the course of man's journey through the night of earth, each of these three elements of the soul becomes dominant for about one-third of his life. This change of dominance provides each third of man's life with a particular, unique character which entails its own set of temptations.

At the first watch, a donkey brays.

During the first third of life the *nefesh* is the predominant force, and man is preoccupied with his life-sustaining drives. This, then, is the period of life when man is most tempted to

3 A particular part of man's spirit, as distinct from the entire spirit which is often referred to as "soul."

misuse his *nefesh* powers and to live for the fulfillment of his physical appetites.

The donkey brays during this "third of the night," for it is the Scripture's symbol of earthy physicality. Describing men who devote their lives to such pursuits, Scripture says that "their flesh is a donkey's flesh."[4] During his youth, then, coping with the "donkey's" wordless demand is man's primary task.

At the second, the dogs bark.

In the second third of life the focus changes. As the urgency of physical appetite wanes, man concentrates on the needs of his inner self, so his main preoccupation is with matters of the *ruach.* The major temptation for abuse now is to devote himself to supplying his *ruach* with the emotional satisfaction of finding favor in others' eyes. One of his major occupations will therefore be enhancing his social position by obtaining wealth and fame. The lust for possession and control demanded by an unharnessed *ruach* is symbolized by the dog's bark, in which the keen ear of the Sages could hear *"Hav, hav!"* — "Give, give!"[5] In this term of life, when man is most likely to covet possessions and status, he too may end up barking "Give, give!"

At the third, an infant sucks from its mother's breast
and a woman converses with her husband.

As old age approaches it is common for man to realize the futility of making mere gratification the goal of his life. As the temptations to misuse the *nefesh* and *ruach* die down, man is free to choose more spiritual goals. And so in the final third of life an awareness of the *neshamah* in him begins to assert itself and he becomes more interested in spiritual matters.

4 Yechezkel 23:20.
5 Zohar III, 124a.

During this period of life, unless he consciously suppresses these stirrings man will find himself first of all turning more and more towards the nourishment of the Torah's wisdom: the spiritual infant, just stirring towards life, sucks from his mother's breast for the first time. Then, as he sucks nourishment into his famished *neshamah,* its powers awaken, and he is filled with the desire to cleave to God and to live by His word.[6] Man living a life of devotion to God's will is pictured by the Torah as a husband and wife living in loving harmony;[7] as the soul moves at last towards love for God, "a wife converses with her husband."

13.2 THE MIRACLE OF EXPRESSION

Man's external self (his body and the *nefesh* that animates it) has the ability to express perfectly the workings of his inner being (his *ruach*). His happiness is expressed by a smile, his sadness with tears, his love and awe for God by the performance of His commandments. This meshing of body and spirit is one of the inexplicable miracles of Creation. When we praise God as מפליא לעשות, "He who does wonders,"[8] it is in appreciation of His binding the physical with the spiritual and causing them to operate in unison.[9]

The partnership of body and soul is also man's greatest source of satisfaction, for nothing is more satisfying than having one's inner and outer being working in tandem. Man is a physical being, for whom reality means physical experience; the inner experiences of the *ruach* lack satisfaction until they are expressed by the powers of the *nefesh* and take on concrete physical existence. Love must be expressed by

6 As in the daily prayers: השיבנו אבינו לתורתך וקרבנו מלכנו לעבודתך — "Bring us back, Father, to Your Torah", first; and then, inevitably, "bring us close to Your service" (Vilna Gaon).

7 *E.g.* Hoshea 2, Mishlei 31.

8 End of the blessing, אשר יצר, "who has formed man with wisdom."

9 This is the interpretation of R. Moshe Isserles (*Rema)* in his gloss on *Shulchan Aruch, Orach Chaim* 6:1.

actions, or at least expressed into words, for it to be a satisfying emotion; ideas and plans are only truly satisfying when they are expressed into the physical world. This is why creative activity — the bringing forth of an intellectual concept into physical being — is such a joy: it is a way of combining *nefesh* and *ruach.*

The fact that only this partnership can create the full human experience is the reason why God, in directing man how to come closer to Him, gave him mitzvos to perform. The well-directed *ruach* recognizes that it must subordinate itself to its *neshamah* and serve God, but only the concrete activity of mitzvos brings His service into the realm of the *nefesh.* For example, it is not enough to believe in Creation; for one's belief to be meaningful, one must act it out by abstaining from labor on Shabbos. It is not enough to know that the Exodus occurred; one must give expression to this knowledge by holding a Seder service and eating *matzah* during Pesach. It is not enough to love one's neighbor; one must give that love reality by expressing it by acts of kindness. Closeness to God, if it gets no farther than the *neshamah* and *ruach,* has no meaning for man; it must become part of experiential existence, which alone he perceives as real.

Even the reward of the world-to-come is not complete until the whole man — soul and body — experiences it. Although there is reward awaiting man after death, the full reward, the direct and unalloyed experience of God's revelation, is not destined to come until after the Resurrection, when soul and reconstructed body are rejoined. Only then can the revelation be experienced in full reality, a reality that for man inevitably includes a physical setting.[10]

10 The "Feast of the Leviathan," which the Sages (Bava Basra 75a) tell us will be enjoyed by the righteous after the Resurrection, is a symbolic Aggadic description of one aspect of this concept.

13.3 A HOUSE FOR THE NEFESH

"Build us a house in the air."

Judaism teaches that man must use his free choice to shape his life, and that life, to be meaningful, must be lived in consonance with the yearnings of his *neshamah.* Man's *ruach,* then, must be directed towards the service of God rather than of himself, and his *nefesh* must be used to express the goals of his God-directed *ruach* in the real world by carrying out God's commandments. In other words, human life can achieve perfection if man will subordinate his entire organism, both his internal and his external being, to carrying out the will of God.

The Elders scoffed at this idea as impossible. It could never be successful, they claimed, for it flew in the face of human history, beginning, as explained below, with the first generation of mankind. The strongest drives of a human being stem from his *nefesh,* the most compelling element of his being. Man cannot live by ideas unless he feels that these ideas will cause him material advancement. No matter how noble an ideal may be, man will not embrace it if it threatens his physical well-being.

In short, argued the Elders, man can never subordinate his *nefesh* to his *ruach* when they are in conflict. The goals of inner man can only be realized if they are also the goals of outer man. How, then, can Judaism profess to do otherwise?

The Elders held the Torah's sublime partnership of body and soul to be unworkable, and so they denied its very existence. In their challenge to Rabbi Yehoshua they used a metaphor employed by the Torah itself: air representing man's *ruach* ("wind" in Hebrew), and a house representing the *nefesh*-based activities by which man fleshes out his earthly existence. Their objection was, how can the "house" of man's *nefesh*-oriented, bodily activities be "built in the air" of his *ruach* aspirations? "We challenge you," they said, "to build such a house in the air."

The Elders claimed that human history demonstrates the futility of the Jewish aspiration to Divine service. In fact, the overpowering nature of the *nefesh* when there is tension between it and the *ruach* is the underlying message of the Biblical account of Kayin and Hevel (Cain and Abel).

13.4 The Brothers' Clash

The strife between Kayin and Hevel was not an ordinary case of sibling rivalry; the strife between them stemmed from a clash between two prototypes of humanity which they exemplified, and therefore has significance for all succeeding generations.

> *. . . Hevel was a shepherd, and Kayin was a farmer. After some time Kayin brought some produce as an offering to God. Hevel, too, brought some of the firstborn of his flock and some of the fattest, and God paid attention to Hevel and his offering. But He did not pay attention to Kayin and his offering, and Kayin was greatly angered and downcast. . . .*
>
> *Kayin had words with his brother Hevel; and when they were in the fields, Kayin turned against his brother Hevel and killed him.*[11]

Kayin and Hevel, the first generation of mankind, are two prototypes of humanity — but of a humanity that has strayed from the path of meaningful activity for which it was created. Each in his way devoted himself to egotistic self-gratification instead of to the service of God.

Kayin's formula for success was to pervert his *nefesh* drives towards gratification; he made his life's goal working the land to insure that his belly would always be filled with food. Hevel, on the other hand, was drawn to the pleasures of a misused *ruach*: he decided to exploit the world for wealth, fame, and power.[12] He therefore chose shepherding as his career, recognizing that, far more than farming, it could be a

11 Bereishis 4:2-8.

12 The Vilna Gaon points out that the name הבל means the same thing as the "הבל" (futility) spoken of in the book of Koheles. The subject of that book is the utter futility of man's pursuit of wealth and prestige (*ruach*-oriented desires).

source of wealth, and would bring in its wake prestige and influence.[13]

The offerings brought by Kayin and Hevel, and the manner in which God related to them, reflect their chosen goals. Kayin brought the poorest of his crops, those which were barely edible,[14] but Hevel brought the very best of his flock: the most precious (the firstborn) and the choicest (the fattest). Kayin could not bring himself to part with what he could eat himself. Hevel, on the other hand, did not mind giving up the best of his possessions — not out of devotion to God, but, as the Sages teach, to gain prestige for himself.

Both offerings were inadequate in God's view: Kayin's was improper in content, Hevel's in intent. Therefore neither offering was acceptable; yet God "paid attention" (וישע) to Hevel's offering. What was preferable about it?

Hevel's acts were superficially correct, despite being motivated by improper intentions. Proper behavior stemming from impure motives has the potential to lead one to serve God with pure motives,[15] and so God "paid attention" to the potential that lay dormant in Hevel's service. Kayin, having refused even to go through the motions of service, unwilling to forgo cramming his belly so as to give honor to God, had no such hope. He refused to sacrifice anything of his desires to serve God, and so God "paid no attention" to his offering.

These are the prototypes of the two paths mankind was to take throughout the ages when it chose self-worship as its goal. Some men of this sort are *ruach*-oriented, seeking wealth, prestige, and power; others are *nefesh*-oriented and direct themselves towards physical gratification.

The story of Kayin and Hevel demonstrates that these two goals are incompatible. Working to acquire power and wealth requires the use of intelligence, whereas concentra-

13 *Cf.* the Sages' explanation of the name "sheep": "Why are they called עשתרות? Because they enrich (מעשרות) their owners" (Chullin 84b).

14 Rashi *ad loc.*, based on Bereishis Rabba 22:8.

15 Pesachim 50b: מתוך שלא לשמה בא לשמה.

tion on sensual gratification blocks the functioning of intelligence. This inherent contradiction makes it impossible to succeed in carrying out the goals of *ruach* where they are opposed to those of *nefesh;* for in the competition between the two, the immediate and concrete pleasure derived from sensory stimulation has a stronger attraction than the need to live by *ruach.* The *nefesh* experience is simply more compelling, and therefore more attractive, to man than the *ruach* experience. Slowly the drive for venality raises its head and takes charge, sabotaging the aims of *ruach*: Kayin slays Hevel.

The Midrash presents this conflict graphically:

> What did Kayin and Hevel argue about? They agreed to divide the world between them; Kayin took all the land and Hevel took all the movables. [But then] one [began to] say: "The land you are standing on is mine," and the other, "Your clothing is mine." One said, "Take it off!" and the other, "Fly!"[16]

Kayin, whose life centered around *nefesh,* claimed the earth as being naturally his.[17] To maintain permanence, Hevel's activities needed a foothold in the world of concrete reality, which required the services of Kayin's *nefesh.* A quarrel — which Hevel was bound to lose — was inevitable.

So it is within every man who has made self-worship his goal. *Ruach* can at best hold sway over his daily life for a while; when it comes to a definite clash of priorities — when Kayin and Hevel are alone in the fields — the *nefesh* drives win out: Kayin slays Hevel.

The same clash of goals between *nefesh* and *ruach* was destined to repeat itself over and over as the generations went by, always with tragic results. One of the most notable examples was that of the Dispersed Generation (דור הפלגה).

16 Bereishis Rabba 22:7, adduced by the Vilna Gaon, *loc. cit.*

17 Kayin's request that Hevel take off his clothing can be explained in accordance with the concept of clothing representing prestige, as explained in §16.3.

13.5 THE TOWER IN THE AIR

> *It happened that while they were travelling from the east they found a valley in the land of Shin'ar, and settled there. They said to one another, "Let us make bricks and bake them in the fire"; for brick served them instead of stone and clay served them for mortar. Then they said, "Let us build ourselves a city, and a tower that reaches to the sky; we will make a name for ourselves, and not become scattered throughout the world."*[18]

During the period of the Dispersed Generation most of mankind had long forgotten God and the purpose for which He had created them, and lived instead for selfish aims. The particular goal of this era was "to make a name for themselves";[19] again, the inevitable tropism of a perverted *ruach* towards prestige, power, and control. If they incorporated spiritual ideals — such as liberty, democracy, and justice — into their declared national aims, this was not because the ideals particularly stirred them. Just as they refused to worship God, they were unable to revere any ideal except that of enhancing their own glory. Any embrace of spiritual ideals was ultimately for the purpose of enhancing their prestige in the eyes of the world by giving themselves a reputation as a noble people. As the Sages put it, the epitome of this generation was those who would "build synagogues and houses of study, and give charity, but not for the sake of Heaven; rather for the sake of their reputation."[20]

The leaders of the Dispersed Generation wanted their citizenry to assist them in the realization of their goals (amassing power, possession, and glory). But if the people's major interests were eating and drinking, then they would be both unwilling and unable to lend their aid. The government therefore understood that if they wanted to succeed, they would have to wean the populace away from their physical

18 Bereishis 11:2-4.

19 Bereishis 11:4.

20 Zohar I, 25b.

drives: citizens would have to be prepared to sacrifice their personal comfort for the advancement of the goals of the state. The awesome "tower that reaches to the sky" was meant to strike fear into any who would oppose their regime and so to daunt the people that they would be willing to make the personal sacrifices necessary to support it.

But the Babylonians were unsuccessful in harnessing the drives of the *nefesh* to support their perverted goals. As the Scriptures tell us:

> *But God came down to see the city and the tower that mankind had built. God said, "They have but one people and one language all of them, and this is how they have begun; shall nothing they plan to do seem impossible to them now? Let us descend there and confuse their tongue, so that one will not understand the other's speech." So God scattered them from there throughout the world, and they ceased building the city. That is why it was called Babylon (*בבל*); for there God confused (*בלל*) the language of all the world, and from there God scattered them throughout the world.*[21]

Had their plans been realized, the hope of mankind to reach its true goal would have been doomed. If man had been successful in creating a society based on the submission of the nefesh to a *ruach* geared to self-worship, he would have remained irredeemably egotistical, forever unable to recognize the true goals of his life. Therefore God in His mercy thwarted their plans and prevented them from building the tower.

The motives which spurred on the leaders of the Dispersed Generation so relentlessly are the motives which spur on any individual who decides to follow the call of his perverted *ruach*. But all attempts to give that *ruach* a real-life existence in the activities of the *nefesh* are equally doomed to failure. This was explained to Zecharyah the Prophet in one of his visions.

21 Bereishis 11:5-9.

13.6 ZECHARYAH'S VISION

> *I looked up, and saw two women. . . with wind (ruach) under their wings, for they had wings like the wings of a stork; and they carried the bushel between earth and heaven. I said to the angel who spoke with me, "Where are they taking the bushel?" And he answered, "To build themselves a house in the land of Shin'ar."*[22]
>
> Said Rabbi Yochanan: These [two women] are flattery and vainglory, which descended to Babylon. . . .
>
> Scripture says, "to build" [not "they have built"].[23] They attempted to build, but were not successful.[24]

In this vision, the two women represent two of the major temptations of the inwardly oriented man, *ruach*, when he is selfishly directed: the desire for flattery and vainglory. The *ruach*-wind under their wings — their motive power — symbolizes the *ruach*-spirit of inner man which gives rise to these temptations. The wings of the women seem like those of a stork — חסידה in Hebrew, a homonym of the word for "pious."[25] This is to teach us that these temptations generally pretend to pious intentions, which makes them that much more difficult to identify and control.[26] The two temptations are represented as women, in accordance with the image used by King Solomon of the *yetzer hara* as a licentious and tempting woman.[27] Like a sinful woman, these temptations promise unlimited gratification if only one will succumb to them.

Zecharyah's prophecy pictures these temptations carrying a bushel basket with which "to build themselves a house in the land of Shin'ar." The women were engaged in the same sort of activity engaged in by the Dispersed Generation

22 Zecharyah 5:9-11.
23 Kiddushin 49b.
24 Rashi *ad loc.*
25 In its feminine form.
26 See §2.1, concerning the "tip of white flame," for a fuller explanation of this concept.
27 *E.g.* Mishlei 2:16.

when they built their vainglorious tower in Shin'ar — another name for Babylonia.

As explained above, the aim of the Dispersed Generation was to create a real-world support for their egotism. In this vision, too, flattery and vainglory still attempted to find a place for themselves in the same land of Shin'ar. They drove men to try to harness the drives of the *nefesh*, and make it "build a house" for the values of the perverted *ruach* in the real world. The bushel which the women carried was held between "earth and heaven," in the domain of the *ruach* which, too, exists between the heavenly *neshamah* and the earthly *nefesh*.

But

> Scripture says, 'to build' [not 'they have built']. They attempted to build [a house], but were not successful.

All attempted societies based on this principle are doomed to failure. And why? Because they are like a house built in the middle of the air, which must inevitably fall.

For the *nefesh* will not of its own accord be harnessed to serve *ruach*. It can be temporarily cajoled into giving up its satisfaction for that of the *ruach*,[28] but inevitably, as the story of Kayin and Hevel teaches, it insists on fulfilling its own appetites rather than working towards man's inner demands.

13.7 AT HOME IN THE AIR

He pronounced a Name of God [by whose influence] he suspended himself between heaven and earth. . .

History and prophecy seem to be on the Elders' side in their challenge of the Jewish goal of creating a partnership between *ruach* and *nefesh*. How, indeed, can a house be built

28 Or coerced, as in the case of the Dispersed Generation; but God will not permit even coercion to work, as their story shows.

in the air? But Rabbi Yehoshua's answer was ready.

If *nefesh* has never been subordinated to the desires of the *ruach,* that was because man's goals were not the correct ones. The culture of the misguided *ruach* — the culture of self-worship — has a fallacy built into it. The goals set by the *ruach* can be realized physically only if the *nefesh* is controlled, prepared to assist in expressing it into real life. However, the *nefesh* can be kept under control only if man has a valid reason and a genuine desire to do so. Herein lies perverted *ruach's* self-contradiction. If the goal is self-worship, what reason is there for self-control? Why should the *nefesh* serve the *ruach?* The irrefutable logic of this question leads life in the end to become a free-for-all among all the parts of man's being, where each seeks its own gratification. Under these conditions, the drives of the *nefesh* will of necessity triumph, as surely as Kayin triumphed over Hevel. When this happens life degenerates into chaos, for once the goals of the *ruach* are not maintained, *nefesh* causes man to follow the instincts of his body aimlessly. In short, societies which set as their goal the acquiring of wealth, fame, and glory are their own assassins; their envisaged life inevitably degenerates into an unproductive life of sensual gratification.

There is only one solution to this dilemma: the *nefesh* will co-operate with the *ruach* only if man ceases to make selfish gratification the goal of his life. This, in turn, can only be accomplished by encouraging the desire to serve God. Only belief in a Being *outside* the self, who is more worthy of man's worship than his own self, can harness the *nefesh* to the needs of the *ruach.*

This, then, is the meaning of Rabbi Yehoshua's lesson: only by the influence of the "Name of God" does it become possible to "hang between heaven and earth" (in the domain of the *ruach*) and to "build a house in the air." Only when life is lived for the sake of Heaven will the *nefesh* willingly subordinate itself to advancing the aims of inner man; only then does it become possible to use one's body successfully as an expression of one's inner self.

This is how Jewish culture is successful in "building a house" for the internally oriented part of man. Torah law is a design for physical life which perfectly mirrors man's inner self. Every experience of intellect and emotion finds its expression in the corresponding mitzvah, and lasting satisfaction is achieved. This is because for the Torah Jew, the inner man is entirely directed towards the Name of God.

13.8 The Inept Builders

[He] told them, "Send me up bricks and mortar from down there."

Bricks and mortar represent the human body: bricks, that make the frame of a building, are its "bones," while mortar, that binds the building together, is its "flesh." If bones and flesh, and the life-sustaining forces that move them, can be directed to serve the *ruach,* then a house can be built for it. Rabbi Yehoshua challenged the Elders: Can you do this? Can you "lift bricks and mortar up in the air"?

They could not, because their view of human life and the use of the soul did not "mention the Name of God"; they had never thought of serving God, and so had no means of bringing the various powers of their soul into harmony. They could not "lift up their bricks and mortar."

"But who could lift them all the way up there?" they asked.
"Then who could build a house between heaven and earth?"

Without the "influence of the Name of God," the "bricks and mortar" — the physically real activities of the *nefesh* — cannot be raised above the man's selfish interest and the "house in the air" can never be built.

14
The Midpoint of the World

[The Elders] asked [Rabbi Yehoshua]: "Where is the midpoint of the world?"

He raised his finger and said, "Here!"

"Prove it!"

He said, "Bring ropes and measure." *(Bechoros 8b)*

14.1 THE END OF DAYS

A person may hold an intellectual belief that there is One God, but a full recognition of God's Oneness means much more than that. It means an unequivocal recognition that there is no other object of human worship, no other goal towards which life should be devoted except that of the knowledge of God and the performance of His will. It was to enable man to reach this full recognition that the world was created. Viewed from this perspective, a belief that materialism and egotism are the goals of life constitute a denial of the oneness of God. Consequently, before man can achieve a true recognition of the One God he must first banish these evils from his life, for as long as alternative gods exist man has not reached his destiny.

The era when mankind will reach this recognition is called by the prophets the "End of Days." As they describe it, that will be a time when truth will be universally acknowledged; when wars and suffering will end; when the world will be full of wisdom "as water covers the sea";[1] and when man will

1 Yeshayahu 11:9.

rise to ever higher levels of spirituality. As man grows, so God will increasingly reveal Himself to him until he achieves his ultimate reward: enjoying the unrefracted experience of knowing God.

14.2 THE THREE ERAS

> The world will last six thousand years [consisting of] two thousand years of Chaos, two thousand years of Torah and two thousand years of Mashiach. Because of our many sins, the years which have gone by, have gone by.[2]

When God created the world, the Sages teach us, He allotted six thousand years for human history. The era of mankind's recognition[3] of God's oneness was to begin after four thousand years had gone by from the Creation. But this would be on condition that they merited the revelation. Unfortunately, when the time arrived for Mashiach their merit did not suffice, and instead of Mashiach coming, say the Sages, "the years that have gone by, have gone by" — in exile from their land, in the long Diaspora.

Of the first four thousand years of human history, the first two thousand were wasted as far as concerns advancing man toward his goal. Shortly after Adam's expulsion from the Garden of Eden, humanity began to believe in uncaring and purposeless gods as the sustaining forces of the universe. Man lost his belief that life might have an ultimate purpose or that he was obligated to any particular pattern of behavior. He saw himself as a helpless bystander in a world which was an arena for competing and often capricious gods. Without any source of instruction as to his true goals (or as to whether there were any goals at all), there was little hope that man could ever extricate himself from his blind wanderings. Because these were years without direction and without

2 Sanhedrin 97a-b.

3 Later, when mankind turned its back on God, the Jewish people were given the task of bringing man to his ultimate goal.

purpose, they are called the Era of Chaos (תהו).

In the year 2000 from the Creation, Avraham, when he was 52 years old,[4] began the great work of his life: bringing to mankind the truth that there is only one God. This event was not merely a milestone in a personal life; it was a turning point in human history, for it meant the end of human chaos. According to Avraham's revolutionary teachings, one God not only created the world but also designed how man should live in it. Reflecting the unity of the Being who created it, life had one purpose: it was meant for "keeping the way of God."[5] With these concepts Avraham gave man the means by which he could begin moving towards his destiny. The Era of Chaos had ended; the new Era of Torah had dawned.

Avraham's children kept to his heritage; they lived by it and taught it to their children and to others until, six generations later, Avraham's descendants were given the Torah at Sinai. The Torah, God's divine plan for human life, taught them how to live as a nation devoted to the service of God, and enabled them to overcome the evil which could hinder man's progress towards his appointed future.

The two-thousand-year era begun by Avraham and climaxed by the Revelation at Sinai ended with the redaction of the Mishna,[6] the Oral Law in which the details of living in accordance with the Torah are spelled out. It was supremely an Era of Torah, and it should have led to man's recognition of one God and to the Era of the Mashiach. But it did not.

Although outwardly the Jewish people fulfilled the Torah's precepts and diligently studied its wisdom, inwardly they failed to carry out its mission. Instead of recognizing God's will they trusted more and more in their own power. Instead of relying on God's Providence, they came to believe that

4 Avodah Zarah 9a.

5 Bereishis 18:19.

6 See Rashi *loc. cit.*, who states that the two thousand years ended 172 years after the Destruction of the Temple and that the date is an approximation. However, Maharsha explains that the date refers to the destruction of the great seats of Jewish learning which taught the Oral law.

they alone were the masters of their fates. A collective selfishness, concomitant with a denial of the sovereignty of God, pervaded the Jewish people. The evil in them prevented the Era of Mashiach from beginning at its appointed time; as the Sages put it, "because of our many sins, the years that have gone by, have gone by." Instead of the Kingdom of the House of David being re-established, the enslavement of the Jews by the Romans became more severe, the Torah centers were wiped out, and the Jews were scattered to the four corners of the earth. The Era of Torah ended but Mashiach had not arrived.

14.3 A Lost Paradise?

"Where is the midpoint of the world?"

"The present time," said the Elders to Rabbi Yehoshua, "is the end of the two millennia of the Era of Torah. Your tradition claims that history will consist of two millennia each of chaos, Torah, and Mashiach. Discounting the two thousand wasted years of the Era of Chaos, the present should be the midpoint between the two productive eras of the world, the Eras of Torah and of Mashiach. This should be the time when we witness the arrival of Mashiach. But obviously he has not come, for you Jews have certainly not been redeemed. We have crushed you and turned you into a nation of ruin, disaster, and despair. The 'midpoint of the world' has manifestly passed by and the Era of Mashiach has not begun. Why, then, do you persist in hoping for his arrival? Why should he come in the future if he did not come at his appointed hour? Is it not clear that the time for his arrival has passed you by forever?"

14.4 The Two Roads to Mashiach

The Elders, however, were unaware of another element of the Jewish tradition concerning Mashiach. For of course the world was created so that man might recognize his Creator — but what if man decides not to carry out his mission? Will God permit His goals for the world to remain unrealized? Not at all. God will not forsake His world no matter how poorly man behaves. The world will inevitably reach its appointed goal: evil will be overcome and mankind will recognize God. Only under these changed circumstances the revelation will arrive not by man's willing choice but by a different path: a choice forced by God's manipulation of history.

God will permit the evils of atheism and selfishness to flourish and He will permit man to follow them. But as the evil in mankind grows, so will its suffering — even to the point of the increased evil threatening the very existence of the world. And then God will force man into the recognition that his choice of selfishness over acceptance of God's dominion was a disastrous one. He will demonstrate to man clearly and inescapably that the source of his ills was his denial of God, and with this awareness his false gods will be smashed forever. Man will then realize that the recognition of God's dominion is his only viable path.

14.5 The Government of Heresy

> The heir of David [Mashiach] will not come until all government has turned into a denial of God [מינות].[7]

When God "takes affairs into his own hands" and begins to manipulate history to expose evil for its true worth, thus forcing man to return to Him, one ideology more than any other will be permitted to take a central position in the world. This is an ideology antithetical to the very purpose of creation: that which denies the existence of God.

When a belief spreads far and wide and comes to be held by most of mankind, and only then is exposed in its falsehood, it is thereby utterly discredited. Therefore, this ide-

7 Sanhedrin 97a.

ology will flourish and be accepted by most of mankind, because human destiny depends on its being totally discredited. Once this "false god" is smashed, then man's way to the recognition of God will be clear. "[Mashiach] will not come until all government has turned into a denial of God," for as long as this ideology holds sway man will not accept God's dominion; but when it has been destroyed few other obstacles will stand in the way of Mashiach.

The Talmud succinctly sets forth this idea in a passage discussed in the next section.

14.6 The Serpent at the Middle

> *All that moves on its belly. . . you shall not eat, for they are loathsome.*[8]
> The middlemost letter of the Torah is the letter "ו" of the word "גחון" (belly).[9]

Just as the center of a circle is the point about which the entire circle revolves, so this particular prohibition was placed in the center of the Torah to teach us that it contains the single idea around which the entire Torah revolves. But is the central concept of the Torah the prohibition against eating snakes? Yes, if we understand the Torah on another level of meaning, that the reptile referred to is the Serpent of the Garden of Eden. That snake, the Sages teach us, convinced man to transgress God's will by denying God's authority over His creatures.[10] In its plain meaning this verse is a prohibition against partaking of the flesh of a reptile. But the "ו" of "גחון" was placed in the center of the Torah to suggest another level of meaning, namely, that the essence of the entire Torah is to have man reject the Serpent's enticements to deny God's sovereignty. On one level the verse teaches us that we may not receive physical nourishment from the flesh

8 Vayikra 11:42.
9 Kiddushin 30a.
10 Pirkey de-R. Eliezer Chap. 13.

of a snake; on another level it teaches that we may not receive spiritual nourishment from the ideas of the Serpent. Both physically and ideologically, then, this verse constitutes the central "point" of the Torah.[11]

14.7 "HERE!"

When the Elders asked, "Where is the midpoint of the world?" Rabbi Yehoshua raised his finger and said "Here!" He was saying that although the Jews had not merited Mashiach's coming by their deeds, nevertheless the Era of Mashiach had indeed arrived at its appointed time. At "the midpoint of the world" God began turning the wheels of history to insure the ultimate arrival of the scion of David.

"You ask," Rabbi Yehoshua was saying, "where is the Era of Mashiach? Your success is the evidence that we have entered this Era. You are a fulfillment of the prophecy that Mashiach can only arrive when the ruling kingdom is completely heretical. No kingdom before yours has been so devoid of spiritual values, so dedicated to materialism. You have been permitted to flourish so that you and the successors to your atheistic culture — who desire little more than naked might and power — may show mankind what havoc you can wreak upon it. Your evil will spread throughout the entire world. You will be so successful that your crass culture will pervade every corner of the earth. But your evil will flourish only to make man appreciate the light of Truth when it is revealed, like light which is only truly appreciated when it follows darkness. When your evil has conquered the entire world, God will reveal Himself to mankind[12] and mankind will realize that there is none besides Him. The world will understand that when you denied man his spirituality, you denied him his humanity; you turned him into a biped beast who left war and pillage, trepidation

11 The explanation as to why the letter "ו," and none other, is the center of the Torah is beyond the scope of this book.

12 Malachi (3:1) says that God will reveal Himself "suddenly in His palace."

and social breakdown in his wake. Mankind will realize that the only way to convert himself back into a true human, a God-like being filled with wisdom, love, kindness, and an exalted spirit, is by the acceptance of God's dominion. And when God demonstrates all this and man recognizes it, Mashiach will finally come."

This process, said Rabbi Yehoshua, was set into motion with the advent of the last third of human history: the Era of Mashiach may not be apparent, but it is "here."

14.8 ZECHARYAH'S VISION

This entire idea is contained in a single passage by the Prophet Zecharyah:

> *In all the earth, says God, two thirds will be destroyed and perish, and the last third will remain. I will put that third in the fire; I will refine them as silver is refined, I will test them as gold is tested. [Then] they will call on My Name and I will answer; I will say, This is My people, and they will say, God my Lord.*[13]

In the final third of human history, God will cause the Jews to learn at last the lesson they were created to learn, so that mankind may reach its goal. They still retain the option to turn to God of their own volition. But if they refuse to learn any other way, the choice will be forced upon them: the lesson will be forged in the fire of suffering. Devotion to materialistic goals will bring tragedy after tragedy, disaster after disaster, until at the end the truth emerges: that mankind can only be successful if it follows God's ways.

What did the Prophet mean when he spoke of two-thirds perishing and one-third being saved? Hidden in this seemingly enigmatic passage is the concept that Rabbi Yehoshua will use to complete his refutation of the Elders.

13 Zecharyah 13:8-9.

14.9 The Rope That Measures Time

"Prove it," they said.
He said, "Bring ropes and measure."

In the Book of Shemuel we are told how King David avenged the cruelty of Moab. Before he put them to death, he laid out his Moabite captives alongside ropes. Those alongside two thirds of the ropes were put to death; those alongside the last third were permitted to live.[14]

King David's test seems quite strange; but in fact he was demonstrating that his judgment of the Moabites was consonant with God's judgment of the world.

The ultimate aim of God's judgment is not cruelty but bringing man to recognize Him and thereby gain eternal life. The recognition of God, then, is the essence of human life and its consummation. During the first two-thirds of world history God waited for men to exercise free choice, to abolish evil from their lives and reach the essence. When mankind as a whole failed, that essence was denied it and the Jewish people took on the task. When they too failed, He withheld His revelation from them; He destroyed their land and sent them into exile. But in the last third — after four thousand years from the Creation — He manipulates history so as to give quintessential life even to those who do not deserve it. Even if the Jews do not choose to seek their God and recognize his rulership, he will nevertheless take them by the hand and lead them to this recognition. Worthy or not, they must be redeemed, or else the ultimate aim of creation would never be realized.

The ropes of King David are the measure of human history. The two-thirds of world history which did not choose to recognize God's dominion refused to choose life. But the last third will be directed towards eternal life by a Providence

14 Shemuel II, 8:2. The crime which engendered this punishment is beyond the purview of this work. See Rashi *ad loc.*

which will lead the Jews step by step to the recognition of their God.

What is the basis of your assertion, asked the Elders, that "here," in the last third of human history, God's mercy is at work and we are in the Era of Mashiach? Answered Rabbi Yehoshua: Remember the ropes of King David and you will learn the ways by which God directs His world. They teach us that God will never abandon His world, that ultimately the good for which God created it will be realized.

15
The Well in the Fields

[The Elders of Athens said to Rabbi Yehoshua ben Chananyah:] "We have a well out in the fields. Bring it into the city."

He took bran and threw it before them, saying, "Make me a rope of this bran and I will bring it in."

They asked, "Who can make a rope of bran?"

"Then who can bring a well from the fields to the city?"

(Bechoros 8b)

15.1 WATER FOR THE UNIVERSE

"We have a well. . ."

There is a life-sustaining substance hidden deep beneath the earth which, although it lies beyond the realm of human perception, man cannot live without. It is called water.

A well is the connection between this hidden treasure of water and man. That which was heretofore concealed, unknowable, is revealed and placed within man's reach in unsuspected abundance.

God is the source of life for the entire universe. He, too, exists beyond man's perception; yet all the same He wants man to have contact with Him. For this purpose He prepared various means by which man can experience a relationship with Him — "wells" which channel the precious, life-giving, revelation of Divinity into the human soul. There are "wells" in time called Shabbos and holy days; a "well" for the intellect called Torah; and a "well" in a man-made structure called בית המקדש, the Holy Temple.

15.2 Adam and Earth

"... out in the fields."

The word for "man" is אדם, which is derived from אדמה, "earth."[1] In the Torah there are no verbal coincidences: the reason for this name is that man is like the earth of which he was formed.

When a seed is planted in it, the earth has the unique power to provide the environment through which the seed's hidden potential for life is expressed in the actuality of fruit.

It is the same with man. He is born with an innate yearning to serve God, a yearning which is the seed of his spiritual life. Man — like earth — has the capacity to express this potential in the actuality of a life full of spiritual activity. In other words, man, אדם, is meant to be God's garden, His אדמה, and bring forth a unique fruit. The "fruit" of his labors is a life of unselfish devotion to the service of God.

Not all earth has the capacity to yield fruit. Only earth which is cultivated retains this power, whereas a fallow field soon loses most of its ability to create produce. Not much can grow in a neglected field, and what little does, unprotected as it is from the ravages of animals and the elements, brings negligible benefit to man. Once again, it is the same with man: a life which does not express man's innate spirituality, because it is directed self-servingly instead of towards the service of God, is compared to a fallow field: unworked, unfenced, and unproductive.[2]

When Adam sinned, he exposed himself to selfish impulses and materialistic desires. These made it much more difficult for him to express his innate spirituality with his life. His אדמה — his potential to engender spiritual living — changed from its natural state of a tilled and tended garden to a wild, fallow field.

When אדם was banished from Eden, the task of human-

1 Bereishis 3:19.

2 Mishlei 24:30-31.

ity throughout the ages became to restore itself to its original "fertility." Most of mankind elected to neglect this task, but eventually certain individuals appeared who took up the challenge. They struggled to remove the wild elements which had entered man's nature and which had blocked his capacity for a life of Godliness.

These were the Fathers of the Jewish people, Avraham, Yitzhak and Yaakov. They were not able to complete the job themselves, but by purifying themselves to the best of their ability from the taint of Adam's sin, they invested their descendants with a special capability. This is the ability of the Jewish people to return man ultimately — at the End of Days — to the state of a "cultivated garden" which was meant to be his. This is why, when Yaakov entered his blind father's Yitzhak's presence, the latter said, "See, my son's smell is like the smell of a field that God has blessed":[3] for in token of his mission to future ages the fragrance of the Garden of Eden entered with him.[4] The rest of mankind, on the other hand, chose to succumb to the selfish, Godless drives which had become humanity's lot and to remain a fallow field. Thus Eisav, the sworn antagonist of his brother, Yaakov, and the archetype of earthiness and self-worship, is called in the Torah איש שדה, "a man of the [wild, fallow] fields."[5] As far as man's ultimate mission in the world is concerned, Eisav's life and that of his descendants is unproductive, useless.

15.3 THE CITY AND THE WELL

"We have a well out in the fields. Bring it into the city."

The well to which the Elders were referring is the most important well of all, the בית המקדש, the place on earth where

3 Bereishis 27:27.

4 Rashi *ad loc.*

5 Bereishis 25:27, which the Targum Onkelos renders as "a hunter, a man who goes out to the fields," where "fields" is used in the sense of the uncultivated wilds where hunting is practiced.

Jews had their closest contact with the Divine Presence. The field is the wild earth of Eisav, "the man of the fields." The city is Jerusalem.

The Elders' argument to Rabbi Yehoshua ran thus: "You say that you have the means (the well) with which to connect yourselves to God. Furthermore, you claim that all of mankind will some day avail themselves of it. But when we conquered you, we stripped you of everything: wealth, land, freedom — and your claim to spiritual greatness. We have destroyed your Holy Temple where you experienced the Divine Presence; we have obliterated Zion from which your Torah went forth; we have razed Jerusalem where the word of God was taught. You claim that our fields are the symbol of man's failure, but clearly you are the failure and not we.

"When we burned your Temple we captured your 'well'; you will never drink from it again, much less spread its water through the world. It will never again return to the city of Jerusalem where your nation gathered to experience closeness to God, 'to be seen by God the Lord of Israel.'[6] Give up your vain hopes of clinging to God, for spirituality is a chimera; material pleasure is the only truth. The well will never be brought into the city, for the man of the fallow fields has triumphed."

15.4 The Bread of Man

God made the universe to serve the needs of His purpose, to bring man close to Himself. If man uses the world rightly, he draws nearer to his goal of closeness. But there is more than that: the world itself draws nearer to its goal of perfection, the banishment of evil and the reign of holiness. And what if man rebels and uses the world for the gratification of his material desires? Then the world itself becomes debased and draws back from its goal, as the Sages say:

6 Devarim 16:16.

> When God made Adam, He took him around to every tree in the Garden of Eden and said to him, "Observe how fine, how lovely My works are! And I made them all for you. Take care not to spoil My world and destroy it."[7]

The physical world, then, was made in such a way that at all times it would reflect the spiritual status of mankind, and of the Jewish people in particular, the only nation actively striving to perfect the world.

We have said that when Adam sinned he was transformed from a cultivated field to a fallow one that lacked the ability to give forth man's intended produce. Man's external world, which was made to reflect his spiritual state, underwent a similar change. The food that the earth brought forth for man became corrupted in a way that parallelled the corruption which had taken place in man himself. Before he sinned, "God the Lord commanded the man, saying, 'From all the trees of the Garden you may eat.'"[8] As Adam's soul-produce was pure, so was the earth's; the earth gave forth edible produce without effort on the part of man, and in a form that was ready to eat without further preparation. But after he had sinned,

> *By the sweat of your brow shall you eat bread;*[9]

and

> *. . . the earth is cursed because of you; by hard labor shall you eat its [produce]; thorns and thistles it will put forth for you.*[10]

This change reflected Adam's spiritual status. Because he had tainted and sullied himself with evil, his produce — the activity which his life brought forth — did not properly express his innate desire to serve God. And so the earth debased and admixed its produce with undesirable growths in the same way

7 Koheles Rabba 7; *cf.* R. Moshe Chaim Luzzatto, *Mesillas Yesharim*, Chap. 1.

8 Bereishis 2:16.

9 *Ibid.*, 3:19.

10 *Ibid.*, vv. 17-18.

that man had done. Whereas at first Adam had only to pluck fruit from a tree, now he must eat "by the sweat of his brow." First man must reap the wheat; then he must thresh it, winnow it, grind it into flour; and then sift the flour to remove the bran. All this work is to remove the various undesirable parts of the wheat, until clean flour is left with which to make bread.

What must be done with the earth's harvest must be done with man's spiritual produce too. His longing for his Creator cannot be fitly expressed until he rids himself of the various drives (collectively known as the *yetzer hara)* which debase his "fruit." Divine service today must be threshed, winnowed, ground, and sifted for it to be acceptably clean from its contamination. The ability to do so, and thereby regain the state of a "fruitful garden," is the heritage of the Fathers to the Jewish people.

It need hardly be said that to the Elders, the idea of sifting out materialism and egotism from the human personality was anathema. Their furious denial of this part of Jewish destiny forms the basis of their exchange with Rabbi Yehoshua.

15.5 CHAFF, STRAW, AND BRAN

He took bran and threw it before them. . .

When the Elders challenged Rabbi Yehoshua to rebuild the Holy Temple, his answer to their challenge revolved around the fact of man's inner corruption, which is reflected in the corresponding corruption of wheat.

When Adam sinned, the first affliction that came upon him was confusion: his ability to recognize truth became impaired.[11] Whereas before God's presence in His world had been clear to Adam, from the moment of his sin his mental vision was clouded. It became possible for man to deny that there is a Creator.

Then the effects of sin spread further, and produced an

11 The Vilna Gaon in his commentary *Aderes Eliyahu* on Bereishis (2:16) explains that the name עץ הדעת, although commonly understood as "Tree of Knowledge," actually means "Tree of Confusion."

affliction in the relationship between man and his body. Now the soul was no longer the undisputed ruler: the aspect of animal nature took precedence. The body's drives for physical survival and sensual gratification began to exert an overpowering pull.

The final stage was that sin produced a personality affliction. Before the sin Adam's natural orientation centered on others: towards serving God or doing kindness to fellow creatures. Now his center shifted towards himself: only activities which enhanced his sense of self gave him satisfaction. His life had become self-centered, directed towards acquiring power, possessions, and social standing.

Nature, that reflects man's spiritual status, took on impurities that corresponded to Adam's defilement. More than any other growth, wheat, man's principal source of food, reflected precisely the three stages of his downfall. Whereas before it had grown in a manner that was ready to eat, now it was intermixed with three excrescences: chaff, the thin covering over the kernels of grain; straw, the fine bits of stalk which are cut with the heads of grain; and, part of the kernel itself, the fast-clinging coat of bran.

As man's eyes became blinded to the truth, chaff grew up over the kernels of wheat, binding itself tightly over the kernel to shut out the light of day. Just as man had shut his eyes to the light of God's Presence, so his wheat was cut off from the sun's light.

As he became inseparably attached to physicality, the stalk upon which wheat grew attached itself firmly to the kernel, thus becoming straw. Just as man had bound himself to his body, so his wheat became bound to its earthy origin.

As his personality became warped, bran insinuated itself into the wheat kernel and became a part of it. Just as man had allowed selfishness to become a part of himself, so bran became an inseparable part of his wheat, irremovable even by threshing and winnowing.[12]

Removing these three impurities thus corresponds to the

12 Although a minute amount of bran is essential for health, the amount of bran that presently is found in wheat is excessive and makes the wheat unacceptable as food until it is sifted.

three steps of man's reconstruction into אדם, the garden that produces unadulterated, pure fruit, the human who fulfills his goal of recognizing his Creator.

15.6 The Fathers' Wheat

As we have seen, the Fathers of the Jewish people bequeathed their descendants the capacity to restore the "earth" in man to its "cultivated" state and enable mankind once again to "bear fruit." By rejecting the evil tendencies of their *yetzer hara* and removing all such impurities from their mentality, they created an ongoing potential in all their descendants for the removal of the undesirable elements in man's "produce." Each individual Jew can make what use he chooses of his potential, whether small or great; he can choose if he wishes to neglect it entirely in his own life. But the Fathers insured that the Jewish people as a whole will never renounce its task. Throughout the ages it continues slowly cleansing its wheat of chaff, straw, and bran, until the job is finished and the world is ready for the revelation of its God and King. Thus it was the Fathers who made it possible for man to rectify the evil with which Adam's sin had infected the world, and who guaranteed that their descendants would carry on the work until that evil was completely overcome.[13]

When Avraham recognized that one God brought the world into existence, he overcame within himself the first evil, man's capacity to deny the reality of a Creator. He attempted to make this victory universal by teaching his truth to mankind, and although most men chose to ignore the message, he left it as a heritage to his children, whom nothing can cause to lose sight of this truth. Avraham winnowed the wheat of mankind and removed its chaff.

His son Yitzhak built on his father's victory and went on to overcome the second evil. He cleansed his mentality of

13 For a fuller discussion of this see Chapter 19.

enslavement to physicality: his message to mankind was that the body is made for man to serve God with, and that man was not made to serve his body. Yitzhak was the first child in history to have this lesson imprinted in his flesh through circumcision.[14] Later he offered his body willingly as a sacrifice to God.[15] Yitzhak's achievements became imbedded in the Jewish consciousness; as a result, throughout the ages no doctrine of sensual pleasure-fulfillment has ever succeeded in seducing the Jews from their Divine service. Yitzhak threshed man's wheat and detached it from its straw.

Yaakov Avinu, with two generations of holiness behind him, overcame the final and greatest evil: man's belief in himself as the pinnacle of Creation. His life was dedicated to uprooting this self-centered belief and its corollaries, man's insistence on relying on his own power, his unwillingness to efface his will before God's, and his refusal to trust God's providence in daily life. Yaakov's life was one of exile and of suffering. He had to flee Eisav's wrath after gaining his father's blessings; he had to suffer Lavan's exploitation for twenty years as he was building his family; he was tortured for fourteen years by what he thought was his favorite son Yosef's death.[16] Despite all this his trust in Divine Providence was not in the least diminished; obedience to the will of God — not his own — remained the sole purpose in his life. Yaakov bequeathed his descendants the ability to efface their will before God's. After a lifetime of struggles, Yaakov insured that the Jewish people would some day proclaim God's glory by their selfless devotion to Him.

The Jewish people have had varying success in implementing the potential bequeathed them by Yaakov; the struggle is a long and hard one. But no force, human or spiritual, can

14 Bereishis 21:4.

15 *Ibid.*, 22:8. Rashi (*ad loc.*), citing the Midrash, points out that Yitzhak was aware of his father's intent to sacrifice him, and all the same went along with him willingly.

16 *Ibid.*, Chaps. 28-45.

hold back this victory forever. Yaakov sifted the bran from mankind's flour.

Yaakov's victory over the final evil is what guarantees the safety, in the long run, of the precious well of the Jewish people. This is the deeper meaning of Yaakov's removing the stone from the well in Haran:

> *He looked, and there was a well in the fields, and three flocks of sheep lying by it; for from that well the flocks were watered. But there was a great stone stopping the lip of the well.*[17]
>
> *. . . Yaakov went over and rolled the stone from off the lip of the well. . . .*[18]

Yaakov saw that some day his descendants, "God's flock,"[19] would be waiting to "drink from the well." This is the Holy Temple, where the knowledge of God flows into the soul. The water of this well can only flow into a soul that is uncontaminated by selfish concerns and desires which cloud the well's water and block the channel. Yaakov saw that one day a "stone" (symbol of the evil inclination within man's heart[20]) would block the well's lip: the *yetzer hara* would succeed in blocking the flow of spiritual experience from entering man's consciousness. When the Holy Temple could no longer function as it was intended to, God would take it away. Yaakov, as the final and culminating Father of the Jewish nation, had as his mission to bequeath his descendants the capacity to "roll the stone off the well" — to remove the final impediment of the *yetzer hara,* the self-serving desires of their hearts — and restore to themselves the ability to absorb the flow of spiritual appreciation into their souls. By removing the last traces of egotistic self-interest from his own heart, totally unblocking and purifying the "well" that was implicit within him, he paved the way for all of his descendants. When the

17 *Ibid.,* 29:2-3.
18 *Ibid.,* v. 10.
19 Tehillim 95:7.
20 Yechezkel 36:26.

Jewish people learns to roll the stone off its heart, then its well will return to it: the Holy Temple will be rebuilt, its "water" will spread forth through the world, and all mankind will drink from it and become familiar with the taste of closeness to God.

The Elders of course would not be satisfied with such an answer. "When is this great victory supposed to come? If your Fathers gave you the ability to do all this, then take back the Holy Temple today! And if you don't, then you have been talking nonsense."

Rabbi Yehoshua addresses this question with his parable of a rope.

15.7 A Rope Has Three Strands

"Make me a rope of this bran and I will bring [the well] in."

The Torah says: "Yaakov is the portion of [God's] heritage [to mankind]."[21] The word for "portion," חבל, is a homonym of the word for "rope." As we have mentioned, the Torah has no verbal coincidences; the word is used to tell us that Yaakov's contribution to the Jewish people is not merely another "portion" of their Divine heritage, it is the "rope" which binds them to God.

A rope must consist of at least three strands, or else it will unravel. Each of the three abilities for overcoming the evil inclination which the Fathers bequeathed their descendants is compared to one strand of a rope — a rope which has the potential to attach the Jewish people inseparably to God in heaven.

By ridding himself of concern with his own will as opposed to that of God's, Yaakov contributed the third strand, the one that completes the rope. Once a three-stranded "rope" of Divine destiny was theirs, the future of the Jewish people was

21 Devarim 32:9.

insured, for now their mission was possible. Man would now have the ability to cleave to God permanently. Yaakov, then, who contributed the final element needed for the world's purification, is "the rope of God's heritage."

What allowed the well to be captured and abandoned in the fallow fields? It was the rampant selfishness of the Jewish people that permitted Rome to overrun it. For the Jews did not carry out their appointed task fully: they reached out to the first two strands and held them tightly, but ignored the third strand. What good is a rope of two strands? The rope was broken, the well's channel stopped, the water fouled with contamination. Their flimsy rope did not suffice to connect all of mankind to its Creator, nor was it strong enough to tie the Jewish people to its well.

What will bring the well into the city? Rabbi Yehoshua's answer to the Elders' challenge is this: You have burned the city of Jerusalem and you have captured its well. But the well will nevertheless return to the city. You ask how? God has promised us that we will ultimately rid ourselves of evil. Some day we will become total and devoted servants of God and not of our own advancement. Either we will repent of our own accord or else He will show us, through the failure of every self-serving endeavor, through exile and suffering, that there is no path for us except service of Him. However it may come to pass, the bran will yet be removed from our wheat; our garden will flourish, and our fruit will be acceptable to God.

Yaakov has made sure that this will happen. The rope will be rewoven, this time with all three of its strands intact. And when it is remade, strong and enduring, then the well from which flows the precious water of knowledge of the infinite God will be brought into the Divine City.

"Who can make a rope of bran?"
"Then who can bring a well from the fields to the city?"

16
The Broken Millstone

[The Elders of Athens asked Rabbi Yehoshua ben Chananyah:] "We have a broken millstone; sew it up."

He took a shard of [the broken stone] and threw it to them, saying, "Unravel some threads from this and I will sew it up."

[They argued,] "Can anyone unravel threads from a millstone?"

[He answered them,] "Then can anyone sew one up?"

(Bechoros 8b)[1]

16.1 FLOUR AND TORAH

If man is to reach his destined goal of recognizing God and cleaving to His ways, then he must be healthy, well-nourished and supplied with his physical needs. It need hardly be said that material well-being is not the goal of human life but a means to reach that goal; all the same, without it man cannot function, and the goal will remain unattainable. The Sages expressed this idea with their customary brevity: אם אין קמח אין תורה — "If there is no flour, there is no Torah."[2]

The Divine Providence which supplies man with sustenance is symbolized by a mill. By grinding wheat into the flour from which bread is made, a mill is in a sense the source of man's nourishment, just as the Providence which brings the flow of sustenance from Heaven to man is the ultimate source of life for all.

1 The reading follows *Ein Yaakov*.

2 Avos 3:17.

> Why are the Heavens called שחקים ["grinders"]? Because there is a mill there that grinds out manna for the righteous.[3]

The use of the image of a grinding mill is intended to express this aspect of Heaven, as the "place" whence life and sustenance descend to the world.

At the end of the Roman Wars the Jewish nation was completely destitute. With the country in ashes and its people in chains, even the merest subsistence was difficult, and life itself was entirely at the mercy of the Romans. Against this backdrop the Elders of Athens posed their question to Rabbi Yehoshua: "Very well, then, you have your spiritual goals. But even you admit that 'If there is no flour, there is no Torah.' Now that we have conquered you and you have no further source of livelihood, how do you expect Torah, and with it the Jews as a separate people, to survive?" Expressed in the symbolic terms of the Talmud, this came out as, "We have captured your mill and broken it. Do you really think you can repair it?"

But the Elders' challenge seems at first to be phrased as nonsense: they asked if the Sages could "sew the mill back together." Why would anyone try to sew up a millstone? To understand the meaning of this odd challenge, and of Rabbi Yehoshua's answer, we must understand more about the mill of Heaven.

16.2 HOW TO RUN A MILL

The Sages customarily hid their profoundest sayings in deceptively simple language. Sometimes their wisdom even takes on the appearance of mere folklore, as in this seemingly trivial statement:

> The sound of a mill in [the village of] Burni means a celebration for a son born there.[4]

3 Chagigah 12b, *q. v.*

4 Sanhedrin 32b. The passage continues: "Lamplight in [the village of] Beror

It was in fact the custom in Burni to grind flour with a loud noise in preparation for a circumcision feast; but this is not the reason that the Sages saw fit to immortalize the custom. They were alluding to a much deeper idea.

The "son" mentioned here is an often-used image for Torah scholars,[5] and the connection between the mill and the birth of a son hints at the deepest causes behind the support of Torah study among the Jewish people. At first glance it would seem that what keeps Torah study going is the financial support of wealthy people. But this is only superficially true. There is a more fundamental force at work here: the will of the Creator that established the law of the universe.

The law of Creation states that Torah scholars themselves are the ultimate cause of their own support. If there are people of means who support Torah study, then this is because there are Torah scholars who have committed themselves unreservedly to their studies. In response to their selfless dedication, God dispatches a flow of prosperity towards those people who have the potential to be supporters of Torah, and arouses in them respect for the Torah and its scholars. The result of this process is that these people use their wealth to support *talmidei chachamim.* The same holds true of the converse situation: if ever the sources of support for Torah dry up, that is because the scholars have weakened in their resolve to study with absolute devotion.

This is why, when the Mishnah states, "If there is no flour there is no Torah," it can state with equal truth that "if there is no Torah there is no flour."[6] The flow of sustenance to the Torah scholars, and on their account to the entire Jewish people,

Chayil means a celebration there." The Vilna Gaon, in his commentary, explains that "lamplight" refers to Torah.

5 For example, in Devarim 6:7, "You shall teach them to your sons," the Sages interpret the word "sons" to mean "students" (Sifrei *loc. cit.* cited in Rashi *ad loc.*). Another example is: "Torah scholars proliferate peace in the world, as it is written, '. . . all your sons will be learned of God; abundant will be your sons' peace.' [Yeshayahu 54:13] Do not read 'your sons' (בניך) but 'your builders' (בוניך)"; i.e., Torah scholars who build the world (Berachos 64a).

6 Avos 3:17.

is ultimately assured by the scholars themselves.

This, then, is the reason behind the seemingly trivial custom of Burni. When "sons" (scholars wholly devoted to Torah study) are "born" — when their dedication reaches the level of being true and selfless, then the "mill" begins to grind — God opens His storehouses of plenty. The mill of Heaven begins grinding manna for the righteous and causes its flow to come to the Jewish people.

16.3 The Honorers of Man

The sense of human dignity stems from the innate human belief that man is nobler than an animal. It is axiomatic that human life possesses a value which cannot be equalled by any kind or amount of animal life. The basis for this axiom is the realization that, unlike any animal, man has a spiritual dimension to his life which gives him the capacity for thought and activities infinitely nobler than the mere survival tactics of a beast.

The need to feel dignity is fundamental to man, and conversely nothing is more shameful to him than to be considered a mere beast, concerned only with survival. This is the reason why humans go clothed. The human body being essentially similar to that of an animal, it does not take too much imagination to conclude on this basis that man is indeed merely another animal species. Thus, nakedness exposes one to the risk of losing his right to human respect. Because man is ashamed at the thought of this loss, he wears clothing. Clothed, his claim to having a spiritual dimension is beyond cavil; naked, that claim is open to suspicion. For this reason Rabbi Yochanan, the Talmudic Sage, always referred to his garments as his "honorers"; they conferred human dignity upon him.[7]

Once this is understood, we can understand further why clothing was not invented until after Adam and Eve ate from the Tree of Knowledge.[8] Before they sinned they had no

7 Shabbas 113a.

8 Bereishis 3:7.

reason to be ashamed of their bodies. Their sexual organs were as honorable an expression of their dignity as their hands. With his hands man could make the Garden of Eden flourish; with his organs of procreation he could reproduce life itself. Given the nobility of human life, what could be a greater source of pride? But after the sin of the Tree of Knowledge, the resultant contamination of materialism and self-serving motivation made it possible to pervert the reproductive drive for the purpose of selfish gratification. Once the sexual organs could be used in such a manner, they became a source of shame to man. They displayed a capacity for mindless, animalistic passions wholly contrary to his essential nature; if he was to maintain his dignity, he would have to hide them from sight. He could not possibly claim nobility while his animal nature was on exhibit. Adam and Eve were thus obliged to invent clothing.

Saving man from the disgrace of nakedness is not the end of clothing's conferral of honor upon man. Clothing is also used to indicate a person's position in society, as a badge of the degree to which he is respected.

Clothing that is a badge of one's social rank usually conveys a message about the wearer's function in society. When the Talmudic scholars adopted a unique style of clothing, it was not only to indicate their position of respect in Jewish society; it also conveyed a unique message about their function and their goals.

The Rabbinic robe (חלוקא דרבנן) was a garment which covered the scholars' arms down to the wrists and their legs down to the ankles, leaving no part of the body uncovered except the face and hands. It was expressive of the life-style of the *talmidei chachamim,* which was unlike that of any other human being.

The Sages were completely devoted to fulfilling the true goals of life. They saw their bodies as instruments for carrying out God's will. Every part of their bodies was dedicated to a spiritual purpose: their legs to take them to mitzvos, their arms to perform the mitzvos, their other organs to sustain life so that they could serve God.

The message of the Rabbinic robe was that its wearer had consecrated his life, and it was conveyed by covering all of the wearer's body. For even after the nakedness of the post-Tree-of-Knowledge body is covered, a partially exposed body displays its animalistic potential; however small, the exposed part can be viewed as a collection of organs whose use is physical survival. To allow their bodies to suffer this implication was intolerable to the Sages, for it would have been a contradiction to the very essence of their lives, which was to reach beyond the animal and cling to the Divine.

The Rabbinic robe expressed this devotion to Divine service by covering all organs which could be possibly construed as animalistic. The message intended was that the true essence of the scholar's body is something that the eye cannot see. Only the face and hands were left visible: the expression of a human face and the motions of a human hand are unique in the world, not susceptible to comparison to animals.

This, then, was the vision of holiness expressed by the Rabbinic robe. But what would happen if that vision became sullied with material leanings?

16.4 The Frayed Robe

> The forces of evil surround us like an earthen moat around the dyke of a vine. The scholars' clothing becomes frayed because of their rubbing against us.[9]

The Talmudic term מזיקין, here translated as "forces of evil,"[10] refers to those innate temptations, and the cultures built on them, which God put into the world to be the antagonists of a spiritual life. It is in their nature to "surround"

9 Berachos 6a.

10 Vilna Gaon, in his commentary. *Cf.* Me'iri, *Beis HaBechirah*, Berachos *ad loc.*, who explains מזיקין as temptations towards heresy.

those who seek to rise in their knowledge of God and His Torah, so as to present constant threats to their spiritual advancement. Their physically oriented beckonings gather round us despite our best efforts to ward them off.

The Jewish people is "the vine of [God's] planting."[11] The vine has a dyke around it to gather the "rain of the Divine teaching"[12] to nourish it, but a muddy moat surrounds the whole, threatening to undermine the dyke and cause its collapse.

The muddy moat is the symbol of Eisav, the earthy "man of the [wild] fields."[13] We have seen that Eisav is the paragon of materialism, who has been attempting to destroy Yaakov and his descendants ever since he lost his father's blessings.[14] If he cannot destroy Yaakov's children bodily, it will suffice to subvert the goals that Yaakov set for them.

The threat of Eisav's malice is a constant factor in the daily fight for spiritual survival. The Torah cannot flourish until this influence has been neutralized. The very destiny of humanity, its recognition of God, cannot be realized until Eisav's descendant and epitome, Amalek, is wiped off the face of the earth. The materialistic temptations of Eisav's earth-culture are a moat threatening the dyke; God's beloved vine is in danger.

Thus, say the Sages, "the scholars' clothing becomes frayed because of their rubbing against us." If the hedonistic and self-serving doctrines of Eisav begin influencing the scholars, their total commitment to a consecrated life becomes weakened. Their "robe becomes frayed" — their nobility is lost.

How does a potential scholar overcome this threat to his goals?

The mill of Burni teaches us that the financial support of Torah depends on the degree of devotion with which Jews

11 Tehillim 80:16 (following Targum and Radak).

12 Devarim 32:2.

13 Bereishis 25:27. See §15.2.

14 See Chapter 10, "The Roman Parade."

commit themselves to it. The same rule holds about Eisav's threats to life and to spirit: absolute, selfless devotion to the Torah is the way to rise above the reach of Eisav's power.

Long ago our Father Yitzhak hinted at this, when in his blindness he attempted to distinguish between his two sons and declared,

> *The voice is Yaakov's voice, but the hands are Eisav's hands.*[15]

The Sages pointed out the deeper meaning of his statement: a prophecy of how the struggle of the two brothers would unfold throughout the ages.

As long as Yaakov's voice is lifted up in the study halls and synagogues, Eisav's hands are powerless; but when Yaakov's voice falters, Eisav's hands gain power.[16]

16.5 THREADS FROM A MILLSTONE

He took a shard of [the broken millstone] and threw it to them, saying, "Unravel some threads from this and I will sew it up."

The meaning of the mill of Heaven, as we have said, is that the ultimate source of Providence's flow of sustenance is neither commerce nor philanthropy but the scholars' commitment to Torah study. Providence is the "mill that grinds manna for the righteous." Expressed symbolically, the mill of Heaven is made of fabric, not stone: it is woven of threads from the "clothing of the scholars." Their total dedication to the Torah's ideals, manifested in the Rabbinic robe, brings the flow of sustenance down from Heaven to them, and so to all of the Jewish nation.

In the days of the Roman conquest sustenance was scarcely to be had, because Torah study was at a low ebb. As the scholars' clothing became frayed, so the fabric of the mill-

15 Bereishis 27:22.

16 Midrash Rabba, Bereishis 65.

stone of Heaven became threadbare, until eventually it fell apart. And what frays the scholars' robes? The forces of evil rub against them — they are influenced by values inimical to Torah and lose their devotion to it.

The Elders challenged Rabbi Yehoshua: How can you resew the millstone when the Torah is dead? We have worn the Rabbis' robes to a ravelling; there are no threads left you to sew with.

Rabbi Yehoshua answered them: The same process which caused the Rabbinic robe to be frayed can be reversed so as to restore it to its original splendor. The worn-out fabric which to you spells despair speaks to me of hope of renewal. We will toil over our Torah and rebuild our dedication to it. When we have recaptured our vision of holiness, when we know that everything in life must be used to express God's will, the thin, rent threads will take on substance again, and then we will be able to reweave the Rabbis' robes. When we have done that, we will take the threads of their robes, now refreshed and renewed, and resew the millstone of Heaven. Its plenty will once again cascade down to our people.

"Can anyone unravel threads from a millstone?" [they asked.]

The Elders were astonished at such a strange assertion. If there is no flour there is no Torah! You cannot indulge this fanatic devotion of yours when you are starving. We control your lives and your sustenance; we will not permit you to return to Torah!

"Then can anyone sew one up?" [was his answer.]

Of course you cannot conceive of resewing the mill of Heaven, because you think that flour is the be-all and end-all; you think the world was created for man to fill his belly. But this is not so. The world was created so that men might devote themselves to carrying out God's will. True, if there is no flour there is no Torah. But there is a more fundamental principle than this: that if there is no Torah, there is no flour.

The world cannot continue to exist without Torah study, for Torah is the life of the world. God has promised that the world will never cease existing until it has reached its appointed goal. But the Torah is the way to that goal. When the Torah's ideals are fulfilled, only then will the world have reached its goal; and so God has promised that the Jewish people will never lose its contact with the Torah. You cannot keep us from our Torah study any more than you can legislate the destruction of the world.

We will renew and reweave our threads of holiness, for the destiny of the world depends upon it. Despite your cruel tyranny, we will reject your tawdry values and restore our devotion to our Torah. And when we have done so, then we will resew the millstones.

17
The Field Of Swords

[The Elders of Athens asked Rabbi Yehoshua ben Chananyah:]
"How does one cut a row of swords?"
"With the horn of a donkey."
"Does a donkey have horns?"
"Do swords grow in rows?" *(Bechoros 8b)*

17.1 LIVING BY THE SWORD

"How does one cut a row of swords?"

The blessing that our Father Yitzhak gave his son Eisav, ועל חרבך תחיה — "You shall live by your sword"[1] — defines Eisav's destiny. As explained previously, the twin brothers, Yaakov and Eisav, have directly opposite world views. Yaakov, the forebear of the Jewish people, measures his success in terms of his closeness to God; Eisav's success is defined in terms of the power he is able to amass for himself. Eisav's most treasured values, therefore, are might and dominion. His culture is geared towards producing individuals who will strive to control others and to amass wealth and power for themselves. The success of his descendant nations is measured in terms of victories on the battlefield.

Eisav is known in the Torah as "a man of the fields," which, as explained previously, means that he himself is compared to a field.[2] As a field gives forth its produce, so do

1 Bereishis 27:40.
2 See §15.2 and next note.

the inner desires of a nation give birth to its culture. If Eisav is compared to a field and his culture is one geared to self-aggrandizement, then his is a field which produces the means for amassing power: it is a field with a "row of swords" growing in it.[3]

Although Eisav's might has brought him success throughout human history, it is destined to come to an end. For when the Era of Mashiach arrives at the End of Days,

> *Swords will be pounded into spades and spears into pruning-hooks, and no nation will raise its sword against another, nor will man be taught [to wage] war.*[4]

In that era the sword will cease to play a role in human life. Eisav's mastery over human affairs will end, as his "fields" are cleared of their rows of swords.

17.2 THE FINAL VICTORY

". . . of a donkey."

How will the ultimate battle be won? How will man bring about God's triumph over evil? Warriors triumph over their enemies by cunning maneuvers and bold attacks; but God's battle with evil is waged in a totally different manner. God created man not so that he might exercise his lust for dominion, but so that he might learn to efface himself before the glory of God, to forego gratifying his appetite for power and to follow humbly in God's ways.

> *[God] does not desire the horse's strength, He is not pleased with man's [mighty] thighs; God desires those who fear Him, those who hope for His kindness.*[5]

3 The comparison in §15.2 to a fallow, wild field, as explained there, is in line with the present idea. A wild, untamed field brings forth only worthless, troublesome weeds which sap the productive power of the earth; similarly, Eisav's doctrine of self-aggrandizement produces a destructive culture devoted to overpowering all other nations. The wild field is thus a "row with swords growing in it."

4 Yeshayahu 2:4.

5 Tehillim 147:10-11.

Thus, the ultimate battle will not be won when man is successful in achieving mastery over others. On the contrary, this is a battle for self-mastery and humility before God. When man learns to control his passions and to efface himself before God, the battle will be won.

For this reason Mashiach, whom God will send to mankind to teach it His ways, is not envisioned by the prophets as a mighty warrior astride a horse, but as a poor man astride a donkey.

> *Rejoice greatly, daughter of Zion! Blow trumpets, daughter of Jerusalem! for your king is arriving. He is righteous and redeemed, a poor man riding a donkey. . .*[6]

Mashiach is "poor" because from his perspective the world does not belong to man but is the possession of the Creator; nothing man owns can be truly called his own. Mashiach rides a lowly donkey because to achieve his goal he uses not power and glory-seeking (whose symbol is the horse, as in the above-cited verse), but rather humility, symbolized by the lowly donkey which faithfully conveys its master to his destination. God repays his humility and trust by "redeeming" him in every battle that he fights against evil.

17.3 CLEARING THE FIELD

"With the horn of a donkey."

When an individual overcomes obstacles or enemies, the Scriptures refer to this as "the raising of his horn." Similarly, the period when the influence of the scion of David (Mashiach) will be ascendant is described as the era when his "horn will rise."[7] When Mashiach's "horn rises," evil will be obliterated, and the sword of Eisav will no longer wield its might. The effective agent by which evil will be removed is the

6 Zechariah 9:9.

7 Fifteenth blessing of the daily Standing Prayer.

"horn of the donkey," the dedication to God's will with which he will invest the world. In the terms used by Rabbi Yehoshua ben Chananyah, the horn of the donkey will clear the fields of Eisav of its rows of sprouting swords.

17.4 THE LAW OF NATURE

"Does a donkey have horns?"

In the Era of Mashiach God will not suspend the laws by which the natural world operates. Even God Himself recognized Yitzhak's blessing to Eisav which promised him a successful living by his sword. This blessing was the reason that God forbade the Jews to engage in war with Eisav's descendants upon coming to their lands after leaving Egypt.[8] No greater proof of the effectiveness of the blessing could be asked than the record of human affairs: they are for the most part a record of the triumphs of Eisav's sword.

God, then, does not suspend the laws of nature in His world, and this will be so, we know, even in the Era of Mashiach. If Yitzhak's blessing has stood by Eisav so steadfastly throughout history, it must be God's desire that brute force rule in His world. Why should this change at the End of Days? How will the power of a donkey suddenly overturn the might of Eisav?

17.5 A FATHER'S HONOR

The answer to this question depends on the answer to another one: What is it which has allowed Eisav such dazzling and prolonged success?

One of the rules which God built into His conduct of the world is that He does not grant material success to a nation unless it has deserved it through the merit of some good deed which it has done. Eisav has been permitted to domi-

8 Bemidbar 21:4 and Rashi *ad loc.*

nate not only the Jewish people but all of mankind throughout world history. What good deeds did the archetype of evildoers perform to merit this?

The Sages tell us that Eisav's merit was his meticulous performance of the commandment of honoring his father.[9] His care in observing this mitzvah is described in the Midrash:

> Said Rabban Shimon ben Gamliel: All my life I served my father, but not even to one-hundredth of the extent to which Eisav served his father. I used to serve my father [even though I might be dressed] in soiled clothing, although when I went travelling I [made sure to be] dressed immaculately. But when Eisav served his father he [put on] garments fit for royalty. . . .[10]

Thus, even one of the greatest Sages of the Mishnah freely admitted that he observed this mitzvah only to a minute fraction of Eisav's degree of observance.

That the merit of this commandment is behind the success of Eisav's sword is hinted at in Yitzhak's request to Eisav:

> *Take your weapons, your sword* (תליך) *and your bow, and hunt me some game.*[11]

Eisav used his sword to serve his father's needs. His reward was Yitzhak's blessing that the same sword would always supply him with his livelihood.

17.6 A VESTED INTEREST

If Eisav lived to serve himself and refused to submit to God's will, how are we to explain the anomaly of his paying such careful attention to the performance of one of God's mitzvos?

The answer is that Eisav is prepared to do God's bidding when it is in his interest to do so. Eisav recognized that the

9 Zohar, Bereishis 146b.
10 Midrash Rabba, Bereishis 65, 12.
11 Bereishis 27:3.

commandment to honor father and mother is a precept which will serve him well in the long run. The son who serves his parents when they are old and needy, and who instructs his children to do the same, will himself be cared for in his old age. It is therefore not surprising that Eisav, the supreme self-aggrandizer, concerned himself with honoring his father, for thereby in the end he honored himself.[12]

Furthermore, Eisav might have had an even subtler self-interest in mind. His aim was certainly self-directed: to derive the maximum personal gain from the world. He saw, however, that civilization, law, and order were necessary to achieve his goals, for mankind cannot prosper midst chaos. This is where the mitzvah of honoring parents fits into his plans.

Honoring the achievements of past generations fosters a respect for tradition. Tradition creates social stability, for it insures that the teachings of past generations will be preserved and revered. To honor one's father and mother means, by implication, to honor one's roots. Thus although Eisav rejected other spiritual values, he inculcated respect for elders into his culture, for it is a value exquisitely fit for advancing his selfish purposes.

Although Eisav's exaggerated care in honoring his father was motivated by self-interest, the merit of his mitzvah has carried him successfully through history. For even a mitzvah done with impure intention deserves a reward, since in the final analysis it too elevates man's spiritual level. In this case, for example, civilized societal life carries more hope for mankind's self-realization than a life of barbarism. Eisav's reward for raising the moral level of humanity was world domination by his sword.

17.7 A BROTHER'S ASCENDANCE

A final question remains. Why is Eisav's reward of world

12 This interpretation of Eisav's motivations is found in Rav E.E. Dessler, "*Michtav Me-Eliyahu*," ed. Carmel and Friedlander, Bnei Brak, 5724, Vol. III, p. 97.

dominion not eternal? Why will he dominate Yaakov only until the End of Days? But when we understand that Eisav's reward was for a selfishly motivated mitzvah the explanation becomes clear.

Eisav dominates Yaakov only as long as his merit is greater. This is expressed in Yitzhak's blessing to Eisav:

> *And when you become ascendant you shall throw off his [Yaakov's] yoke from your neck.*[12]

Eisav overpowers Yaakov — he "throws off his yoke from his neck" — when he "becomes ascendant," i.e., when his merit is not counterbalanced by Yaakov's even greater merit. But when Yaakov commits himself fully to Torah and to mitzvos and his own merit is the greater, then Eisav has no power.

Although Eisav deserved reward for honoring his father, selfishly motivated mitzvos can grant him dominance over Yaakov only when they measure favorably against Yaakov's mitzvos — that is, when Yaakov's mitzvos share the same nature and are done to a lesser degree. In other words, Eisav's merit might be found to be superior to that of the Jews only as long as the Jews perform their mitzvos too out of selfish considerations, such as for gaining social status, prestige or money. Measured against deeds of equal selfishness, Eisav's merit for his scrupulous honoring of his father can outweigh the mitzvos of the Jews.

But this will no longer apply when "the poor man on the donkey" arrives. When the sole motivation of the Jewish people is submission to God's will, Eisav's mitzvah no longer grants him superiority. Measured against a purely motivated mitzvah, Eisav's merit ceases to outweigh that of the Jewish people.

How does the "horn" of the donkey upon which Mashiach arrives clear the fields of Eisav of his swords? Because this sword can exist only before the poor man arrives on his

12 Bereishis 27:40.

donkey. But when he comes upon the human scene and his teachings exercise their full force, the fields of Eisav will be cleared of their swords. The swords exist only as long as the Jews live a superficial life, for then their merit does not match that of Eisav. But when they realize that their lives are given to them for acquiescence in God's will, Eisav has no merit compared to that of the Jewish people, and his power will pass from the world.

"Does a donkey have horns?"
"Do swords grow in rows?"

18
Of Eggs and Cheese

[The Elders of Athens] brought two eggs before [Rabbi Yehoshua ben Chananyah]. "Which will be a white hen and which a black?" they asked.

[Rabbi Yehoshua] brought two cheeses before them. "Which is from a white goat and which is from a black goat?" he said.

(Bechoros 8b)

18.1 THE CHOSEN CHILD

Yitzhak prayed to God across from his wife, for she was barren. God answered him and his wife Rivkah conceived. The [unborn] children struggled within her until she said, "If so, why did I [pray for a child]?"; so she went to seek the word of God. God said to her, "There are two peoples in your belly; two nations shall separate from your innards. . ."[1]

RASHI: "Struggled": Whenever they passed the entrance to a house of Torah study, Yaakov strained to leave; and whenever they passed a house of idolatry, Eisav strained to leave.

"Will separate from your innards": . . . one to his wickedness and the other to his righteousness.

While the mother lies upon the chicks or the eggs. . .[2]

"The Mother" — the nourishing Presence of God

"lies upon" — that Presence is close to

1 Bereishis 25:21-23; the translation follows Rashi's commentary.

2 Devarim 22:6.

"the chicks" — the young children of the Jewish people
"or the eggs" — it is close even to their unborn children.[3]

When Rivkah, the wife of Father Yitzhak, conceived twins after many years of prayer, the sensation of their development within her caused her great distress, as the above-cited Midrash relates. Even before their birth, one child was drawn to the worship of idols and the other to the study of Torah. When Rivkah asked God's prophet[4] to explain the phenomenon, he told her that she would soon give birth to two sons and that one would be wicked and the other virtuous. And so it came to pass: she bore Eisav and Yaakov, and when the children grew up Eisav became a hunter and a "man of the fields,"[5] interested only in earthly affairs, while Yaakov became a *tzaddik*, a righteous man who sat in the tents of Torah at the feet of the wise.

The Elders, challenging as always the Jewish claim to uniqueness, sought to demonstrate that the Jews' belief in their status as a chosen people was absurd. Their argument took the following lines:

"You profess that God loves you and has chosen you to be His people because you are spiritually more apt than other nations. Your claim would be reasonable if it were based on the fact that God gave you the Torah. Through the Torah you know more than any other nation about how to carry out God's will, and you can keep His commandments best of all people. For that reason God might well love you more than any other nation.

"We might be able to accept this argument, but not your conception of a chosenness unrelated to carrying out God's will. The story of the unborn Yaakov and Eisav, as well as your interpretation of the mother bird lying on her eggs,

3 *Tikkunei Zohar, Tikkun 6,* fol. 17a, interpreting the verse on its exegetical level of meaning.

4 The Sages tell us that this was Shem, the son of Noah.

5 See Chapter 14, "The Well in the Fields," for a full explanation of the concept of "a man of the fields."

indicate that your belief in your chosenness extends to even a Jewish fetus. We refuse to accept this, for how can it be true?

"Chosenness is comprehensible only as a function of closeness to God. Can a fetus (or even a young child) who cannot even understand what God is, let alone perform His commands, be considered intrinsically closer to God than anyone else? Does it make sense to say that God loves an unborn Jewish child (or even an infant) more than He loves a non-Jewish one?

"If we show you two eggs, can you tell us which will produce a white hen and which a black? How, then, can you claim to know that a Jewish infant will develop into a righteous man and a non-Jewish one into a wicked one? Obviously, your definition of chosenness is nonsense, and all the more so your pretention to enjoy a chosenness of this sort."

18.2 THE SEED OF HOLINESS

[Rabbi Yehoshua] brought before them two cheeses. "Which is from a white goat and which is from a black goat?" he said.

You dissolve me like milk and harden me like cheese.[6]

With these words Job praised God for the miracle of his conception. In his chosen symbolism, his mother's ovum and his father's seed are represented by "milk" and "cheese," to which they bear a certain physical resemblance. Rabbi Yehoshua, in his retort to the Elders, uses Job's metaphor of "cheese" to refer to the seed from which the Jewish people was conceived.

Can a fetus or an infant be considered chosen by God? Yes, says Rabbi Yehoshua, because holiness is not necessarily a function of the performance of mitzvos; it is stamped into

6 Iyov 10:10.

the Jewish people at an even earlier stage, in the seed of which they are born.

> This [Jewish] nation has three signs: they are merciful, they have a sense of shame,[7] and they do kindness.[8]

It is no mere figure of speech that Avraham, Yitzhak and Yaakov are called the "fathers" of the Jewish people. Fathers pass on their genetic code to their offspring; so did these Fathers, too, invest their descendants with their spiritual essence. To them a yearning for closeness to God was an inherent trait of their soul, and as a result a Jew is born with an innate affinity for matters of holiness. This affinity is expressed by a special set of characteristics which all Jews possess, characteristics transmitted from generation to generation, which engender in the Jewish people a tropism towards spiritual matters.

These three characteristics, as the Sages teach us, are that Jews are merciful, they have a sense of shame which makes them morally restrained, and they are kind and generous. No nation is as concerned with the needy, the underprivileged and the downtrodden as the Jews are; no nation is as faithful to spouse and family as the Jews; no nation is as generous of self and wealth as the Jewish nation.

These distinctively Jewish traits are not a product of one's observance of the laws of Torah. Even non-observant Jews have these same characteristics, if not at their highest peak of development, then at least to a greater degree than any other nation. Nor are these traits a product of one's environment, for they have been part of the Jewish nature throughout history, irrespective of the thousands of cultures in which they lived in the course of the ages. These innate tendencies are the reason why to this day Jews, in every corner of the

7 ביישנים — lit., bashful, modest.

8 Yevamos 79a. "Merciful" is the trait by which one seeks to alleviate another's suffering out of pity. "Kindness" is the trait by which one desires to benefit others out of altruistic feelings.

world, are at the forefront of every movement for human rights (because they are merciful), are more committed to their families than any other group (because they are morally restrained),[9] and are the least violent element of the populace (because they are kind and generous). These Jewish qualities could not possibly be so ubiquitous unless they were part of a heritage innate in the seed of the "fathers."

One does not have to go back to Rivkah's bearing of Yaakov to see Jews struggling to get to the house of worship: one can see it to this very day. No matter how little learned a Jew may be, no matter how estranged he is from his heritage, something within him relentlessly pushes him to strive for ideals of the spirit. All over the world, wherever there is a struggle for a cause of justice or kindness, Jews — observant or not — are at its forefront.

Of course, the ideals being fought for are not necessarily Jewish ones, but the very fact that Jews seek such causes indicates their natural spiritual thirst. Thirst does not insure that one will end up drinking water; one might be driven instead to attempt to quench his thirst with saltwater, which will increase it. Similarly, to satisfy his longings a Jew might take up ideals which are ultimately unfulfilling. But in any case, in the final analysis a Jew is a spiritually thirsty person, and this is so because of the intrinsic nature of the Jewish seed.

A Jew's innate sensitivity to non-materialistic values gives rise to an attitude of refusing to accept selfishness and materialism as a goal of life, and of questing for alternative goals. Spirituality, by definition the antithesis of selfishness and materialism, becomes the sought-for alternative. The character traits mentioned above are the expression of this attitude.

This, then, is the definition of Jewish chosenness. It does not mean physical or mental superiority; it simply means that Jews feel the need for spiritual content in their lives.

9 Ironically, one of the reasons for the high rate of intermarriage is that Gentile women prefer Jewish men, knowing that they make more faithful husbands.

If Jewish chosenness were a function of the people's performance of commandments, the Elders' argument would be valid, for then certainly infants and the unborn would have no claim to being chosen. But this premise is incorrect. With respect to Jewish chosenness the Torah itself explicitly states:

> *It was not because you are more numerous than all nations that God desired you and chose you, for you are the least of all nations. It is because of God's love for you, and to keep His vow to your forefathers, that He took you out [of Egypt]. . . .*[10]

> *Not because of your righteousness and your heart's honesty are you coming to inherit [the Canaanites'] land. . . but so as to keep the vow that God gave to your forefathers, Avraham, Yitzhak, and Yaakov. For you must know that not because of your righteousness is God giving you this good land as your inheritance, for you are a stiff-necked people.*[11]

The Jews' chosenness is unrelated to merit; it is part of the inherent character which the Fathers bequeathed them. They have not earned it, nor can they escape it. It is part and parcel of their essential being.

The cheese made from the white goat's milk is distinct from that made from the black goat's milk, though this is not visible to the eye. The difference between them is a genetic one. The same is true about the difference between the Jewish people and the rest of the nations.

"Which [egg] will be a white hen and which a black?"
"Which [cheese] is from a white goat and which is from a black goat?"

10 Devarim 7:7-8.
11 Devarim 9:5.

19
The Blocked Entrance

Said [the Elders of Athens to Rabbi Yehoshua ben Chananyah:] "Show us a utensil not worth the damage it causes."

He took a reed mat and unfolded it: it would not go through the doorway. "Bring a pickaxe," he told them. [With it] he broke open the wall.

"Here," he said, "is a utensil not worth the damage it causes." *(Bechoros 8b)*

19.1 A Poor Exchange

"Show us a utensil not worth the damage it causes."

The Torah teaches us that the very soil of the Holy Land cannot tolerate evildoers.[1] So it was that because of the sins of the Jewish people God caused the Land to vomit them out. The Romans took complete possession of the Jewish land and turned it into a Roman colony. Considering their philosophy of self-adulation and their rabid jealousy of the Jews, it was only natural for the Elders to argue that their successful conquest and colonization of the Land of Israel proved that they were a more worthy nation than the Jews.

Their argument ran thus: "If, as you say, the land cannot tolerate evil, and because of your evil it spat you out, then would it be likely to put up with another nation which be-

1 Vayikra 18:28.

haves no better — or even worse? Yet the land has not ejected us. Does this not prove that your standards of behavior are erroneous? For who would keep in his house a utensil that does more damage than it is worth? Why would the Land of Israel keep within it a nation that does more evil than good? Surely, if the Land permits the Roman nation to dwell within it, then that is because the Roman nation is superior to yours. Our philosophy of the worship of man is better than your unrealistic piety, and our selfishness is better than your foolish ideas of altruism."

Their challenge to Rabbi Yehoshua is, then, that if he wishes to see the Romans as morally inferior to the Jews, then he must explain why a householder (God) would keep in his house (the Holy Land) a utensil that does more harm than good (the Roman nation with all its purported wickedness).

Rabbi Yehoshua's answer to the Elders explains some basic facts regarding the nature of the world, of which the Elders were unaware.

19.2 THE TWO DOORS OF THE WORLD

> Why was this world created with the letter ה? Because it is like [the shape of a ה]: a three-walled portico [since one side is completely open]; whoever wishes to leave can drop right out [into sin].
>
> And why is there a gap between the leg of the ה and the roof?
>
> So that if man repents he will have a way to return.
>
> Why shouldn't he return the way he left?
>
> It wouldn't work.[2]

The Torah tells us: אלה תולדות השמים והארץ בהבראם — "This is the story of heaven and earth when they were created."[3] The Sages say that the word בהבראם suggests the reading ב"ה" בראם

2 Menachos 29b.

3 Bereishis 2:4.

— "With [the letter] ה He [God] created them."[4] This world was patterned according to the spiritual reality expressed by the letter ה, a reality tersely described by the Sages in the heading of this section.

The letter ה, in the script used for writing sacred texts, is formed by combining two other letters, ד and י, with the י turned upside down and placed inside the ד. These two letters by their shapes represent the respective realities of physicality and spirituality. A י symbolizes the idea of a point, a thing which has neither length nor breadth, which exists only as an idea in the mind. Spirituality, too, has no physical dimensions, and cannot be perceived by the senses. It can only be apprehended by the mind. Therefore its best representation is a geometric point, or a letter י, which consists essentially of a point of ink. The letter ד, on the other hand, consists of two spreading perpendicular lines, symbolizing the axes of a geometric plane, length and breadth. Thus ד represents the reality of the physical world.

ה is a combination of ד and י, representing the idea of spirituality (י) entering into physicality (ד). The purpose of creation is to imbue the material world with the sanctity of the Divine. To fulfil this purpose, the Torah — the blueprint for a spiritual life — was specifically given to human beings, who were created to live in a material world, and not to angels.[5] It was given to inhabitants of a three-dimensional physical world, possessed of animalistic instincts and drives, and it commanded them to use their free choice to develop, in spite of their physical limitations, a sense of closeness to the Divine. Because the purpose of creation was that there be a world where the spiritual י meets and enlightens the material ד, the world was "created with a ה."

The significance of ה extends further, to every detail of its

4 Bereishis Rabba *ad loc*. This might be why the ה is written superscript.

5 *Cf.* Shabbas 89a, where it is told how Moshe Rabbenu convinced the angels that the Torah must be given to humans and not to them, because angels have no predilection towards sin.

shape. The Sages explain that the wide opening at its bottom teaches a lesson about sin. Although the world was in fact created to be used to worship God, man has the free choice to disregard this purpose and, instead, to use it to worship himself (i.e., to sin) by fulfilling his appetites wantonly and satisfying his lust for glory. However, when man lives so, he fills himself with spiritual impurities which make contact with God impossible for him.[6] If the world of ה is a world of contact with the spiritual, then illicit use of the world drives man out of it.

The wide, unobstructed opening of the ה is meant to show how easy it is for man to leave his world. The world is like a portico of three walls with the fourth side wide open for all to leave by. Most significantly, in this case the exit is at the bottom; man need only give in to his natural gravity and he will be drawn down and out.

If one has left the realm of God's influence, how, when he regrets his evil, can he re-enter the world? He can do so by removing the impurities which caused him to leave the world in the first place: by repentance. But this does not come easily, for he has to struggle against more than mere gravity. The Sages tell us that "one sin brings on another"[7] — that sin itself makes it easier to sin again. One must overcome the qualitative change that the violation of God's will has brought about in his nature. Sin increases the power of lust and material drives, making them dominant in his character. Sin mutes a person's spiritual longings; whereas before his instincts drew him towards God and Torah, now he must struggle against his corrupted nature to reach spirituality.

Before man sinned, the doorway to the world was wide open. Now that man has left his world, when he turns back he finds it blocked before him. Through misuse of his free choice he has warped its pattern; the straight way back is closed for him. How then will he re-enter the world?

6 *Cf.* Chapter 13, "The Well in the Fields."
7 Avos 4:2.

To achieve repentance, the individual must overcome the inclinations now implanted within him which have caused him to feel at ease with sin. He must raise himself up to an even higher level of attachment to holiness than he had before he sinned in order to uproot these compromising inclinations. To return to the world that was created with a ה, he must rise from the outside to the narrow aperture near its roof and force his way through it. Returning through the wide opening at the bottom "would not work."[8]

19.3 THE RECTIFICATION OF THE WORLD

The shape of ה tells the story of human history. As we have seen, the world was made to be a tool with which mankind might achieve its goal: complete closeness to God within a material setting. Man needed a place where the physical could become totally pervaded by the spiritual, and so with ה as its design the world was created.

But Adam sinned, choosing to reject God's will and to follow his own instead. The world became invested with impurities which blocked him from full contact with the Divine. Expulsion from the Garden of Eden was the way God chose to force man to eradicate the evil with which he had filled the world. If he removed that evil and chose to follow God's will rather than his own, he would be allowed back into Eden.

It was to be a difficult climb back into the Garden. Man would have to reject an evil which was now part of him; he would have to seek a new entrance to the ה-shaped world and squeeze his way back into his lost domain.

Twenty generations after the Expulsion, Avraham took up the challenge of returning man to Eden, of living according to the values for which man was created. Jewish history, which is the story of Avraham's descendants, is the account

8 The Vilna Gaon goes on to explain that the letter ק (whose leg is drawn towards the right) represents the blocked entrance of the ה.

of how this nation moved mankind towards its ultimate goal.

Each era of Jewish history represents a test for the Jewish people in the abolition of another element of the evil which has become part of man's nature. These tests have often been extremely difficult; at times the Jewish people were successful and sometimes they failed. When they failed, the only solution has been for the Jews to be placed in a situation where they would be forced to make an even greater effort, so that they might finally succeed. For once one has fallen out of the bottom opening of the ה, far greater spiritual effort is needed to rise up to the aperture at the top in order to climb back in. The Jews would undergo suffering, exile, and dispersion until they finally eradicated the particular evil which it was incumbent upon them to overcome in that particular era.

The cumulative effect of all these tests will move the world towards the elimination of evil from man's mentality and his society. This will sufficiently weaken the power of evil in the world to enable mankind to recognize its Creator as King. And this will usher in the Era of the Mashiach, the great return to the Garden of Eden.

19.4 Opening a New Door

He took a reed mat and unfolded it: it would not go through the doorway.

The reed mat that Rabbi Yehoshua spread before the doorway represents the Roman Empire, whose foundation, as the Rabbis tell us, was a reed driven into the sea bottom:

> When King Solomon married Pharaoh's daughter [who continued to worship idols, and Solomon did not reprove her for this], the Angel Gavriel drove a reed into the sea bottom. [As time went on] it collected a bar of silt [which grew until] on it was built the great city of Rome.[9]

9 Shabbas 56b, following the Vilna Gaon's reading, which is implicit in the text, *q. v.*

King Solomon's failure to meet the test of his days paved the way for future and greater trials. The idolatry which he failed to eradicate from his palace provided the seeds for the creation of a nation — Rome — whose idolatries would dominate the entire world.

The doorway in which Rabbi Yehoshua unfolded a mat represents the wide-open doorway of the letter ה, which is blocked by sin. Rome, the empire founded on a reed, blocked that doorway. With its armed might it destroyed the Temple, expelled the Jews from their land, and proceeded to attempt to swallow them up in its godless culture. It closed the door to spirituality before the Jewish people.

He broke open the wall.

The Elders asked, Why would a householder keep a utensil which causes more damage than good? What is the purpose of God permitting Rome to replace the purported Chosen Nation in the Holy Land?

The assumption behind the Elders' argument is that the expulsion of the Jews from their land was a punitive act on the part of God, indicative of His having rejected His people. If this were the case, then it would certainly follow that the Romans, having inherited the Land, must be a more worthy nation: for why would God dismiss one evil people only to take on another even more evil?

But, explains Rabbi Yehoshua, the truth is that God drove the Jews from their land as an act of love, to cause them to return to Him and to fulfil their destiny. The Romans are a mere tool with which God will realize this hope.

If the Romans existed only to enjoy the holiness of the Land of Israel, the fact of their conquest of the Land would be a disproof of Jewish destiny. But the Romans' conquest of the Land of Israel was not intended to enhance its spiritual potential (which indeed they are incapable of doing) but rather to block access to it. This very blockage was their unintentional service to God, making the repentance of His people, when it comes, complete and final. For only when they are surrounded and dominated by the godless Roman culture and yet reject it will their repentance be complete.

When Rabbi Yehoshua broke through the wall he formed a new entrance into the blocked house. He was saying, "Observe! I have blocked the door with a reed mat. But note that this obstruction has caused me to break through the wall and open a new doorway. Were the doorway not blocked, I would never have found it necessary to break through the wall. In the same manner, Rome's successes challenge those who have left the world of the ה to force their way back in through the entrance at its roof."

The reed mat causes damage by blocking the principal doorway, but this very damage is its great accomplishment: the obstruction forces anyone who would re-enter the building to break open a new entrance. This service is surely worth more than the temporary damage of the reed mat blocking the doorway; if not for that impediment, the second door would never have been made. If the Land were not blocked before them, the Jewish people would never be able to eradicate evil; they would never achieve full repentance and would never push upwards to the second doorway of the ה.

The Elders did not know that ה is the true shape of the world. They did not know that the world exists to overcome evil and to imbue the physical with the spiritual. Measured against the usefulness of the open entrance which it blocks, the reed mat is in fact a utensil not worth the damage it does. But once the wall is broken open and the rightful tenant has come back into his home, it will be clear to all that the utensil was worth its damage, that it fully served its owner's purpose.

20
The Hooves Of Rome[1]

For what was the First Temple destroyed? For [the] three [cardinal] sins that were rampant then: idolatry, sexual immorality, and murder. . . . But in the time of the Second Temple [the Jews] kept busy studying Torah, and performing mitzvos, and doing acts of kindness; for what then was it destroyed? Because of their unwarranted hatred of each other. From this one may learn that unwarranted hatred is as great a sin as idolatry, immorality, and murder all together.

. . . Said Rabbi Yochanan: Better the claws of earlier generations than the bowels of our own generations. [And if you would say that we are better than they, consider that] the Temple was rebuilt for them and has not been rebuilt for us.

(Yoma 9b)

20.1 THE FINAL TEST

Jewish history, we have said, is the story of how Avraham's descendants have faced trial after trial to overcome every aspect of evil, thereby paving the way for the coming of the Mashiach.

Thus Nevuchadnezzar and the Babylonian Empire attempted to force their idolatry upon the Jewish people, but the Jews resisted and remained faithful to their God. The Persian Empire tempted them with sensual pleasures, but

1 In the Hebrew text, this text is part of the previous chapter, "The Blocked Entrance."

the Jews met the test, and commemorate their victory on Purim. Greece sought to seduce the Jews into cultural assimilation; that the Jews successfully met the challenge is celebrated by Chanukkah. Each era presented its own test, each of which was successfully overcome.

The Roman period was the culmination of this process. The long and weary road had been travelled successfully, and there only remained one ultimate evil to be overcome. Not the urge to idolatry, not the temptations of the flesh: the challenge of this era was to face the deepest-rooted evil of them all, man's collective selfishness.[2] Man's instinctive drive to believe in his own power, his fantasy that human accomplishment is the result of man's own efforts, had to be overpowered. At last the Jewish people must efface itself completely and finally before God, trusting His providence absolutely.

The challenge was not met. Instead of rejecting collective selfishness utterly, the Jewish nation allowed itself to be infected with this peculiarly Roman disease, and became caught up in worship of the self and, its corollary, the search for dominion and power over other men. Inevitably the selfishness created a society of mutual competition which penetrated to the individual level. The ambitions of each individual for mastery and control over others caused him to see the other's existence as a threat to the fulfillment of his own goals. These ambitions caused Jews to begin to hate one another, with an unwarranted hatred which had no cause except resentment of the other's very existence. When this hatred had become so firmly implanted in them that there was no hope of overcoming the evil of selfishness, God took back his gifts of the Holy Temple and the Land of Israel. The long exile had begun.

20.2 Claws and Hooves

A kosher animal has two signs of its *kashrus:* it chews its cud and its hooves are cloven. These two signs have a com-

2 For a fuller discussion of this aspect of evil, see Chapter 13.

mon element: they are a clear indication that this is not a beast of prey, and that it is content with its lot. A hunting animal does not chew its cud, since it eats no vegetable matter, and meat is digestible without rumination. Once the prey is digested, the predator seeks new food, ever discontent and ravenous, whereas a ruminant is content with whatever is already in its stomach and makes it do double service. A hunting animal possesses claws with which to tear its victims apart; a kosher animal is satisfied with the food its Creator brings forth for it from the ground. Having no victims, it needs only its hooves.

The commentaries explain that non-kosher animals are forbidden as food because eating them subtly influences man towards the undesired characteristics of a beast of prey: discontent with one's lot and the resultant exploitation of other creatures. Nothing is more antithetical to spiritual health than these character traits. The last of the Ten Commandments is לא תחמוד — "You shall not covet," and it is the foundation for them all. Dissatisfaction with one's lot stems from a lack of true faith in God's providence.

Nearly all non-kosher animals lack both of these signs. The Torah details just four animals that have one sign but lack the other: the camel, the rabbit, the hare and the pig. The first three chew their cud but do not have cloven hooves. The last, the pig, has cloven hooves but does not chew its cud.

These four are singled out by the Torah not only because of their impurity for the Jewish table but because they also represent four forms of spiritual impurity. The first three animals have the internal sign of *kashrus* (chewing the cud) but not the external one. Thus they represent the various manifestations of a frustrated spiritual nature, when one's inner essence is amenable to holiness, but is prevented from realizing itself by one's inappropriate external behavior. If one's behavior is exploitative of others (like that of a predator), then one's "hooves" — his outer nature — have become "claws," even though one's inner nature remains potentially "ruminant," i.e., satisfied with its lot.

The fourth animal, the pig, has the external sign of *kashrus* but not the internal one. Thus it represents a worse form of impurity: a person whose outer behavior is expressive of holiness, but who inwardly denies the dominion of God. This person has "cloven hooves" instead of claws, but his inner nature is that of a beast of prey; claws would suit him better.

The four forms of spiritual impurity which these animals represent, say the Sages, represent as well the four great kingdoms that in the course of history subjugated the Jewish people: Babylon, Persia, Greece, and Rome. The first three, respectively, are represented by the camel, the rabbit and the hare; the fourth, Rome, by the pig.[3]

Like the non-kosher animals mentioned in the Torah, the first three kingdoms demonstrated the behavior of a beast of prey, seeking wealth and self-aggrandizement at the expense of others. But within their hearts they believed in God and His providence. The Roman Empire, however, displayed all the external signs of commitment to spirituality: on the surface it was civilized, looked after human welfare, and preached justice and human rights; but inwardly it believed in nothing but self-worship.[4]

20.3 Claws and Bowels

Better the claws of earlier generations than the bowels of our own generations.

External behavior that exemplifies impurity but in fact hides an essential inner purity is better than inner defilement hidden by a veneer of piety. Following this principle, Rabbi Yochanan explains why the earlier generations of the Jewish people, who wallowed in the three cardinal sins of

3 Vayikra Rabba 13.

4 *Cf.* §17.6, and the discussion there of Eisav's care in honoring his father.

idolatry, sexual immorality, and murder, were preferable to the later generations, who appeared to be pious, diligently studying the Torah, and obeying its commands. The earlier generations, says Rabbi Yochanan, suffered from serious evil in their external behavior, but in their hearts they acknowledged God's kingship. It was simply that they could not govern their lusts. Later generations (specifically those of the Roman period) led a satisfactory external life; but their society was filled with clandestine hatred and jealousy, because their hearts were rotten with selfishness and the resultant denial of God's dominion in human life. They did not really trust that He would provide them with their needs, and imagined that man alone was in charge of his fate. Worst of all, they believed that any other human being was a potential threat to their own success, and thus made him the object of their hatred.

Following the symbolism of the kosher and non-kosher animals, the earlier generations were like animals that have claws but chew their cud, whereas the later generations were like the pig: they showed their cloven hooves, but inwardly were unclean. Rabbi Yochanan's comment says, Better one who behaves like a beast of prey but whose heart longs for God than the most pietistic of men who in his heart worships only himself.

How fitting, then, that when the inner corruption of the Jews became so great that God was obliged to drive them from their land, the nation to which they were enslaved was none other than Rome: the nation that proclaimed human values, justice, responsible rule, whose symbol the Torah gives as the pig, and which demonstrated all the external signs of *kashrus*; all the time inwardly worshiping nothing but itself and its own glory. It was a nation that was the externalized mirror of the values the Jewish nation had taken for its own.

Since they had not rejected this culture, they were made its slaves. The reason was simple: since they had not overcome human selfishness the easy way, they could now only do it the hard way. While living a life of suffering, dispersion, and enslavement, they would have to reject the Roman value system from within its very midst. If they succeeded in this awesome task, they would have undone the evil for which they were expelled from their land.

The test of the Roman dominion is the most difficult the Jewish people has ever faced — and it faces it to this very day. For it comprises the most difficult struggle of them all: man's rejection of his self-worship.

The struggle has gone on steadily for the last nineteen hundred years, as the Roman heritage of the Western world continues to dominate Jewish life in one form or another. It is carried out under the most difficult conditions which have ever challenged the Jewish people. However, there is good reason for all these difficulties, for on this struggle hangs the fate of the world. When this last evil has been eradicated, Adam's sin will be fully rectified, the Mashiach will come, and humanity will finally realize the goals for which it was created.

תושלב"ע

בהלי"כ ולאאע"י

Appendix

An Essay on the Aggaddos[1]

מאמר על ההגדות

by

Rabbi Moshe Chaim Luzzatto

(5467-5507 / 1707-1747)

The Aggadic passages can be divided into two classes; didactic and interpretive. The didactic passages are those which teach the principles of ethical or Divine wisdom; the interpretive ones are those which elucidate a verse of the Holy Scriptures.

There is no need to discuss here the didactic passages dealing with ethics, for their benefit is well-known and their importance obvious. No one can argue with them, nor can even the most stubborn of people misinterpret them. But we shall discuss here the didactic passages concerning Divine wisdom.

It is well-known what moved the Sages to commit the Oral Torah to writing, even though their tradition taught that "Oral teachings may not be taught in writing."[2] It was because they saw that what with the lengthy exile and the vicissitudes of the times, people's minds were becoming weaker and weaker, their memory was becoming shorter, and their understanding was decreasing, so the Torah might be forgotten.

1 Published 1) as an appendix to *Derech HaShem* (Warsaw, 5696); 2) as part of the introduction to the Vilna (Romm) edition of *Ein Yaakov* (the standard omnibus of Aggadata); 3) in *Sefer HaMaamarim* (Jerusalem: Levin-Epstein, 1972).

2 *Cf.* Gittin 60b.

Therefore, basing themselves on [the verse], "It is time to do [something] for God; [therefore] disturb the Torah,"[3] they decided to set down the entire explanation of the mitzvos in a book so that it would endure for all time. This is the Mishnah and the Gemara.

After further consideration they realized that their apprehension for the mitzvos[4] applied equally to the hidden wisdom of the Torah and the principles of Divine knowledge. However, the solution they had devised for the Torah's laws would not suit its esoteric section. This was because it is no harm to anyone if the explanations of the mitzvos and laws are set down in writing, clear and plain for every reader. But it would not be fitting to deliver the esoteric part [of the Torah] to everyone who wants to pretend to wisdom.

This is both on account of the great value of these concepts and on account of their depth. As for their value, it would be disrespectful towards the Creator, blessed be He, to give over His secrets to men of bad character, even if they be brilliant scholars. As for its depth (and these ideas are indeed extremely deep), only persons of clear mind, who have been well trained in correct logical analysis, will succeed in [understanding] them. Dense individuals and those untrained in correct logic, if they should come across them, would so interpret these true and precious concepts as to make them erroneous and harmful.

Therefore [the Sages] decided on a compromise: they would commit [the Torah's hidden concepts] to writing so that they would not be lost to succeeding generations, but [they would do so] in an obscure form or in various riddles, so that no one could understand them unless he had been given the proper keys — that is, the rules by which the allusions can be understood and the riddles explained. For one not privy to the keys, [these cryptic sayings] would be like something written in a sealed book, or as if they had

3 Tehillim 119:126.

4 I.e., that they might be forgotten.

never been written at all. These keys were put into the hands of the Sages' disciples, who had received the [interpretations of the hidden wisdom] from their teachers, and [the Sages] relied upon them to transmit this wisdom only to those among their disciples who were as worthy as they themselves. And so it continued, generation after generation.

They furthermore admonished (with the force of a command) everyone who understood and taught [this wisdom] to caution and inform everyone that the Sages' teachings and their enigmas need careful study, and that anyone who approaches them without having the keys [to their understanding] is deliberately exposing himself to harm. Once this warning has been given, anyone who rushes in to this study without having the keys and then falls back crippled has no one but himself to blame for the disaster, and the Sages are absolved of responsibility.

* * *

Now, the Sages used various methods to disguise their ideas. One is the method of metaphor and parable. These are the literary devices of expert writers and speakers, with which by way of simile and parable they ascribe phenomena and functions to entities for whom such phenomena and functions are completely inappropriate.

Another method is that of [deliberate] obscurity: that is, suppressing any mention of the conditions in which a statement is true. The Sages may make an absolute statement, when in fact the statement is true only within limits, for example, only in one aspect or one subject, or only at a certain time or in a certain situation. Whoever takes that statement as being general and absolute will become snared in error and confusion. Thus there are many statements [of the Sages] which appear mutually contradictory because their limiting conditions have not been spelled out; but someone who knows the limits defining each one of them will find them correct and not in the least contradictory.

We may observe that this same situation prevails in many of the Sages' statements about Halachah and mitzvos (though the intent in this case was not the same). For one finds in the Talmud statements or Baraisos which, if they were understood as absolute, would be either false or contradictory; but they are interpreted in the Talmud by remarks [such as] הכא במאי עסקינן ("what is the context of this case?"), and once each statement is defined within its limits, all is clear and well-reasoned.

The third method is [deliberate] triviality, namely, that some great and noble principle is alluded to by means of a statement which appears trivial or inconsequential, as it were a folk tale. But the Sages are actually referring to noble and lofty concepts, and this seemingly trivial statement provides a clue to them for someone who knows how to detect such a clue and who can think abstractly so as to deduce the implicit from the explicit and abstruse concepts from lowly ones. Examples [of this method] are their statements, "Youth is a crown of roses; old age is a crown of weeds," and "I search for what I have not lost,"[5] and many similar statements.

One must also know that many fundamentals of the hidden wisdom are alluded to by the Sages by [statements about] natural or astronomical science, in which they used whatever the scientists in those generations were presenting as facts. What mattered to the Sages, however, is not the natural or astronomical concept but the esoteric concept that they wished to allude to. Thus the truth or falsehood of the parable with which the Sages cloaked their ideas has no bearing on the truth of the idea to which they alluded, for they only wanted to disguise the hidden wisdom in a commonplace idea of that generation's science. The same concept might as well have been cloaked in some other form in accordance with whatever was accepted as fact in other times,

5 Shabbas 152a. The second citation ostensibly refers to the stooped posture of an old man, which gives him the appearance of searching for a lost coin.

and so the author of that very statement would have framed it had he been making his statement in those generations.

Besides all this, one must know that our Sages hold to their principle: that all physical objects are empowered by, and follow the direction of, the various spiritual forces, namely the angels, the demons and the harmful spirits *[mazikin]*. Everything in the physical world acts in accordance with these supernal influences; but equally, physical things make their impression upon the spiritual forces. Someone who is unaware of this principle will be completely unable to understand even the slightest bit of the Sages' wisdom.

* * *

Until now we have discussed the Sages' didactic statements; now we shall discuss their interpretive statements.

There are three types of interpretive statements. One is intended to explain the direct meaning of the verse, where the significance of the verse is, in their opinion, what they state here.

The second type is not intended to give the actual meaning of the verse. Rather it follows the tradition that the Sages received about how the Creator, blessed be He, dictated the Torah, the Prophetic books, and the Hagiographa. For in addition to what He wished to be written explicitly, with the words plainly saying just so, He wished to suggest many other true concepts by each written story or passage. He did not wish that these other ideas be written explicitly, only to allude to them by a few letters or words. The Sages of blessed memory received as a tradition both these ideas and the methods by which they are alluded to in the Scriptures. Of course, a Scriptural verse cannot possibly be understood to be speaking in its plain meaning about these matters, for the Creator, blessed be He, did not wish to have the verses speak of such concepts openly, only to allude to them.

The third type follows a further tradition of our Sages:

that the Creator dictated the Holy Scriptures in such a way that their text would contain many aspects of truth. With His wisdom He encompassed all the concepts that are true regarding each subject [spoken of by the Scriptures] — although they are not [all] true from the same perspective but from many different perspectives, as we shall explain with the help of Heaven. Thus God wrote the Torah in such a manner and style that when all the possible interpretations which the words will allow are worked out (in accordance with certain rules and methods) then all the aspects of truth which God in fact desired to include in the text would be revealed. And this amounts to the totality of all the ideas which are in any way (even partially) relevant to that subject. It follows, then, that God caused the entire Scriptures to be written in such a way that everything which can be understood from its words by following the rules we have mentioned will be true regarding that particular subject.

However, much study is still needed, and great wisdom too, in order to know in what sense each of these [derived concepts] is true. For, as we have already said, they are not all true from the same aspect and in the same way; rather from different aspects and in varying ways. Some may be true only when viewed from a unique aspect; some only in a metaphorical sense; some only as regards a corollary that can be derived from them; some only as regards God's ways of giving just reward. (This last is exemplified by the statement "מעלה עליו הכתוב" ["Scripture views him as if. . ."] so often found in the Sages' teachings.[6] For when it comes to merit and blame, reward and punishment, what is lacking can be deemed present and what is present deemed lacking, and likewise a little can be valued as a lot or a lot valued as only a little — all according

6 E.g., Avos 3:6. This expression is used to explain why a great reward or punishment is given for a relatively minor act. Because "the Scriptures consider the person as if" his act was of major importance, he deserves an equivalent reward or punishment.

to the prevailing circumstances.) This is what the Sages meant when they said

> Just as the later generation did not [destroy all the idols] yet Scripture credits them for it, so the earlier generation did not [build all the idols] yet Scripture blames them for it.[7]

* * *

These matters have so many details to them that they cannot all be assembled here. But what one should know is that a statement [of the Sages] can be approached in one way out of all the above and found to be true, whereas by every other approach it will not be true, as we might expect[8] of an absolute statement. Consequently, one need not be upset upon encountering a statement which at first glance seems false or inaccurate, for if we can but muster enough wisdom to discover what sense it was meant to be understood in, we will see how it is true and gain satisfaction from it. But someone who already knows the principles of Divine wisdom will know the limiting conditions of all these things.

Now I have already mentioned that when we say that everything which can be understood from the words of Scripture is true in some way, this is not a blanket statement. For there are methods and rules involved, namely the rules governing Aggadata. One could easily fall into error by interpreting a verse without employing these aforementioned rules; for then the derived interpretation might be a total falsehood, completely unconnected with the truth. What is more, even if the interpretation were essentially true, it might be inappropriate to this particular verse, whose words might not have been intended to reflect that particular matter.

7 Shabbas 56b.

8 The *Ein Yaakov* (Vilna) edition has כ"ש here, which was expanded (apparently mistakenly) to כל שכן in the *Derech HaShem* edition. However, in *Sefer HaMaamarim* (Jerusalem, 1972) the reading is כמו שנאמר, which is the basis of the present translation.

This is the reason that we occasionally find one of the Sages declaring another's derivations to be mistaken. This is because in this Sage's opinion, the other Sage had made incorrect use of the rules of Aggadata (with which they were all familiar) while deriving his interpretation. Although we cannot make out from their arguments what the interpreter's error was, the Sages [needed only to] hint briefly to each other to indicate the error, or to rebut arguments [posed against an interpretation]. All of this followed the rules which were so familiar to them, but not to us, and so it is hard for us to understand their premises, their arguments, and their rebuttals. But someone who truly understands these methods will find everything to be perfectly clear and orderly.

For example, when Rabbi Meir interpreted the verse, "The king was still at his feast"[9] in a way which disparaged the Jewish people, the other Sages said to him, "Shir HaShirim is not to be interpreted in a disparaging manner, only in a complimentary one."[10] This was because the rule they had received [about Shir HaShirim] was so, in which case anyone who interprets its verses disparagingly is straying from the intention [that] the Divine spirit [had for this book].

Similarly, when Rabbi Levi interpreted Scripture to say that Avraham was born circumcised, Rabbi Berechyah tells us that "At that point Rabbi Abba bar Cahana spoke to Rabbi Levi without respect."[11] This was because of the rule they had received, that in a [Scriptural] story about the righteous everything applicable must be interpreted in a complimentary manner, and vice versa in a story about an evildoer. For this was their received tradition: that the Creator's intention, blessed be He, in causing His words to be written down, was to allude to every detail of evildoers' wickedness and to make plain every bit of their disgrace; and vice versa with the righteous, [His intention was] to avoid disparaging them as much

9 Shir HaShirim 1:12.

10 Midrash Rabba, Shir HaShirim *ad loc.*11.

11 Midrash Rabba on Bereishis 47:9.

as was possible and to make plain whatever redounded to their praise. Now whoever wishes to make a true interpretation [of a text] must follow the author's method, for only then will he be in harmony with his intent — but this is obvious.

The Sages had a further tradition, that in addition to alluding to the topics related to the story being told, Scripture also is alluding to various future or past topics. Accordingly, each Sage interpreted them in his own manner, in accordance with the laws and rules which they knew of.

* * *

It was in fact possible that someone might err in his derivation, and on account of this the Sages who arranged the Talmud and the Midrashim (who were outstanding wise men of their generations) went to such great trouble to gather together all such statements and assess [their truth] in consultation with all their fellows. All statements that were found worthy, and which yielded truth according to the approach which ought to reveal their truth, were entered into the Midrashim they were compiling.

It therefore becomes apparent that all that is written in the Aggadic interpretations of the Sages is true, every concept in its own way, for they have all been tried in the crucible of investigation and found trustworthy by the aforementioned Sages who arranged the Midrashim. We can rely on them that they would not enter into their works anything that they had not investigated and found fitting, each matter in the manner proper to it.

Subject Index

שונדין ופונדיון הוא ב' איסרין. כמ"ש כי מעה ד' איסרין ואמרו (פאה פ"ה) אלימתי כ"א מתרין בלקט כו' שלא כדי שיהא העני יוצא ולא יהא מביא בארבעה איסרין. שהוא מזונות לו ולאשתו ליום אחד כמ"ש הר"ש ור"ש ע"ש שהוא ששנו מככר בפונדיון כו' ע"ש. וזהו מעלה גרה שהוא מדת מזונו בלתלום לעני ביום א' כמ"ש כל מי שיש לו פת בסלו ואמר מה אוכל למחר כו' וכמ"ש (שמות י"ו) דבר יום ביומו כו' כידוע. וגמל וארנבת ושפן סימן טהרה שלהם מעלה גרה וסימן טומאה שאינו מפריס פרסה ובחזיר להיפך. והענין כמ"ש במדרש רבה (שמיני פ' י"ג) גמל זו מלכות בבל ארנבת כו' ע"ש היטב כמ"ש (תהלים פ') יכרסמנה חזיר מיער כמ"ש (פסחים קי"ח) ע"ש. ואמרו (יומא ט':) ראשונים עדיפי או אחרונים עדיפי ואמרו ראשונים עדיפי אדרבא אחרונים עדיפי דעסקי בתורה ואמרו תנו עיניכם בבירה כו'. והענין כי ראשונים שנתגלה עונם נתגלה קיצם. אחרונים כו' והטעם כי הראשונים היו מעשיהם הטובים טמונים. ועונותיהם גלוים. כי לבם היה טוב. ואחרונים להיפך ורמנא ליבא בעי כמ"ש (סנהדרין ק"ו:) רבותא למבעי בעי בשני דרב יהודא כו'. ע"ש ואמרו ראשונים שהי' בהם ע"ז וג"ע וש"ד אלא שתלו בטחונם בהקב"ה. נמצא כי מעשיהם רע מאוד שבולן ביהרג ועל יעבור עבירות חמורות שבתורה ולבם הי' טוב מאוד שמעלת הבטחון על כולם כנ"ל. ואחרוני' עסקו בתורה ובג"ח ומפני מה חרבה מפני שנאת חנם ללמדך ששקולה שנאת חנם כו' כמ"ש (ברכו' ס"ג) איזה פרשה קטנה כו' ואהבת לריעך והוא מחוסר הבטחון שכל הקנאה והשנאה ממנו ולכן ראשונים הגלו בג' מלכיות שסימן טהרה שלהם מבפנים וסימן טומאה שלהם מבחוץ ואחרונים בגלות ישמעאל שנמשלה לחזיר שהוא בהיפך והוא פושט טלפיו להראות סימני טהרה שלו. ושבע תועבות בלבו. וכן הוא בגלות הזה מדתן של ע"ר ונעשה לנו שם כנ"ל. וענין סימני טהרה בטלפיו לא השדים ולודה לי ליד בכיבוד אב אבל כי ליד הוא סימן טומאה לד וטורף כנ"ל בפיו שאינו מעלה גרה כו' ח"ש טובים נפרכן של ראשונים סימן טומאה שלהם מכריסן של אחרונים והבן. נמצא כי בגלות הזה עשו פושט טלפיו רגל הקו"ף ושיט מניח ברגלו הה"א ליכנס והוא סית קנה. וזה בודיא פתר לתרעא פתח הה"א ויש לנו תקוה לכנס בפתח קטן של תליית ה"א שגם הקו"ף מניח זה כנ"ל. ויצה"ר אינו מניח לשוב והוא סית דמאן כנ"ל סית קנה. וז"ש (בזוהר ס"א) עיקרן בב' אותיות אלו חי"ת קו"ף. וזה שאמרו (ברכות י"ז) רבון העולמים גלוי וידוע כו' אלא ששאור שבעיסה שהוא היצה"ר מ' שסותם תליית הה"א כנ"ל. ושעבוד מלכיות עשו רגל הקו"ף לכנס מלמטר יהי רצון שתשבור מעלינו ונשוב לעשות רצונך בלבב שלם ואז יעשה ה"א הנה הנס:

פירוש המאמר ששון ושמחה. כ'...

סוד יפה נוף משוש כל הארץ. הם ד' מינים שבלולב שהם ד' אותיות הוי' כידוע. יפה הוא אתרוג. פרי עץ הדר. נוף הוא הדס ענף עץ כו'. משוש הוא ערבי נחל שהם אפיקי מים כמ"ש בתז"ח פ"ג ע"ג ושתית מאשר ישאבון הנערים דאינון ברהטים בשקתות המים ר"ל ברהטים ידועים שהם הרגלים. ואמר שם תרין נביאי קשוט אפיקי מים. ולכן נקרא' ערבי נחל וגדלים על הנחל. והוא נהר דנגיד ונפיק. נביאים מגינה. ואמר שם ויעמד שם שעורים וישת עלי' דא ביעורא דתרין שוקין וכן בתז"ח רנ"ח אמר שם שאינון שית סלקין. וזהו ניסוך המים לשיתין. ואמרו (סוכה מ"ט). חמוקי ירכיך אלו השיתין. שהם ירכין כידוע. ולכן כל השמחה הי' בשאיבת המים וזהו משוש. כל הוא הלולב לדיק כידוע. הארץ שהיא כולל הכל כמ"ש בס"ד והארץ תנינא לאו במושבן כו' והוא כורסייא קדישא דרגא חמישאה ברזא דאלקים בסוד המאור הקטן כמ"ש בפ' בראשית והוא סוד בשמחה לאודם כמ"ש במעשה מרכבה בזו"ח יתרו ובתיקונים בהקדמה וגלא נקרא בשון והוד נקרא שמחה ונגדן בס"א והרגלים ילאו כו' כמ"ש בזוהר ואפיזתם שם כמ"ש באד"ר. והאמת גבוה מן השנית (כאן חסר שורה בהעתק) שנבנמי' אמת נלא גבוה ובנבמי' א' הוד. וז"ש (סוכה מ"ח) א"ל ששון לשמחה אבא עדיפנא כו' א"ל שמחה כו' חד יומא שנקיך ושייך פרונקא. כי הם הרגלים כנ"ל ולע"ל רעו זרים צאנכם. א"ל חד יומא שנקיך ומלו בך היא כנ"ל שהם אפיקי מים. ולע"ל מעורו של לויתן יעשו סוכה וז"ש הפשטת עור כאן ואז זמן שמחתינו. ונו"ה הם משט' לגבורה. שלכן שניהם כרובים זהב וזהו ירכתי צפון. ומשם ישאבון מים גבורות ממותקות שהם נקר' ישועות כמ"ש בפ' בראשית ד' ע"ו ע"ש. וזהו ושאבתם מים בששון ממעיני הישועה:

כי חזא שיתין ביסתרקי סבר כולהו חבראי לדהבא אתו א"ל לספונא שרי ספינת' בהדי דאתי איתי עפ'מעפרייהו כי מטה לבי בליעי אית ביה תלת צלמון חד מטי ידיה ארישי' והד מטי אליביה ובתרא דכולהו מחוי בידיה לאחוריה שקל כוזא דמיא מבי בליעי כי אתא אוקמינהו קמי' קיסר וחזנהו דחוי מענו אמר ליה לאו הני אינהו שקל מעפרייהו שדא עלייהו אקשו לאפי מלכא אמר ליה כל דבעית עביד להו איתו הנהו מיא דאתי מבי בליעי שדינהו בתיגדא אמר להו מליוה ואיזלו לבו מלו שדו ביה קמא קמא הוה קא בלע להו מלו עד דשמיט כתפייהו ובלו ואזול:

רש"י

וכי חזא שיתין ביסתרקי. סבר כל חברי לחדר זה יבואו: **א"ל רבי יהושע. לספונא.** רב החובל: **שרי ספינתך.** התר ספינתך ולך: **לבי בליעי.** מים שבאוקיינוס שבולעין כל מים שנופלין בו ומבליעין אותן עד תהום ופולטות אותן דכתי' והים איננו מלא: **דהוו מענו.** מעונים ושפלים לפי שלא היו באהלם: **אקשו.** העיזו פניהם ודברו קשות את המלך כשהריחו את ריח אהלם והיו סבורים להיות קרוב לאהלם: **בתיגדא.** בכלי ל"א בסילאה בחביות: **דשמוט כתפייהו.** נשמטו פרקי שכמם: **ובלו ואזול.** כלו והלכו לאבדון:

בי' הגר"א

בזוהר. ואמרו מ"ט שקרא לא קאי שקר אין בו רגלים ופירשו דקאי אחד כרעא של קוף שיורד למטה ואמרו (שבת ק"ד) ק' קדוש ר' רשע. אבל בזוהר פ' בראשית כתב דקו"ף רי"ש הן אותיות דאתחזיאו על ס"ס בישא כמ"ש (שם ב' ע"ב). עאלת אות ש' קמיה כו'. אבל הואיל ואתוון דזייפא כו' מכאן תאן דבעי למימר שיקרא כו'. וזה שאמרו כל שקר שאין אמת בתחלתו אין מתקיים. לפיכך בשקר אות ש' בתחלתו. אבל קשר רשעים אינו מן המנין שהוא באמצעי. ומפריש בין קו"ף לר'. וענין ק' ר' הוא רשע כנ"ל וקו"ף הוא שטן הוא יצה"ר כמ"ש כמה פעמים בזוהר. שהוא קו"ף בפני אדם. ורגליו יורדות מות וכמ"ש (בז"ח כ"ג ס"ה ע"ב) בשעתא דאיהי אתרת בזכירה דוליך מיין אידכרת דהא ערלה כו'. ואות קו"ף אתפשט כו' ע"ש ושם בסוף העמוד והוא מקטרגא פשיט זנביה כו'. ע"ש כל המאמר. ובזה יתפרש המאמר בזוהר (פ' פנחס רנ"ב ע"א) שם גער חית קנה דא חיה דאתאחד בה עשו. ת"ח בתלרים איהו שלטה כו' כל המאמר עד הנה הנס. ושם בר"מ ובגין דא ק' דאיהו קוטא זעירא חבר לה וייעול ה' באתרא כו' עד מנשר אתן ע"ש היטב. והענין כי ה' מורה על שליטת הקדושה שנעשית ה'. כמ"ש הרבה פעמים בזוהר ובז"ח שם. כדין אתפרש מגו מקדשא ועריק וכלה נפקא לגבה דרחימא כו' ועיילת באות ה'. וכן שם בסוף העמוד ע"ש וכמ"ש הא לכם זרע וקוף הוא אות של ס"א ויתחבר רגלה ומתעביד ה'. וכן ת' ויתחבר קוטא זעירא ואתעביד ה' בסוד חמץ מלה כמ"ש בזוהר ור"מ שם. והענין כמ"ש (מנחות כ"ט:) מפני מה נברא העוה"ז בה"א מפני שדומה לאכסדרא שכל הרוצה לצאת יצא מ"ט תלא כרעא דה' דאי הדר בתשובה מעיילי לי' וליעייל בהך לא מסתייעא מילתא כו' ע"ש. והענין שאמרו לא מסתייעא מילתא ליעול בפתח שלמטה כיון שחטא נעשית מה' קו"ף שהוא יצה"ר שאחריו הר' שהוא רשע. שקו"ף רודף אחר הר' וכיון שחטא נמתח רגל ה"ה ונעשה קו"ף. וזה ההפרש שבין ה' לקו"ף לכך מנים בשניהם תליית רגל ה' וקו"ף. כמ"ש בשבת ובמנחות בשניהם מפני מה רגל הא' וקו"ף תלויה דאי הדר ביה ליעול בהך. ולעתיד לבא יחבר רגל הקו"ף ויכנסו בפתח רווחה מלמטה שעכשיו לא מסתייע מפני יצה"ר וע"ש במהרש"א. עמ"כ לעתיד וז"ש הקב"ה לישראל פתחו לי כחודה של מחט ואני אפתח לכם פתח שיעברו גמלים וקרונות. ר"ל שיכנסו בו התליית רגל הקו"ף כחוד של מחט ואני אפתח לכם כו' מלמטה שאתבר רגל הקו"ף ויעול בהך שהקוף רגליו יורדות מות כמ"ש רגליו יורדות כו'. וזהו מתיחת רגל הקו"ף והוא חית קנה כנ"ל. וענין הקו"ף הוא עשו שפושט טלפיו ומראה סימני טהרה. וכן ביצה"ר שמראה סימני טהרה לאדם ואינו מניח לשוב. וענין פשיטת הטלפים כי ענין סימני טהרה שני סימנים מעלה גרה ומפרסת פרסה. והענין כמ"ש הקדמונים כי בעוף אמרו כל עוף הדורס טמא וענין כי מאכילת הדבר כפי מזג המאכל כן יהיה טבע האוכל. כי אבר מחזיק אבר וז"ש נפש הבהמות שבאדם ונפש המוספת וסוד הקרבנות כידוע. וכל העבירות והחטאים הכל מחמדה כמ"ש כי לא תחמוד כולל כל הדברות וכל התורה כמו שהאריכו בזה. ועיין בדבריהם וכל העוף הטורף טרף הוא סימן שאינו בו מדות ההסתפקות. וכמ"ש (מכות כ"ד) בא חבקוק והעמידן על אחת ולדיק באמונתו יחיה (חבקוק ב') והוא ההסתפקות וכן הוא בבהמה סימן מעלה גרה שמסתפק במאכל שבקרבו וכן מפרסת פרסה הוא סימן שאינו דורס וטורף טרף אלא גדל על אבוסו. ז"ש מעלה גרה וכ"ל למה גרה והענין כי ודאי מי שיש לו הרבה מאוד יותר על מידת סיפוקו והוא מסתפק בהם בודאי אינו ממידת הסתפקות רק מי שמסתפק כדי סיפוקו זה הוא מדת הסתפקות ונאמר (שמות ל') עשרים גרה השקל ומתרגמינן עשרין מעה ואמרו כי מעה הוא שני

פנדיון

אייתי איהו תרי גביני א"ל הי דעיזא חיוורתא והי דעיזא אוכמתי. אמרי ליה ודציצא דמיית בביעתיה בהי נפקא רוחיה אמר להו בהיינו דעאיל. אמרו ליה אחוי לן מנא דלא שוי לחבליה אייתי בודיא פשטוה לא הוה עייל בתרע' אמר להו אייתו מרא סתרו היינו מנא דלא שוי לחבליה אייתינהו כל חד וחד

כי

זגתא. תרנגולת: ודליילה דמית. אפרוח שמת בתוך קליפתו: אחוי לן מני דלא שוי לחבליה. הראנו כלי שאינו שוה הפסד שהוא מפסיד: בודייא. מחללת: לא עייל בתרעא. שהיה ארוך ורוחב יותר מן הפתח: לייתו: מרא. פיש"ר בלע"ז וסתרו בנין הפתח והכותל עד שיכנס: לייתינהו. למיכל בספינתא הואיל תכינהו והיה מביא א' א' בפני עצמו ומכניסו לחדר:

וכי

וזה ששאלו האיך אפשר בבטן אמם וכשהם קטני' לחלוק זה לקדושה וזה לס"א כמ"ש ויגדלו הנערים ויהי עשו כו' ויעקב איש תם כו' שאז הם אפרוחים זה חיוורתא וזה אוכמתא. אבל בגים האיך אפשר: (אייתי ליה איהו תרי גביני א"ל הי דעיזי אוכמתא והי דעיזי חיוורתא) הענין כמ"ש (חולין ק"ה) אכל גבינה מותר לאכול אחריו בשר אכל בשר אסור לאכול אחריו גבינה. והענין כי הטעם על לא תבשל גדי בחלב אמו כמ"ש לעיל שבעוונותינו אין נגמר מלשיו. ומפלת כ"י את משים הכינו חלנו כו' (ישעיה כ"ו) וידוע שזרע הזכר נקפא דומה לגבינה. וזרע נקיבה נלול דומה לחלב. וכשאשה מזרעת תחילה אז גובר זרע הזכר ויולדת זכר. וז"ש (איוב י') הלא כחלב תתיכני זהו אשה מזרעת תחיל' וכגבינה תקפיאני זהו אח"כ זרע הזכר ואח"כ יולדת הולד. עור ובשר תלבישני אמו מזרעת שממנו עור ובשר כו' ובעצמות וגידים תסוככני זהו זרע האב שממנו עצמות וגידים. ואח"כ חיים וחסד עשית עמדי. זהו מה שנותן בו הקב"ה כו"ן. ואם ח"ו מפלת אותו ונימוח בבלי' אז נימוח הבשר וחוזר לחלב זהו לא תבשל גדי בחלב אמו שיחזור לחלב אמו זרע האם. וז"ש אכל גבינה מותר לאכול אחריו בשר שזה סדר הלידה. אבל אכל בשר אסור לאכול אחריו גבינה שזה ח"ו סיבת הנפל. וביה"כ כאמר (ויקרא י"ו) ושני שעירים א' לשם וא' לעזאזל שהן א' ישראל שה פזורה ישראל (ירמי' נ') וא' עשו הן עשו אחי איש שעיר (בראשית כ"ז) ושניהם שוים במראה ובקומה ובדמים ושניהם מזרע א' של יצחק מאב אחד שהוא גבינה. וא"ל איזה דעיזי חיוורא ואיזה דעיזי אוכמא. מאחר שהן מטפה א' שנחלק כידוע בתאומים. שזה יותר פלא מאפרוחי' על בגים ואם א' אלא כמ"ש (תהלים נ"ח) זורו רשעי' מרחם (ירמי' א') בטרם תצא מרחם הקדשתיך: (ודליילא דמיית בביעתא בהי נפקא רוחיה בהי דעייל) דאיתא בחלק (ד' ק"י) קטני בני א"ה לכ"ע אין באין לעה"ב. שנאמר (מלאכי ג') כי הנה היום בא בוער כתנור והיו כל זדים וכל עושי רשעה קש ולהט אותם היום הבא אמר ה' צבאות אשר לא יעזוב להם שורש וענף שורש בעה"ז וענף לעוה"ב וכן כתיב (דברי' כ"ה) תמחה את זכר עמלק וכתיב (מלכים א' י"א) עד הכרית כל זכר באדום ואמרו (ב"ב כ"א) אנן זכר קרינן בצירי' ושאלו לו ע"ז אם גדולי' חטאו קטני' מה חטאו כמ"ש וירב בבת על עסקי נפש כו' וזהו רלילא בעודם קטני'. ואמר בהי דעייל כידוע שהקטני' מתים בעון אביהם. כמ"ש (שמות ל"ד) פוקד עון אבות כו' וז"ש בהי דעייל בהי מי שעייל רוחו בו והוא האב ובסיבתו יכלו ג"כ כנ"ל: (א"ל אחוי לן מנא דלא שוי לחבלא) כי הגלות של ישראל בעבור מעשיהם שאינו שובל אדלס. כמ"ש (עזרא ט' י"א) ארץ נדה היא ושאלוהו ע"ז האיך אתם אומרי' שאתם עם קרובו אף בגלות יותר. האיך הורים אתכם והושיב את עשו במקומכם. הלא הם גרועים יותר מכם. כמ"ש (אסתר ז') כי אין הצר שוה בנזק המלך. (משלי ל') תחת שלש רגזה ארץ תחת שנואה כי תבעל כו':

אייתי בודיא פשטוה לא הוה עייל בתרעא. א"ל אייתו מרא סתרה. היינו מנא דלא שוי חבלא). וכ"ה אף שעשו אינו כדאי. ונ"מ בשביל למרק עונותינו הושיב אותם. וז"ש (משלי ל') תחת שלש רגזה ארץ תחת עבד כי ימלוך כו' כנ"ל. וז"ש (דברים ט') אל תאמר בלבבך בהדוף כו' בצדקתי הביאני וברשעת הגוים כו' לא בצדקתך וביושר לבבך כו' כי ברשעת כו' ולמען כו'. הענין כי אם היו אומרים כן לא היו חוטאין מלחטוא כמ"ש (ויקרא י"ח) ולא תקיא אתכם הארץ כאשר קאה את הגוי אשר לפניכם. והם לא היו חוטאין כיון שלא הושיבו אותם אלא מחמת צדקתם וא"כ אפשר שלא ימלא אומה צדיקים לא יחוטו. לכן אמר לא בצדקתך רק ברשעת העמים ולמען כו'. וכמ"ש (סנהדרין נ"ח:) היינו דאמרי איגשי רהיט ונפל תורא ואזיל ושדי ליה סוסיא באורייה. והענין הבודיא שהוא מחללת של קנים שאינו יכול ליכנס בפתח מפני הקנים. כמ"ש (פסחים קי"ח ע"ב) ועוד עתידה מצרים שתביא דורון כו'. א"ל הקב"ה לגבריאל גער חית קנה שדרה בין הקנים. וענין גער חית קנה ואמירה דוקא לגבריאל. כמ"ש (שבת נ"ו) בשעה שנשא שלמה את בת פרעה נעץ גבריאל קנה בים ועלה בו שרטון ועליו נבנה כרך גדול של רומי. לכך אמר הקב"ה גער אותו קנה ויאבדו וכן מלאתי אח"כ

בזוהר

זנאמר (בראשית כ"ז) הקול קול יעקב והידים ידי עשו כשהקול קול יעקב אז אין הידים כו' וכשפוסק הקול יעקב נתורה אז והידים ידי עשו. אז מקוים בעשו ועל חרבך תחיה ומשמני הארץ מושבך מי גרם לכל זה שאין מחזיקי ידי ת"ח בישראל אז נמסר המזונות להם וזהו הגלות. כמ"ש (בזוהר קע"א) וירא כי לא יכול לו ויגע בכף ירכו שהן ברכי ת"ח שמחזיקי' בהם. והם מזונות של הת"ח והם הרימיים עומדות שהן נקראו שוקים כידוע למבין. וז"ש (ישעיה כ"ד) וכל בניך למודי ה'. שבוע הבן סימן הרימיים וד"ל. ויקח יעקב לחם לאכול ובגד ללבוש. וענין הבגדים כמ"ש (יחזקאל י"ו) ואת עירום ועריה שאין לה תורה ומע"ט. פלוקא דרבנן כל המתלבש

עיסרא דסכיני במאי קטלי לה. ערוגת סכינין במה גוזזין וקוצרין אותה: זגתא

לימיני' גדדי ואיחייטי' אמרי ומי איכא דיכול למיכרך גרדי מריחייא אמר להו ומי איכא דחייטא ריחייא. מישרא דסביני במאי קטלי ליה בקרנא דהמרא ומי איכא קרנא להמרא ומישרא דסביני מי הוייא. אייתי ליה תרי ביעי א"ל הי דוגתא חיוורתא והי דוגתא אוכמתי אייתי

בטלית של ת"ח כו'. וזהו והאבדתי קול רחיים ואור נר שהוא התורה כי אם אין קמח אין תורה והוא אור נר כי נר מצוה ותורה אור (משלי ו') וז"ש ונפלו הטוחנות כי מעטו וחשכו הרואות בארובות שהם עיני העדה כמ"ש (יחזקאל ג') צופה נתתיך לבית ישראל. וז"ש (ברכות ו'.) הני ברכי דרבנן דשלהי מינייהו. שאין מחזיקים ת"ח והוא מן העכו"ם אותן שהם המזיקים והן עומדים עלינו ככסלא לעוגיא שהוא איש שדה. הני מאני דרבנן דבלי מחופיא דידהו. ויתערבו בגוים כ"ש (תהלים ק"ו). וז"ש אית לן ריחייא דתבירא את הרימיים שלכם שנשברו. אית לנו עכשיו. זיל חייטיה שישוב לכם. (אמר כרוכי מיניה גרדי ואיחייטיה.) ועיין רש"י הוליאו מוטין. שמאחר דבלו שיוכלו לקיים התורה ואז איחייטיה גם לרחיים. (אמרו ומי איכא דיכול למכרך כו') כי אחרי שאין קמח אין תורה. (א"ל ומי איכא דחייט ריחייא) כי אם אין תורה אין קמח אחרי שאין לנו מוטים ללבוש אפי' מסיורי האריגה שבלו שהוא התורה כמ"ש לעיל. (מישרא דסכינא במאי קטלי) ר"ל עשו נתברך בו על חרבך תחי' ונקרא איש שדה. משמני הארץ מושבך. ופרנסתו וזריעתו הוא חרב וזה אמנתו בהליך יפול. וכתי' במשיח בן אפרים שימשול על כל העולם ויכלה אותם בכור שורו הדר לו וקרני ראם קרניו בהם עמים ינגח יחדיו והם רבבות אפרים (דברי' ל"ג) אבל עשו לא יפול בידו. כמ"ש (סנהדרין ל"ח) עד שתתפשט המלכות ט' חדשי' על ישראל שנא' לכן יתנם עד עת יולדה ילדה ויתר אחיו ישובון על בני ישראל ר"ל מלכות יהודה ישוב על מלכות ישראל שהם מלכות אפרי' ויבואו עם גוג ומגוג על ה' ועל משיחו כי ברכת אביו על חרבך תחי' עומדת לו. כי זכות כיבוד אביו קיימת שא תליך כו' ונודה לי ליד. וזאת החרב קיימת לו וזהו ועל חרבך תחי' כידוע שכל קיומו בשביל כיבוד אביו ולכן הזהירה תורה לישראל בבואם ממצרים (דברים ב') אתם עוברים בגבול אחיכם בני עשו ונשמרתם מאוד. אל תתגרו בם כי לא אתן לכם מארצם עד מדרך כף רגל כו'. (בקרנא דחמרא.) ר"ל ביד משיח בן דוד. שהוא עני רוכב על החמור ועל עייר בן אתונות (זכרי' ט') וכתיב (בראשית מ"ט) גור אריה יהודה כו' עד כי יבא שילה ולו יקהת עמים אסרי לגפן עירה ולשרקה בני אתונו כבס ביין לבושו ובדם ענבים סותה והענין כי אצל עשו כתיב (ישעי' ס"ג) מי זה בא מאדום חמוץ בגדים מבצרה מדוע אדם ללבושך ובגדיך כדרך בגת פורה דרכתי לבדי כו' ע"ש כל הענין. וכמ"ש (דברים ל"ב) כי מגפן סדום גפנם ומשדמות עמורה ענבימו ענבי רוש אשכלות מרורות למו. חמת תנינים יינם כו' הלא הוא כמוס עמדי כו' לי נקם ושלם לעת תמוט רגלם. ר"ל פתחלם זכות עשו אותו החרב וכמ"ש (ישעי' ב') וכתתו חרבותם לאתים כו'. ר"ל זכות החרב ואומנות החרב של עשו. ואז אוסרי לגפן שהוא עשו כנ"ל עירה אותו עיר בן אתונות. ואז ויז נצחם על בגדי וכל מלבושי אגאל. בדם ענבי' של התורה. וזהו כבס ביין לבושו ובדם ענבים סותה. וכמ"ש תוס' בשמעתא דסוקריקן (גיטין נ"ה ע"ב) בשם ירושלמי קבלה בידם שאין נופלת אלא ביד יהודה. וכמ"ש (מיכה ד') קומי ודושי בת ציון וז"ש עד מדרך כף רגל עד היום שידרכו ברגל אותם פורה דרכתי כו' וזהו בקרנא דחמרא: (ומי איכא קרנא לחמרא) הא באפרי' כתיב וקרני ראם קרניו שנמשל לשור אבל משיח ב"ד נמשל לחמור ומי אית ליה קרניי: (ומי איכא מישרא דסכיני) ר"ל אז מי יהא מישרא דסכיני הלא כתיב לעת תמוט רגלם. וכתתו חרבותם לאיתים וחניתותיהם למזמרות לא ישא גוי חרב. שאז ישלם חרבי של עבו העשו ינס חרבו כמ"ש דהכתי לבדי: (אייתי ליה תרי ביעי א"ל הי' דוגתה אוכמתא והי דוגתא חיוורתא ר"ל שנאמר (בראשית כ"ה) ושני לאומים ממעיך יפרדו כו' שחלקו יעקב ועשו בבטן אמם יעקב נטלה עוה"ב ועשו נטלה עוה"ז ויתרוצצו הבני' בקרבה כמ"ש רש"י שם. וידוע שעוקר בבטן אמם וכשהם קטני' נקראי' בלים. וכשינדלו קצת נקראי' אפרוחי' כמ"ש (דברי' כ"ב) והאם רובצת על האפרוחי' או על הבני' שרומז שהשכינה יש לה מנוח בגלות בזכות הקטני'.

וזו

שפושט טלפיו סימן טהרה שלו. וכמ"ש נגע לבעת זה אדום וכיון שנעשה כולו לבן בא משיח. וז"ש הבא בבא תלוי מליעת העולם וביאת משיח והם כולם מינים (א"ל ומי יימר אייתו אשלי משמו) הענין כמ"ש (זכרי' י"ג) פי' שנים יכרתו והשלישי יותר בה. והבאתי את השלישית כו' ולרפתים כצרף את הכסף והענין כי שני חלקי העולם ב' אלפים תוהו וב' אלפים תורה חלפו ועברו שהסרו כנ"ל והשלישית יותר בה שלים של ימות המשיח וכן נאמר (במדבר כ"ד)

דרך כוכב מיעקב ומחץ פאתי. מואב כו'. ונאמר (שמואל ב' ח') וימדד שני חבלים להמית ומלא חבל אחד להחיות והוא כנ"ל: וזה שאמרו (אייתו אשלי ומשחו) ואמר אשלי על ענין ג' גוונים שתתהפך כולו ללבן שלישי מגוונים דזה מוכח הבא כנ"ל. (אית לן בירא בדברא עיילי' למתא). הענין כמ"ש (בראשית כ"ט)

דעלמא היכא זקפה לאצבעתיה אמר להו הבא אמרו ליה מי יימר אמר אייתו אשלי ומשחו אמרו ליה אית לן בירא בדברא עיילו למתא אייתא פארי שדא להו א"ל איפשילו לי הבלי דפארי ואעיילו אמרי ליה איכא דמפשל הבלי מפארי אמר להו ומי איכא דמיתי בירא מדברא למתא. אית לן ריחייא דתביר' הייט' שקל פיסקא מינא שדא להו אמר להו כרכו לי

מפארי. סובין עשו לי חבל מסובין ואם אין אתם עושים שאלתי אף אני לא אעשה שאלתכם: ריחיא. רחו' אוחה: כרוכו לי גרדי מינה. הוציאו לי ממנה חוטים כדרך הנשים שמוציאין חוטין מן הבגד ותופרים אותו בהן: גרדי פרנס"י:

משרא

וירא והנה באר בשדה ר"ל באר מים חיים שנאמר (ירמי' ב') אותי עזבו מקור מים חיים לחצוב כו' ונאמר (שיר השירי') שמוני נוטרה הכרמים. מי גרם לי להיות שמה לע"ז. ונמסר הכל לחיצונים כנודת כו' וזהו בשדה בחלקו של איש שדה. ואין קיום לישראל וגאולתם אלא בזכות ג' אבות כידוע. וכמ"ש (בראשית ו') ובגפן שלשה שריגים אלו ג' אבות. והוא כפורחת עלתה נצה. מן הבאר כו' והאבן גדולה על פי הבאר. הוא אבן נגף יצה"ר (יחזקאל ל"ו) והסירותי את לב האבן מבשרכם ונאספו שמה כל העדרים כי אין הגאולה באה אלא עד שיזכור ברית שלשת אבות כמ"ש. (ויקרא כ"ו). וזכרתי את בריתי יעקב ואף את בריתי כו'. והענין כי מאברהם יצא ישמעאל ומיצחק עשו שהן מוץ ותבן להטה. כמ"ש בר"מ פ' משפטים דף ק"ך ע"ב. ומס"ע דתבואות ה' מיני כהמה כו' עד בני בכורי ישראל ע"ש היטב: וזה ששאל עשו לאביו האיך מעשרין תבן שהיה גם לעשר התבן שהוא עשו ואין בן דוד בא עד שיתבררו מן העכו"ם ויהיו כמוץ אשר תדפנו רוח. ולכן יבואו ב' משיחים שהן דרגא דאברהם ויצחק. ויבררו מוץ ותבן. ועדיין אינם יכולים עד שתתברר הסובין מן הקמח. שהן דבקים בסטה מאוד והן ערב רב שהם הפסולת מס"ע דיעקב כמ"ש בר"מ. וז"ש והאבן גדולה. שכל העכוב הזה מן האבן הנ"ל. ולכן ויגש יעקב ויגל את כו'. וזהו הבירור בעלו בעו"ה בגלות שדבקים מאוד הערב רב בנייהם והם העשירים עליזי גאותך וזהו ובטלו הטוחנות כי מעטו. (קהלת י"ב.) ולכן אם אין קמח אין תורה שעדיין הסובין דבק בסטה. וזהו כל הגלות חבריין בגלותא עד שיברר בשלשת ימי האפילה. כמ"ש. (הושע ב'.) הנה אנכי מפתיה והולכתי' המדבר. ושם יבררו ויומתו כל רשעי ישראל:

וז"ש ולרפתים כצרוף את הכסף מס"ע דאברהם. ובחנתים כבחון את הזהב מס"ע דיצחק כידוע והוא יאמר ה' חלקי ישראל מסט' דיעקב: וז"ש (דברים ל"ג) וישכון ישראל בטח בדד עין יעקב שיהו מנוקים מתבלבל או דק שבענין שהן תערובות ישראל בע"ר. אל ארץ דגן ותירוש שיבררו וכן יין כמ"ש בר"מ פ' משפטים שם. ונאמר יעקב חבל נחלתו. ועיין רש"י שם שהוא חבל המשולש בג' אבות. ואין יכולין לגאול אבן מע"ש הבאר עד יעקב חבל נחלתו בג' כנ"ל. וז"ש אית לן בירא. שהבאר נהפך להם בדברא כנ"ל באר בשדה עשו איש שדה. ויעקב איש תם יושב אהלים. וז"ש אייתי למתא שאתם אומרים שעדיין אתם דבוקים בקדו"ה. א"כ אייתו למתא לאיש יושב אהלים אל עיר דוד שיה ציון. שישבה בדד העיר עכשיו. (וא"ל אפשילו לי חבלי מפארי.) ואי תפשלו החבל יעקב בעוד הסובין בנו. (ואז עיילים). וז"ש פארי בביאה עניותא בביאתא. כי אין עני אלא בדעת. אלו עניות דתורה ואם אין קמח אין תורה כו' (א"ל ומי איכא כו') ר"ל מי יכול זה וא"ל ומי איכא כו' ר"ל שלכן ב"ז א"י. (אית לן ריחייא דתבירא) הענין כמ"ש (ירמיה כ"ה) והאבדתי מהם קול ריחיים ואור נר כו'. והענין כמ"ש (סנהדרין ל"ב) קול רייחים בבורני שבוע הבן שם אור הנר בברור סיל משתה שם משתה שם. והוא כמ"ש (חגיגה י"ב:) שחקים שבו רחיים עומדות וטוחנות מן לצדיקים. כמ"ש (תהלים ע"ח) ויצו שחקים ממעל ודלתי שמים פתח כו' ודגן שמים נתן למו והוא שמזונות שחסרו בגלות כמ"ש (קהלת י"ב) ובטלו הטוחנות כי מעטו. ואמרו (פ"ג דנדה) זכר זה כל ככרו עמו נקיבה נקייה באה. ולפיכך ריחיים סימן לבן

ונאמר

לארעא אמר להו אסיקו לי ליבני וטינא מהתם אמרי ומי איכא דמצי לאסוקי התם אמר ומי איכא דמצי למבני ביתא בין שמיא לארעא. אמרי ליה מציעתא דעלמא

מגדול של דור הפלגה שנאמר ויאמרו נקבה בארץ שנער כו'. והענין כמ"ש שהאדם (עולם קטן) דומה לבית כמ"ש (איוב ד') שוכני בתי חומר אשר בעפר יסודם. ור"ל הבשר הוא החומר והעצמות הן הלביני' כמ"ש אביו מזריע לובן כו' שהם קיומו של אדם והבשר החומר קיומו שלו מאכילה. כמ"ש מרבה בשר וכו' והעצמות קיומם משתי' כמ"ש בפ"ב דנדה השותה יין חי עצמותיו שרופין. מזוג כו'. וכל ששתייתו מרובה מאכילתו עצמותיו שרופין. וזהו וימררו את חייהם בחומר ובלביני' ובכל עבודה בשדה (שמות א') שהם ענייני' גופני' איש שדה כנ"ל. נמצא שכל עסקי העוה"ז בעצבון תאכלנה. משא"כ בעה"ב כי קרוב אליך הדבר מאוד בפיך ובלבבך כו' (דברים ל') ובעלי מדות של הרוח ראו שאין קיומם אלא שיבריאו מאכילתם ושתייתם למדה הזאת ורצו לבנות בית לה וז"ש נלבנה לבינים ונשרפה לשריפה ותהי להם החמר לחמר והלבנה כו' ואמרו השריפה לשריפה כי הלבנה קיומה בשתיי' וכל ששתייתו מרובה עצמותיו שהן הלבנים שרופין. ונבנה לנו עיר שהוא העוה"ז הגוף. כמ"ש (קהלת ט') עיר קטנה כו' וראשו בשמי'. כמ"ש (איוב כ') אם יעלה לשמים שיאו. כגללו לנצח יאבד וכן בעשו נאמר (עובדי' א') אם תגביה כנשר משם אורידך נאום ה'. זדון לבך השיאך מרום שבתו שהוא הגאוה של עשו איש יודע ציד כנ"ל כמ"ש לקמן משם אורידך שאין לה קיום כנ"ל וכמ"ש לקמן ונעשה לנו שם בבתי כנסיות הכל לשם ולתפארת כמ"ש בזוהר. פן נפוץ על פני כל הארץ שלא יהי' להם תקומה באויר. אבל הקב"ה מכלה מחשבתם ודעתם שא"א להם זה ונתפרסם מפלתם. ויפץ אותם שחזרו למדות של הארץ. וז"ש (שם) דיקא נמי דכתיב לה שלא נתקיים בנין זה של הבית באויר בין שמים לארץ. וזה שאלו אותו שאתם אומרי' שקר אין לו רגלים שאין לו אלא רגל אחת של הגוף כמ"ש המפרשים שאין להם יסוד על מה לעמוד ענייני הגוף שהוא הרגל השני משא"כ אמת מלבן לבוני' שיש לו קיום הלביני' כנ"ל ולכן ועצמותיך יחליץ כגן רוה. ברשע עונותיו מקיפים לו על עצמותיו. והמשיל היצה"ר של המדות לחיים כנ"ל. וידוע שעיקרן של כל המדות הם הקנאה והתאוה והכבוד שמוציאין כו'. והקנאה והכבוד הם במדות הרוח ולכן קין אין לו אלא תאומה אחת התאוה. משא"כ בהבל לו תאומה יתירה וז"ש בני לך ביתא באיזה דעלמא שכל מעשיהם של העכו"ם אינם אלא להתייהר. כמ"ש (ב"ב י':) מ"ש צדקה תרומם גוי (משלי י"ד) ע"ש: ואמר בני לך ביתא כו' שאנשים שלהם הי' שאנו אומרים שפת אמת תכון לעד שיש קיום לאמת בשמים אמת מארץ תצמח כו' והלא באויר א"א לבנותו אמר שם. שאמר לשם שמים ולא דיפתוהו בפיהם ותלא בזה בין רקיע לארעא. ואמר אסיקו לבנא וטינא משם. שתעלו מדות הגשם חומר ולבנים משם מן הארץ אז אבנה לכם בית שם. ואמר שאין אתם יכולים לעשות אין קיומם קיום וזה הגרס' בקצת נוסחאות (ומי איכא דמצי לאסוקי התם אמר ומי איכא דמצי למבני ביתא בין שמיא לארעא) משא"כ בנו אמת מארץ תצמח וצדק משמים נשקף. לכן שפת אמת תכון לעד: (מציעתא דעלמא היכא.) והענין כמ"ש על פסוק כעת יאמר ליעקב מה פעל אל (במדבר כ"ג): ר"ל כעת מתחלת העולם עד המשיח כן ימות המשיח (בניסן ותשרי שהן זמן הגאולה לר"א ור"י). וכמ"ש שמתו כימות עניותו שלכן היום והלילה שוין הגלות והגאולה וז"ש (סנהדרין צ"ז) העולם שתא אלפים שנה ב' אלפים תהו ר"ל שאינו נחשב בכלל העולם. וז"ש תוהו ב' אלפי' תורה ב' אלפי' ב' אלפי' משיח רק בעונותינו שיצאו מה שיצאו והוא סימן לימות המשיח שהלילה מרובה מהיום. וז"ש שראה אדה"ר בתקופת טבת שהימים מתקצרים אמר שמא ח"ו עולם חשך בעדי. שחשב שלא יהיה יום כלל. שלא ידעו ח"ו מאבלות כו' כשראה ימים טובים הוא קבעום לש"ש והם קבעום לע"ז. שראו שהלילה מרובה מהיום. וזהו ראשון לכל אלידים. וז"ש מציעתא דעלמא היכא שראה אמצע של ימות העולם. א"ל הכא כו' (שם) אין בן דוד בא עד שתתהפך המלכות כולה למינות ואמר רבא מאי קרא שנאמר כולו הפך לבן טהור: (פ"ק דקדושין) ז' דבגון אמצע של תורה. שהתורה הוא העולם כידוע ואמר הולך על גחון זה נחש שאין לו רגלים שקבלו רגלי שקר אין לו רגלים ושפת הגשם שכפל באלקים מאכל כו' כדאי' בפרקי ר"א. ואמרו המן מן התורה מנין שנאמר המן העץ. והענין כמ"ש במגילה כי המן ומשלת בניו הם הס"א הגשם וי' כתרין דמסאבותא. ואלו אותו כל עץ על מיתת עץ הדעת. וזו מיתת מיתתו. ואמרו ר' דווייתא צריך למתחסינהו. וזהו גורל הודיו שצריך למתחסינהו. ועיין במלב"א. ואמרו הפך לבן כי האדם מורכב מד' גוונים אדום שחור לבן כמ"ש ויעש אלו"ל ר"ח ג' גוונים כיון שיתהפך לפיתת שהוא לבן החתוך מכלא סימני הצרה והוא אדום שחור אימר שחיכם

דז"ש נפש רחבה. והרוח זה הכבוד והקנאה כמ"ש ורום גבוה גבה רוח. ורוח נכאה שהוא הקנאה תייבש גרם כמ"ש (משלי י"ד) ורקב עצמות קנאה וכל הכבוד ומדותי' תלויין בהבלי עולם. ותשמרה לאשובה בתחלת ילדות שואף לתאוה כי הילדות והשחרות הבל ואמר דברים שעושים בילדותו מרדים הבל בזקנותו. כמ"ש בס"י על תאות המשגל וכן על כל התאוות וזהו שמור טעד שהוא בעל תאוה אשר בשר שמורים נפרס והבל עניני השומר. ובאמצעית. האדם הולך ורודף אחר הכבוד והעשירות ככלבים שלועקים הב הב ובמשמרה הג' שרואה שליפתו מסרה אז בתשובה ואז מתגוללת הנשמה. ואז תינוק יונק משדי אמו כמ"ש (שם ה') דדיה ירווך בכל עת באהבתה כו' ואשה מספרת עם בעלה כמ"ש (הושע ב') ואשובה אל אישי הראשון שחוזר להקב"ה שהתורה מביאה לידי מעשה. כמ"ש בתפלת השיבנו אבינו לתורתך וקרבינו כו' והוא ענין של שלשה בנים של אדה"ר קין והבל ושת קין עסק בעבודת האדמה לפס לאכול לשבוע. והבל עסק בעבודת הצאן כמ"ש ועשתרות צאניך כו' שמעשרות את בעליהן בקניינים המדומים ושת בדמותו בצלמו מכלל דעד השתא אוליד רוחין בישין ושדין והם קין והבל כידוע וידוע שסנ"ן הם בראש ובטן וגוי' שהם כנ"ן בגמ' לב וכבד כידוע שהם נגד שמים וארץ ואויר כמ"ש בס"י ולכן קין איש האדמה ואמר להבל למה אתה עובר על אדמתי פרח באויר כי כל עסקו בעניינים חומריי' עסקי הגוף אבל הבל עסקו בענין הבלים ובונה בתי כנסיות להתגדל ולהתפאר בם וכן לדקות להתגדל כמ"ש בזוהר ע"פ ונעשה לנו שם וכל זה הבל כמ"ש בקהלת הבל הבלים מה יתרון לאדם בכל עמלו שיעמול תחת השמש ואמרו תחת השמש אין לו אבל למעלה כו' ותחת השמש הוא באויר וכל הענין של קהלת הכל הוא ענין של הבל כמ"ש כי מה הוה לאדם בכל עמלו וברעיון לבו שם מקום הרוח בכל שהוא עמל תחת השמש כי כל ימיו כו' גם זה הבל הוא ולחוטא נתן ענין לאסוף ולכנוס לתת לטוב לפני האלהים גם זה הבל ורעות רוח של הרוח איש אשר יתן לו האלהים עושר ונכסים ולא ישליטנו כו' גם זה הבל וכהנה רבות כל הספר מדבר מזה וכל מטאים של התאוה הכל בנפש והנפש אשר תאכל ואמרו נפש לרבות את השותה ויבא קין מפרי האדמה. מן הפסותין שאינו נותן לשם רק אותן שא"ל לאכילתו המשוייר וז"ש זרע פשתן שאינו נאכל והבל הביא מבכורות צאנו כו' שכל עניינו לקנות שם ותפארת בארץ ויהי בהיותם בשדה ויקם קין אל הבל אחיו ויהרגהו הענין כמ"ש בעשו איש יודע ציד איש שדה

דעלמא אמר שם קם ותלא בין שמיא לארעא

שזה מדה של קין איש יודע ציד לרמות כמ"ש כי ציד בפיו כמ"ש בס"י ועל מדתו של הבל ואמרו כל מעשיך יהיו לש"ש אפי' בעניינים הגשמים והזהירו על מדת התאוו' ביותר שכל אכילה ושתיה יהי' לשם שמים הענין כמ"ש הביאה לי ציד ואוכלה ואברככה לפני ה' כו' וכן אכילת השבתות והמועדים וקראת לשבת עונג הענין כמ"ש הרשב"א באגדת לויתן ושאר המפרשים כי אין הנשמה שלימה אא"כ באכילה ושתיה שיתיישב הגוף וזהו סעודת לויתן לע"ל וכן כל הסעודות של מצוה כמ"ש על רופא כל בשר ומפליא לעשות שקושר רוחני בגשמי במאכל כי הגוף נהנה במאכל והנשמה בכוונת האכילה לשמו כמ"ש בגלגולים ואין חיזוק לשום דבר אלא באכילה ושתיה והנשמה גר בעוה"ז במדותי' ע"כ כל מעשיך יהיו לש"ש ואז תתיישב הנשמה בעולם והנשמה מדורה בראש ושמים כנ"ל וז"ש לש"ש בשביל הנשמה ואז חיבור לשמים וארץ וז"ש הגיע השמים על הר סיני וכן ברשע שאוכל לתאוות גופו זה המדה מתקיימת לו אבל מדת הרוח אין לו קיום כי אין לו יסוד בגוף באכילה ושתי' כי הכל למדת הנפש לכן מדות הרוח אין לו קיום מ"ש שיקרא לא קאי ואמרו שקר אין לו רגלים כנ"ל אמת מלבן לבוני' כמ"ש לקתן וכן אמרו האי מאן דיהיר אפי' אאינשי ביתי' לא מקבל וכן כל החונף סוף נופל בידו כל מחלוקת שאינו לש"ש אין סופו להתקיים וכן החונף ניכר מעשיו מפרסמין את המכנפים כו' וכ"ז שאין לו קיום וז"ש ויהי בהיותם בשדה עוסק בעניני גופו איש שדה כנ"ל ויקם קין אל הבל אחיו ויהרגהו שאז אין לו שליטת הבל לכן ויהרגהו שאין לו קיום כנ"ל כי הצדיק כובש יצרו של התאוות ולאכול בשביל להיות לו כח למדותיו של הקב"ה אבל הרשע שאינו עושה לש"ש א"א לכבוש את התאוה כי מי יאכל ומי יחוש חוץ ממני וז"ש והנה שתים נשים יוצאו' ואמרו (קדושין מ"ט) אלו חניפה וגסות הרוח שידו לבבל שהן מדות הרוח כנ"ל. ועיקר החניפה במעשיו כידוע וז"ש על הנהו ורוח בכנפיהם ואמר ולהנה כנפים ככנפי החסידה. שמראות בעלמן כחסידה. ודימה אותן בנשים כו' כמ"ש זאת הרשעה. ואמרו שהיא היצה"ר כי נופת תטופנה שפתי זרה. אשה זונה שית זונה כו' כידוע שהנוקבא מפתה לאדם. כמ"ש בזוהר וז"ש ותשלכה את האיפה ויאמר זאת הרשעה. כי המדות נושאות את היצה"ר שמשכנו אצל מדות הקבועות בנפש ורוח. ולב כסיל לשמאל בין הארץ ובין השמים כנ"ל. שהמדות אלו הן בין שמים וארץ בלב ואויר לבנות לה בית בארץ שנער. והוא ענין בנין [מגדול

מילחא כי סריא במאי מלחי ליה בסיליתא דכודנתא ומי איכא סילתא לכודנתא ומילחא מי סריא: בני לן ביתא באוירא דעלמא

יחזרו הבני' אליה עוד כמאמרם אסוה דמרכא זייפנא כנ"ל וזהו ששאלו וכודנייתא מי ילדה וא"ל הי' כיהו כו' וזהו הכזב שלכם שע"כ היא יולדת כמו שמוכח מכל הנ"ל מלידתה ומפיתקא הנ"ל: (מילחא כי סריא במאי מלחא לה) הקב"ה בא עם ישראל בברית כמ"ש אצל כהני' (במדבר י"ח) ברית מלח עולם וכן אצל דוד נאמר (ד"ה ב' י"ג ה') כי ה' אלקי ישראל נתן ממלכה לדוד על ישראל לעולם לו ולבניו ברית מלח. וכן בא עם כל ישראל בשלש בריתות כמ"ש בסוטה ע"ש והענין הברית שהי' לו לאשה כמ"ש אצל אשתו של אדם (מלאכי ב' י"ד) והיא חברתך ואשת בריתך כו'. וכמ"ש (סנהדרין כ"ב:) אין האשה כורתת ברית אלא למי שעושה אותה כלי כו' בעלה הראשון וז"ש ואשובה אל אישי הראשון כו' ביום ההוא תקראי כו'. והענין של ברית מלח הוא שלא תופר הברית כמו שא"א לעולם בלא מלח כי א"א לדבר להתקיים בלא מלח שלא יסריח וע"י מלח נתקיים לעולם כן הוא ברית מלח שמתקיים לעולם ושאלו כיון שברית מלח שלכם נקרא בזה אתם הלפים שתבוא ותתחזק הברית כמ"ש (ירמי' ל"א ל"א) הנה ימים באים נאום ה' וכרתי את בית ישראל ואת בית יהודא ברית חדשה לא כברית אשר כרתי את אבותם ביום החזיקי בידם להוציאם מארץ מצרים אשר המה הפרו את בריתי ואנכי בעלתי בם נאום ה'. ור"ל אין האשה כורתת ברית כו' כנ"ל כמ"ש כי זאת הברי' כו' (שם) והברית שאנחנו כורתים עם הקב"ה הוא התורה כנ"ל בי"ג בריתות וכמ"ש (ירמי' ל"ג) אם לא בריתי יומם ולילה כו' ואנחנו הפרנו תורתו כנ"ל אשר המה הפרו את בריתי כו' כי זאת הברית כו'. נתתי את תורתי בקרבם ועל (ליא) לבם אכתבנה כו' ע"ש כל הפרשה: אמר להו (בסילתא דכודנייתא כודנייתא כו') כנ"ל ובשלייתא היולדת מבין רגליה מתרגמינן ובזעיר בנהא וכ"פ רש"י ואמרו אין העולם מתקיים אלא בהבל פיהם של תינוקות בית רבן וז"ש והאם רובצת על האפרוחים (דברים כ"ב) או על הבינים על התינוקות שנשנילן אין השכינה מסתלקת מישראל בגלות ורובצת בתוכם והם מקיימין העולם שנאמר אם לא בריתי יום ולילה כו' וענין השליא כמ"ש למעלה דמשיח אקרי בר נפלי לפי שהפלת אותו בכל פעם והענין כמ"ש קטן שלא כלו חדשיו תלמיד שלא הגיע להוראה כו' ואם היו כל ישראל עוסקי' בתורה ומצות אז היה משיח ג"כ בגמר עיבורו אבל בשביל שאינם עוסקים רק הקטנים לכן לא כלו חדשיו ג"כ למשיח ומפלת שליא וז"ש (ברכות ד'.) שעסק ד"ז בשפיר ובשליא לספר האשה לבעלה: (ומי איכא שליא לכודנייתא ומילחא מי סריא) שאלו אותו אשר שכ"י מקרה בגלות ונתגרשה מבעלה כמ"ש (ירמי' ג') לאמר הן ישלח איש את אשתו והיתה לאיש אחר כו' ואת זנית רעים רבים כו' האיך אתם מולידים קטנים לקב"ה הלא בריתכם של התורה מופר מכל וכל. והשיב להם מילחא מי סריא וכי אפשר לברית מלח שתופר כי עדיין אני אשתו כמ"ש (ישעי' נ' א') אי זה ספר כריתות אמכם אשר שלחתיה או מי מנושי אשר מכרתי אתכ' לו הן בעוונותיכם נמכרתם ובפשעיכם שולחה אמכם וכמ"ש היתה כאלמנה ולא אלמנה ממש אלא כאשה שהלך בעלה כו' ונמכרנו בעוונות. לכן כיא מתקיימת על תינוקות של בית רבן שאין בהם חטא כמ"ש דידי ודידך מאי א"ל אין דומה הבל ש"ש בו חטא להבל שאין בו חטא לכן והאם רובצת על האפרוחי' ועדיין הברית קיי' אלא שתתחדש לע"ל כמ"ש (ירמי' ל"ג) כה אמר ה' אם תפרו את בריתי היו' כו' גם בריתי תופר כו' הלא ראיתי מה העם הזה כו' כה אמר ה' אם לא בריתי יומם כו' גם זרע יעקב כו' אלא שאין לנו בני' של קיימא להקב"ה בשביל מעשינו כמ"ש בזוהר חדש בשיר רכיכין כו' ול"ל תוקפא אלא בחינן ינוקין וכן נאמר (ש"ה א') אם לא תדעי לך היפה בנשי' שהיא שואלת איכה תרעה איכה תרביץ בצהרי' בגלות ואמר לה הקב"ה ורעי את גדיותיך אלו תינוקות של בית רבן ועליה' תתקיי' וגם בגלות אנחנו יושבין ומלפין לו כמ"ש הושע ג') ימי' רבי' תשבי לי (שם ב') ואשובה אל אישי הראשון וארשתיך לי לעולם כו': (בני לן ביתא באוירא דעלמא אמר שם תלא בין שמיא לארעא א"ל אסיקו לי ליבני וטינא כו') והענין כמ"ש (זכרי' ה') וארא והנה שתי' נשי' יוצאות ורוח בכנפיה' ולהנה כנפי' ככנפי החסידה ותשאנה את האיפה בין הארץ ובין השמי' כו' ויאמר אלי לבנות לה בית בארץ שנער ואמרו לבנות לה הכלל דלא אתקיי' שם כמ"ש (סנהדרין כ"ד) דיקא נמי דכתיב לה. והענין בארץ שנער היא ענין של דור הפלגה שרצו לבנות בית וכתיב וימצאו בקעה בארץ שנער כו' הבה נלבנה לבני' ונשרפה לשריפה והחמר הי' להם לחמר כו' נבנה לנו כו' וראשו בשמי' ונעשה לנו שם פן נפוץ וכו'. וזה הענין אמר שם כו' ואסיקו לי ליבני וטינא כו'. וענין הבנין ההוא כמ"ש פ"ק דברכות שלש משמורות הוי הלילה. וכתבו המפרשים שהוא על שלש נפשות של אדם כנ"ן. נפש בה התאוה לעניים הנוטים,

וז"ש

לן מילי דכדיבי אמר להו הוה לן כודנייתא וילידת והוה תלי לי' פיתקא וכתיב ביה דמסיק בבי אבא מאה אלפא זוזי אמרו ליה וכודנייתא מי ילדה אמר להו הי ניהו מילי דכדיבי. מילחא

מילי דכדי. דברי רוח ל"א דכדיבי דבר כזב: כודנתא. פרידה: תלי פיתקא. שטר בצוארה של פרד': הי ניהו מילי דכדי. אלו הן דברי רוח: פיליפס. פיליפ: מפסרי

ואמרו (תענית ז':) אם ראית תלמיד שתלמודו קשה עליו כברזל בשביל משנתו שאינה סדורה לו כראוי מה תקנתיה ירבה בישיבה. וכמ"ש שסבירך יקיימיה בידך וכ"ש אם משנתו סדורה לו מעיקרא כו' וע"ש כמנא כי צריך קודם ללמוד המתניתן ואע"פ שאינו יודע לפרש המתני' ילמוד כולו ואח"כ ילך לגמרא וכתיב (שם ו') איש אשר יתן לו אלקים עושר ונכסים וכבוד ולא ישליטנו אלקים לאכול ממנו זה בעל משנה. כי איש נכרי יאכלנו זה בעל הגמרא (מ"ע והביאו רש"י בקהלת) ואעפ"כ ילמוד המתני' כנ"ל בשני משנתו שאינה סדורה לו כו' כנ"ל. כי במה יתרץ קושיתה בגמ' כמ"ש ד"ת עניים במק"א ועשירים במקום אחר. וז"ש כאן גברא דאזיל לאגמא קטל קנא טונא ולא מלא ביה. הוא לימוד המתני' קטל קניא באגמא כנ"ל ואינו יכול לפרשם קטל ומהם עלוי' שלומד עוד מתני' כנ"ל עד אתרמי אינם מדלי ליה עד שלומד הגמרא כי אינו יכול ללומדה עד שלומד כל המתני' כמנא כי באחר יעזר על חבירו אף כאן כמ"ש (יבמו' כ"ד) עשו משמרת למשמרתי משל דר"א למה הדבר דומה לאדם שאמר הפרדס ומה ר בתוך כלה משתמר כו' והא דר"א בדותא התם כו'. כמנא כי ע"י ד"ת מתקיים ד"ת כן כאן חוזר ומלוה לו שיכול לשלם לו עם מה שהלוה לו בראשונה:

א"ל אימא לן מילי דכדיבי. דאיתא (בעכו"ם י"א) עוד אחת לשבעים שנה כו'. ואמרי סך קירי פלסתר אסוהי דמרכא זייפנא א"ר אשי פיהם הכשילם כו' מרכא גונבא זייפנא. כמנא כי אנשנו מסולקים מאשם שהם אומרים יעקב זייפנא שברכותיו לא נתקיימו כמ"ש בזוהר שהקשה הנכרי על פסוק שפת אמת תכון לעד ואנשנו אומרים שהם כוזבים בברכתם כנ"ל מרכא גונבא זייפנא. וזה שהקשו אימא לן מילי דבדיאי הראה לנו דבר כזב שאנשנו כוזבים הלא ברכתינו נתקיימה ולא שלכם כמו שהקשה הנכרי הנ"ל (א"ל הוה לן כודנייתא וילידה והוי תלי ליה פיתקא וכתו' ביה דמסיק בבי אבא אלפי זוזי) כמ"ש (ברכות י') א"ל ההוא מינא לברורי' כתיב (ישעי' נ"ד) רני עקרה לא ילדה משום דלא ילדה רני א"ל שטיא שפיל לסיפא דקרא כי רבים בני שוממה מבני בעולה אמר ה' אלא מאי לא ילדה רני כו' שלא ילדה בנים לגיהנם כוותיבו. והענין קשה דמ"מ הדרא ק"ל דא"כ מאי עקרה הלא ילדה. ועוד מאי כי רבים אלא ד:דאי ילדה ומאי עקרה לא ילדה שנשארה בלא בנים. כמ"ש אבל טור (שם כ"ג) בושי צידון כי אמר ים מעוז הים לאמר לא חלתי ולא ילדתי ולא גדלתי בחורים רוממתי בתולות. ונאמר אבל ציון (שם מ"ט) שאי סביב עיניך כולם נקבצו באו לך כו' עוד יאמרו באזניך בני שכוליך צר לי המקום כו' ואמרת בלבבך מי ילד לי את אלה ואני שכולה וגלמודה גולה וסורה ואלה מי גדל כו' וכמ"ש בברכת מתנים שוש תשיש ותגל עקרה בקיבוץ בניה לתוכה בשמחה וכמ"ש (תהלים קי"ג) מושיבי עקרת הבית אם הבנים שמחה ונאמר (דברים ל"ב) אם לא כי צורם מכרם זה אברהם אביהם שנאמר עליו (ישעי' נ"א) הביטו אל צור חצבתם זה אברהם כמ"ש (שם) אל אברהם אביכם והוא מכרם לגלות שאמר לו הקב"ה מה תברור או גלות או גיהנם ובירר הגלות כי בגיהנם יכלו ח"ו משא"כ בגלות ולכך אברהם יושב בפתח גיהנם ומוציא מגיהנם כי הוא מסרם לגלות בשביל שלא ירדו לגיהנם וז"ש רש"י כי שדומה לעקר' שלא ילדה בני' לגיהנם שאם לא היתה עקרה בגלות היתה מולדת בני' לגיהנם כי רבים בני שוממה כנ"ל עוד יאמרו באזניך בני שכוליך צר לי המקום כו' הרחיבי מקום אהלך כו'. וההבטחה על שלא יכלו בגלות נאמר בשיר השירים (ח' י"א) כרם היה לשלמה בבעל המון נתן את הכרם לנוטרים איש יביא בפריו אלף כסף כרם אלו ישראל נתן לנוטרים מסר אותן לאומות וכולם ינחו אותם: האלף לך שלמה כו'. כמ"ש (שבועות ל"ה) מלכותא דקטלא חד משיתא בעלמא לא מיענשא שנאמר האלף לך שלמה כו'. כמנא כי יש לנו חוב על א"ה שיוציא מגלות האלף כסף הנ"ל וז"ש הוה לן כודנייתא עקרה הנ"ל שכולם הלכו בגלות ואח"כ ילדה אותם והוציאם מגלותא הוה תלא פיתקא בצוארה חוב על אבא אלפא זוזי האלף לך שלמה כנ"ל (ואח"כ דאיתי בגמ' כו' מאה אלפי זוזי והענין כי כל כסף האמור בתורה הוא סלע צורי ד' דינרין ונאמר תחת הכסף אביא זהב ושל זהב ד"ה סלע כסף שהן מאה זוזים כמנא א"ל כי האלף הנ"ל יביא תחת מאה אלפי זוזי) א"ל וכודניתא מי ילדה א"ל הי ניהו מילי דבדיאי. והם סוברים כדעת המיני' שהיא עקרה ממש שלא

יחזרו

גברא דאוזיף ומריף מאי הוי דהדר אוזיף אמר להו אזיל גברא לאגמי קטיל קמא טונא ולא מצי ביה קטל ומנח עליה עד דמתרמי ליה אינשי דסידלי ליה אימא לן

רש"י

בעבי אכן מינך: אי זכיתו לי. אם הגלמודי: דמדלי מינה. שפיותם' מראשונה ושואל אותה הלא יש לו ללמוד תושיל ולא נסבו לו ראשונה כל שכן זו: סיכתא. קני"א: דלא לאתאי. דלא השפיל ידו במקום שאין חור בכותל ולא אעל: דלי דלא. הגביה ידו ונעלה במקום נקב ועאל: דאוזיף ועריף. שהלוה מעות לסחור ולא נפרע ממנו כי אם בקושי שערף לקוחות: מאי שני דהדר אוזיף לאחריני ולא נתייאש מן הראשון: לאגמא יער: קטל קמ' טונ' אוחד הבילא ראשונה ולא מצי ביה להרימו על שכמו. הדר קטיל ומנח עליה. הואיל וצריך סיוע לאחרים עד דמתרמי איניש ומדלי ליה והאי נמי הואיל והפסי' באמנה ראשונה חוזר ומאמין לאחרים עד שמזדווג לו אדם נאמן ומשתכר בו:

מילי

בי' הגר"א

מוכן למזגו ואותו השעה דוחקת לו לפי שאינו שעתו המוכנת לו לשבעו ואמרו אשרי מי שנולד בשעתו המוכנת לו וזהו אדם שיש לו מזל ושעתו עומדת לו והכל כפי מה שהיה בגלגול שדחק הוא את השעה שעה דוחקתו וכל הדוחה מפני השעה שעה עומדת לו. וז"ש הכל תלוי במזל בשעה שנולד אפי' התורה ג"כ לפי שנולד בשעה המוכן לתורה כמ"ש בתקונים ובמדרש שאלה היתה מטרוניתא לר"י מהו שכ' יהיב חוכמתא לחכימין כו' לשוטים מיבעי ליה. א"ל אם אתה מלוה מעות למי אתה מלוה לעשיר או לעני א"ל לעשיר א"ל אדרבה לעני צריך להלוות. א"ל לפי שאינו בטוח. א"ל כן יהיב חוכמתא לחכימין ע"כ. והענין כמו שאינו רוצה ללות מעות לעני לפי שאינו בטוח שאינו בר מזל לזה. כן בתורה מי שאינו נולד במזל של תורה אינו נותן לו כי לא ישאר בידו אחר שאינו במזלה. וז"ש דברי חכמים כדרבונות וכמסמרות כו' מה דרבן מכוון את הפרה לתלמיה להוציא חיים לעולם אף ד"ת מכוונים ללומדיהם מדרכי מיתה לדרכי חיים אי מה דרבן מטלטל אף ד"ת מטלטלין ת"ל וכמסמרות כו'. והענין שמשל לדרבן שמשם כל העשירות והחיים של עוה"ז. כמ"ש ורב תבואות בכח שור כן בד"ת. יכול כשם שהעשירות אינו עומד במקום א' אלא הולך לאחר כמ"ש גלגל חוזר בעולם כן בד"ת. לכן נמשל למסמר שאינו זז ממקומו כן בד"ת. כי הש"י אינו נותנה אלא למי שישאר בידו וכמ"ש ותקעתיו יתד במקום נאמן ר"ל במקום אשר לא ימוט. וז"ש (שקל סיכתא ודלה לאתאי לא עאל) שחכמה המשלה ליתד שאינו נכנס למקום שפלים במדריגה לשוטים (דלה לעילאי ועאל) יהיב חוכמתא לחכימין לפי שהוא בר מזלו כנ"ל. כן הוא בנתינת התורה שלא קבלו העכו"ם שאינה בר מזלם. שנאמר לא תרצח לא תנאף. ושמו חותמו על החרב ויתמעאל ידו בכל עד דאתרמי ליה בר מזליה: (גברא דאוזיף וטריף מאי טזא דהדר אוזיף) הענין כמו במשל הנ"ל שהמשיל נתינת התורה להלוואה. וכמ"ש ר"א יזיף ופרע וכמ"ש שאמר הקב"ה לישראל מי מערב אתכם כו' ערבייך ערבא צריך. ואמרו בנינו בנותינו כו' הא ודאי. והענין כי א"א להיות ערב אא"כ הוא אינו חייב בשביל עצמו ובטוח בשלו. וז"ש ערביך ערבי כו' משא"כ קטנים שאין חייבין עדיין במצות. ואמרו כשחרב בהמ"ק בשביל שלא קיימו את התורה עמדו וגדרו על עצמן כמה גדרים וכל מד"ס נתקנו אז וכמ"ש בירושלמי מי גרם להיות משמר ג' ימים בשביל שלא שמרת שבת יום אחד מי גרם להפריש ב' חלות כו'. וכמ"ש חדשים גם ישנים אלו ד"ת ואלו ד"ס וז"ש גברא דאוזיף כו' שלא פרעתם ד"ת והוספתם ד"ס. והענין הערבות שמשלם מה שלא שלם הלוה ואמרו האבות יערבו עלינו. כמ"ש יצחק פלגא עלי ופלגא עליך ואמר ערביך ערבא כו' כמ"ש שם שיש להקב"ה דין עליהם אברהם אמר במה אדע כו'. וז"ש אין העולם מתקיים אלא בשביל הבל תינוקות של בית רבן שהם הערבות והם משלימים ביטול תורה שלנו שאלמלא כן היה העולם חרב כמ"ש (ירמיה ל"ג כ"ה) אם לא בריתי יומם ולילה כו'. וז"ש (תהלים ח' ג') מפי עוללים ויונקים יסדת עוז למען צורריך להשבית אויב ומתנקם שלא יהיה להם שום קטרוג עלינו בשביל התורה. וז"ש הוא ללמוד ובנו ללמוד הוא קודם לבנו כי אין נפרעין מערב תחילה עד דל"ל ללוה ולכן היא קודם: (אמר להו גברא אזל לאגמא קטל קמא טונא ולא מצי ביה קטל ומנח עלוי' עד דאתרמי אינ' מדלי ליה) וכמ"ש (ב"ב קמ"ה:) מסיע אבנים יעצב בה' אלו בעלי' גמ' ובוקע עצים יסכן בהם אלו בעלי משנה. וקשה הא אמרו העוסק במשנה מדה בגמרא אין לך מדה גדולה הימנו וכן אמרו התנאים הם מבלי עולם כו'. ונ"ל העוסקים בגמ' לבד עליהם נאמר מסיע אבנים כו'. אבל העוסקים קודם במתניתין ועוסקים ג"כ בגמרא עליהם נאמר ובוקע עצים שהעוסק בגמ' לבד הוא כמו מסיע אבנים כמו שחצבן מן ההר בלי שום תיקון ואין בהם הנאה אבל העוסק קודם במשנה הוא כמו החוטב עצים מקודם כורת (עצים) מיער והוא לימוד המתני' ואח"כ בוקע אותם והוא לימוד הגמרא מפי' המתני' ולכך דימו אותו באינו יודע לפרש המתני' לקטלא קניא באגמא כמ"ש בשבת רבך קטל קניא באגמא ועיין רש"י שם ואמר קניא שא"ל לביקוע כמ"ש (פסחים נ') המשתכר בקני' כו' מ"ט משום דנפיש אספייהו.

ואמרו

בי' הגר"א

ושכתיב ויעקב איש תם ובעשו כתיב כי ציד כו'. ושירך יעקב אע"כ נתחכם יותר. כמ"ש בא אחיך במרמה ומתרגמינן בחוכמתא כו' ויעקבני זה פעמים כו' וזה שכתוב אני חכמה שכנתי ערמה. כמ"ש חז"ל כיון שלמד תורה נכנס בו ערמומיות.

וז"ש לו כאן אנן סבימין מינייהו וז"ש אם אחד מששים בניהם שהיא דרגא דעשו. וכן אחשנו בגלות שנסתלקה ממנו הנבואה בגלות ואמרו אעפ"כ בחלום אדבר בו. חלום אחד מששים בנבואה וכן השיב' שאנו ישנים בגלות אחד מששים בעוה"ב. וכמ"ש בשוב ה' את שיבת ציון היינו כחולמים כמ"ש בזוהר שהכל הן שיתין דרגין דנבואה כו' וכן הוא בכולם:

א"ל ההוא גברא דאזיל ובעי איתתא ולא יהבו ליה מאי הוי דאזיל היכא דמדלי מיניה. הענין שכל הנילוס שלהם היה על מעלות ישראל והאומות שאמרו לו האיך יתכן כמו שאתם אומרים שישראל הן למעלה מכל עכו"ם וישראל עם קרובו והייתם לי סגולה מכל העמים ולתתך עליון כו' וכהנה רבות. וידוע שע"י התורה נתקדשו ישראל להקב"ה ונעשו לו לאשה כמ"ש קח לך אשה אהבת ריע וכתיב לאמר הן ישלח איש את אשתו. ואיה ספר כריתות אמכם. וכן וארשתיך לי לעולם שהקידושין הראשונים היו לא לעולם. כמ"ש לא כברית כו'. וכן ואמונה של אישי הראשון ביום ההוא תקראי לי אישי כו' וכהנה רבות. ואמרו ה' מסיני בא וזרח משעיר למו הופיע מהר פארן כו' מאי בעי בשעיר מאי בעי בפארן אלמד שהחזיר את התורה לכל עכו"ם ולא קבלו ממנו. ובזה היתה תשובה וכי אפשר שאתם יותר במדרגה עליונה הי"כ אחר שלא רצו להיות לו לאשה אחר הם יותר שפלים ממכם האיך ילך אח"כ לכם (אחר כיתבי זאת מצאתי בתוספ"ת שהתחיל ג"כ כנ"ל). (שקל סיכתא דצה לתתא לא עאל לעילאי עאל. אמר האי נמי מתרמי לי' בת מזלי') אמרו שהכל תלוי במזל ואפילו ס"ת שבהיכל והענין קשה להאמר. והענין הוא כמ"ש (תענית כ"ה) ר"א דפיקא לי' שעתא כו' ואמרו בזוהר ובתקונים לפי שבגלגול הראשון פגם את המזל לכן דפקא לו שעתו. והענין דפיקא שעתא הוא כמ"ש בתקונים שאינו נולד בשעה שמיכה לו ושכר

מוכן

רש"י

בהמה: ואנא רישא דחיותא אמרי לך בהמיה: סגי. לעוד ולך לפני: דרי כריכא דקני. טול חבילה של קנים: וכי מטית להתם. כנגד הפתח: זקיף. החבילה: במאן דמתפח. כאדם העומד לפוש: אזל רבי יהושע: אשכח דרבנאי. אורבים מאנדראי. שלא יצא א' מן הזקני' לחוץ: מגואי. שלא יכניסו אחד ליכנס: וכי חזו. הנך סבי' כרעא דעיילי קטלי לבראי. שהיתה אסקופת החדר לרע והשפכין סובין או אפר עליה וניכרת בה פסיעות אדם וכי חזו כרעא דעיילי קטלי לשומרים בראי שהניחו לבא וכי חזו כרעא דנפקי קטלי לגואי שהניחו לצאת והשומרים לא היו הורגים שום אדם אלא א"כ נכנס כולו לפנים על כרחו או אחד יוצא כולו לחוץ: אפכי. רבי יהושע לסנדליה ועמד על האסקופ' ונראי' פסיע' א' נכנסת ופסיעה אחת יוצאה והחבואו השומרי' ויצא וכשבאו הזקנים וראו כן ודמו ששני בני אדם הן אחד נכנס ואחד יוצא וקטליניהו לכולהו שומרים ואח"כ נכנס רבי יהושע: וינוקי מלעיל. בעלייה להרע נתכוונו שהנותן שלו' לעליונים תחלה הורגין אותו התחתונים ואמרו לנו הזקנים ולא היה לך ליתן שלו' לבחורים תחלה והנותן שלום לזקנים הורגין אותו הבחורים ואומרים הלא ראיתנו חשובים מהם שאנחנו למעלה והם למטה: מאי עבידתיך. מאי בעית הכא: אי הכי. דחכימא

ניבעי

גמרא

על לבי טבחא אשכחיה לההוא גברא דקא עביר חיותא א"ל רישא אית לך לזבוני א"ל אין א"ל רישא בכמה א"ל בפלגא דזוזא יהב ליה לסוף א"ל הב לי רישך יהב ליה חד רישא דחיות' א"ל אנא רישך אמרי לך אמר ליה אי בעית דאישבקך סגי אחור לי פיתחא דבי אתונא א"ל מכתפינא דכל דמחזי להו קטלי ליה א"ל דרי כרובא דקניא וכי מטית להתם זקפה במאן דקא מתפח אזל אשכח דרבנאי מגואי ודרבנאי מבראי דאי הזי כרעא דעיילי קטלי להו לבראי ודנפקא קטלי להו לגואי אפכיה לסנדליה קטליה להו לגואי אפכיה לסנדליה קטלינהו לכולהו אזל אשכח ינוקי מלעיל וסבי מתתאי אמר אי יהבינא שלמא להני קטלי לי הני סברי אנן עדיפנן דיתבינן לעיל ואינהו לתחת אי יהבנא להני קטלי לי הני סברי אנן עדיפנן דאנן קשישי ואינהו דרדקי אמר להו שלמא לכו אמרו ליה מאי עבידתיך אמר להו חכימא דיהודאי אנא אתאי למיגמר חכמה מיניכו אמרי ליה אי הכי ניבעי מינך מלתא אמר להו להוי אי זכיתו לי כל דבעיתו עבידו בי ואי זכינ' לכו אכלו נהמ' גבאי דידי בספינ' אמרי האי גברא דאזיל ובעי איתתא ולא יהבו ליה מאי הוי דאזיל להיכא דמדלי מינה שקל סיכתא דצה לתתאי לא עאל דלי דצה לעיל עאל אמר האי נמי מתרמיא ליה בת מולידה

גברא

אמר *ליה קיסר לר' יהושע בן חנני' נחש לכמה מיעבר ומוליד א"ל לשבע' שנין והא סבי דבי אתונא ארבעינהו ואוליד לתלת הנהו מעוברין הוו מעיקרא ד' שנין והא משמשי שמושי א"נהו נמי משמשי באדם והא חכימון אינון אנן חכימן מינייהו אי חכימת זיל זבינהו ואייתינהו לי א"ל כמה הוו שיתין גברי א"ל עביד לי ספינתא דס' בתי וכל ביתא שדי בה ס' ביסתרקי עבד ליה כי מטא להתם על

* בכורות דף ח' ע"ב

רש"י

לכמה מיעבר ומוליד. כמה שוהא עוברו במעיו: דבי אתונא. מקום: והא משמשי שמושי. ואי הוו מעברי לא הוו משמשי שדרך חיה ובהמה לאחר שנתעברה אינה מקבלת זכר: והא סבי. הנהו סבי וילדו לסוף המעשה: זבינהו. נלאם בממון: ביסתרקי. כסתות: כי מטא להתם. לכרך שלהם: עביד חיותא. מחמת בהמה

בי' הגר"א

אמר ליה קיסר לריב"ח נחש לכמה שנים מיעבר ומוליד. באלוהו על חבלי משיח שמדמה הכתוב לעיבורו של אשה והגאולה ללידה כמש"כ הרינו חלנו כמו ילדנו רוח ישועות בל נעשה ארץ. ונאמר שאלו נא אם ילד זכר מדוע כל גבר ידיו על חלציו ונהפכו כל פנים לירקון ואמרו שזהו בחבלי משיח ואמרו אין בן דוד בא עד שתתפשט המלכות על ישראל ט' חדשים שנאמר לכן יתנם עד עת יולדה ילדה ויתר אחיו ישובון על בני ישראל מי ראה כו' היוחל ארץ ביום אחד אם יולד גוי פעם אחד האני אשביר ולא אוליד אם אני המוליד ועצרתי כו'. וזהו חבלי משיח חבלים של אשה כו'. ונאמר כי משורש נחש יצא צפע ופריו שרף מעופף כו' ויצא חוטר מגזע ישי ונצר משרשיו יפרה כו'. כי ישי נקרא נחש כמ"ש אשר בא אל אביגיל בת נחש. ושאלו כמה ימי העיבור וא"ל לשבע שני כמ"ש (סנהדרין צ"ז) שבוע שבן דוד בא בו שנה ראשונה מתקיים מקרא זה והמטרתי כו'. וזהו התחלתו וגמר של ביאתו כמו העיבור ללידה. וז"ש (ישעי' כ"ו) הרינו חלנו שהיה לנו כל הצרות אבל ילדנו רוח שלא בא עדיין. וזהו קושיית רב יוסף בגמרא הא כמה שביעית דהוה כן ולא אתא ע"ש. ואם זכה כיון שיעברו עליו משך מן הצרות נגאלו כמ"ש בזוהר וז"ש בטרם תחיל ילדה בטרם יבא חבל לה והמליטה כו' וכיון שלא זכינו עדיין אע"פ שנתעבר כנסת ישראל ממשיח לעפ"כ מפלת אותו כמ"ש בתז"ח (דף ע"ד) ע"ד הכשל לאו איהו בר קיימא והא הוא דלא כלו לו חדשיו כו' דאתמר בהון אין ב"ד בא עד שתתפשט מלכות ט' חדשים על ישראל בירחא קדמאה איהו משיח אין בירחא תניינא עביד ליה עם תלין. בירחא תליתאה מוסיף בי' בינה. בירחא רביעאה גמיל עמיה חסד דעאל לי' פרנסא מטבורי' דאמא. בירחא חמישאה יהיב בי' תוקפא דגבורה לאתגברא על יצה"ר מס"ט דכ"ת שלא שלט עליה בבטן אמיה למעבד ליה נפל לקטלא משיח כו' ע"ש. והענין כמו בחבלי משיח שהן ט' חדשים שתתפשט מלכות שהן חבלי משיח שהן העיבור לישראל כן למעלה במשיח בבטן כ"י ואם ישראל לאשה מתרפין מאורייתא שע"ז נאמר וארץ רפאים תפיל. כמ"ש שם בתז"ח לעיל מזה וארץ רפאים תפיל אילין דאתמר בהון רפאים בל יקומו ואילין איכון דמתרפין מאורייתא עיין שם כל המאמר אילין דאתמר כו' ע"ש כי בכל עת ועת מתעברת ממשיח ואם היו ישראל קדאי כבר נולד משיח אבל בעונינו מפלת אותו כל פעם ופעם בעבור שאנו מתרפים מד"ת. וז"ש שם בגמרא אימת אתי בר נפלי א"ל בר נפלי קרית לי' א"ל אין. דכתיב כו'. ויש עיבור ט' ויש עיבור ז' וכולהו איתנהו במשיח כידוע. ושם בתז"ח חשיב עיבור של ט' חדשים וכאן בגמרא הוא של שבעה. וידוע שרוב המפילים מפילים לה' וכמ"ש בתז"ח בירחא חמישאה יהיב לי' תוקפא כו'. וז"ש שם הא כמה שביעית דהוה כן ולא אתא א"ל אביי בששית קולות בשביעית מלחמות מי הוה כו'. ר"ל שלא נגמר העיבור אלא בחמ' והפילה (והא סבי דבי אתונא אמרי לתלת הנהו הוי מעברי מעיקרא) הענין שהם ששנו התחלת הגאולה ועיבורה משנה בשמיטים כמ"ש בשמיטית שובע גדול ואוכלין ושותין ושמחין ותורה חוזרת על לומדיה. בששית קולות ובשביעית מלחמות כו'. וא"ל רבי יהושע העיבור מתחיל מעיקרא מעת התחלת הצרות כמ"ש אגרא דכלא דוחקא (ר"ל ישראל נקראו כלה) כשרוצה הקב"ה לגאול את ישראל כדי שיגאלם מהר. ועיין בזוהר. וכך היה במצרים קודם הגאולה תכבד העבודה על האנשים כו'. וזהו עיקר הגרם לגאולה. (והא סבי אינון שהן חכימי עלייסו) שהסבי דבי אתונא היו מאדום שימי החורבן כו' כל הגדולה והיקר והחכמה נטלו אדום שע"ז נאמר ביום ההוא נאום ה' והאבדתי חכמים מאדום ותבונה מהר עשו והיו ששים נגד ששים גבורי ישראל כולם אחוזי חרב כו'. וכן בעשו זה לעומת זה כידוע ובהם ועל חרבך תחי'. וזהו מספר בלילות שהן ס' דעשו כידוע. ואמר קיסר שעשו הוא חכם יותר ממנו כמ"ש כי ציד בפיו. וביעקב נאמר איש תם וישב ובההוא שאלה ששאל ההוא מלך לשר נצחו על מה שמצא בדברי ימים קדמונים שאין חכמה כחכמת ישראל ושאל לו והכתיב

רשב"ם
בי' הגר"א

רב דימי אמר כל הפורש עצמו מד"ת נופל בגיהנם שנאמ' אדם תועה מדרך השכל בקהל רפאים ינוח ואין רפאים אלא גיהנם שנאמר ולא ידע כי רפאים שם בעמקי שאול קרואיה:

(דברים ל"ג) מימינו אשדת למו. ופסוק הוא בירמיהו: רפאים בעמקי שאול. כפל לשון הוא: לכמה

לנפש הרשע מה דבעי ורצה הוא נראות בצדיק. אדרבה נהפוך הוא שירצה הצדיק כ"ז ברשע. כי הצדיק יהיי' בתכלית ההצלחה והרשע בתכלית השפלות ואמרו (אריי א"ר כל הפורש מד"ת אש אוכלתו שנאמר כו' כי אתא רב דימי אמר כל הפורש מד"ת נופל בגיהינם) הם אמרו תיקון נב' מדות רעות שאמר למעלה ער תואב ובעלי בנות והם תאוה וגאוה כאשר באתגר ושניהם אינם באים כ"א מחמת ביטול תורה והרפואה להם היא התורה כחז"ל בראתי יצה"ר בראתי לו תבלין וכתש"כ ברמב"ם אין ההרהור מצוי אלא בלב הפנוי מן התורה וכן דרכי ענוה אינו רק מן התורה כמו שאמר במעלות דפב"י וז"ש כל הפורש מד"ת אש אוכלתו ר"ל אש היצה"ר מן התאוה ולכן אש של גיהנם אוכלתו ונגד הגאוה אמר כל הפורש כו' ניפל בגיהינם והוא ג"כ מדה כנגד מדה במחשב שהוא גדול ורם מהכל ולכן נופל לגיהנם מאיגרא רמא לבירא עמיקתא וע"י התורה ניצול משניהם וזוכה לאור באור החיים:

כי תצור אל עיר וגו'. דרשו בזוהר שכל זה דבר הקב"ה למ"ה. ואמר ימים רבים כמ"ש ימים רבים הם שלשה ולפי שהן של צער נקראו ג"כ רבים. וידוע שבשלשה חדשים אלו והן תמוז אב וטבת שבהם יש שליטה לס"א ג' ימים ידועים כמ"ש בזוהר. שבהם שולט מ"ה ביותר והם עשרה בטבת שבו צרו על עיר הקודש. ובי"ז בתמוז גבר האויב במלחמה והובקעה העיר. ובתשעה באב לכדוה והן ימים רבים הנ"ל. וזהו לפי דברי הזוהר כי הצור בי' בטבת על עיר הקודש. להלחם בי"ז בתמוז. לתפשה בט' באב או לתפשה בי"ז בתמוז שכבשו העיר בו ביום. ולהלחם עליה בין המצרים. עד רדתה בט' באב. שבו ירדה הכבוד מראשיתו ירידה תשחית. אותו תשחית וכרת ובנית מצור. הוא בזמן בין המצרים. שאז נהרגו חסידיה ושפכו דמם סביבות ירושלים עד שהספד הקב"ה את שמתו על בהמ"ק בט' באב כמ"ש במזמור לאסף וכה"א על כל דור ודור שאלו הימים יש לו שליטה ורוצה לצור על ישראל והן נקראין כל אחד עיר קטנה. כמ"ש בקהלת עיר קטנה וכו' כי תצור על עיר ואמר ימים רבים כנ"ל. להלחם עליה בקטרוג. לתפשה בעונותיו להמיתו. ואמר עליה בלשון נקבה כמו שנקרא עיר קטנה בלשון נקבה ועניינו תפיסת המ"ה אינו אלא את הגוף. וכן אמרו בזוהר הכסיל חובק את ידיו ואוכל את בשרו הוא הגוף והוא נקרא קץ כל בשר ולכן נאמר להלחם עליה בלשון נקבה. כמ"ש במדרש הנעלם שהגוף נקרא נקבה ונשמה זכר. לא תשחית את עצה היא נשמתא ונקראת דעץ החיים שהוא עץ מאכל והוא התורה שנקראת עץ חיים היא למחזיקים בה. לנדוח עליו גרזן כנ"ל שלא יטול רק את הגוף ולא הנשמה לכן נאמר עליו לשון זכר. והוא שלא ישחית הנשמה כידוע בשמיעתו בסכין פגום נפגם הנשמה וזהו גרזן. ואמר כי ממנו תאכל. כמ"ש אם רעב שונאך האכילהו לחם ואמרו (סוכה נ"ב) מלחמה של תורה. כי גחלים אתה חותה על ראשו וה' ישלם לך אל תקרי ישלם אלא ישלימנו לך. ועניינו כענין שעיר לעזאזל בסוד קרבן. ותורה במקום קרבן שנהנה ממנו אפי' הס"א מאברים ופדרים כמ"ש זאת התורה לעולה כו'. וז"ש קודם שיאכל אדם יש לו שני לבבות לאחר שיאכל אין לו אלא לב אחד. כי טרם יאכל האדם ר"ל מלחמה של תורה כמ"ש לכו לחמו בלחמי יש לו שני יצרים אחד מיעטו לטובה כו'. ואח"כ משלים עמו היצה"ר ונעשה יצ"ט כמ"ש בכל לבבך בשני יצריך. וז"ש כי ממנו תאכל אתה המ"ה ג"כ ולכן ואותו לא תכרות. וזהו וה' ישלימנו לך. ואמר לא תשחית ולא תכרות וכן לעץ שאינו מאכל אמר תשחית וכרת. כמ"ש בזוהר תשחית בעוה"ז וכרת בעוה"ב ועניינו כי כרת הוא רק שאינו חוזר לשרשו ונכרת לגמרי מן השורש כמו שכורתין עץ מן השורש והשחתה הוא שנשבת מן הגוף ולא יצלח עוד כמ"ש בירמיה נשחת האזור ולא יצלח וגו'. כי האדם הוא הת"ח שנקרא אדם כמ"ש וזרעתם זרע אדם וזרע בהמה. עץ השדה הוא עץ הנ"ל. והוא עץ של השדה הידוע שנאמר כריח השדה אשר ברכו ה' ומתרגמינן חקל תפוחין כידוע. לבא מפניך במצור כמ"ש אשרי שאל יעקב בעזרו שברו על ה' אלהיו ואמרו בזוהר שנשבר גופו בשביל ה' אלהיו. שלא יפול בחלקו של ס"א וסובל מצור ודוחק. ז"ש לבוא מפניך. שבורה מפניך. שלא יהי' בחלקך כי הקב"ה מדבר לס"א בלשון נכח. במצור כנ"ל שסובל רעב ודוחק. רק עץ אשר תדע כי לא עץ מאכל הוא. שאין בו תורה והוא מס"ט דעץ הדעת טוב ורע. שאסור לאכול ממנו שנטעוהו אדם הראשון עליו אותו תשחית וכרת כנ"ל. ובנית מצור כמ"ש ובנה עליו מצודים וגו'. על העיר אשר היא עושה עמך מלחמה. כמ"ש רשעים אפי' בשעת מיתתן מקשים שאומר לו בא קיצך והוא אומר עדיין. כמו שכתבתי בביאור מגילת אסתר על פסוק אשר לא עשתה את מאמר המלך וגו' עיין שם. עד רדתה. את עיר הקטנה. הוא הגוף דקבר שכל לת"ם לא תשחית:

ולהבה מקרית סיחון. מקרית צדיקים שנקראו שיחין. אכלה ער מואב. זה המהלך אחר יצרו כעיר זה שמהלך אחר סיחה נאה. בעלי במות ארנון. אלו גסי רוח דאמר מר כל אדם שיש בו גסות הרוח נופל בגיהנם: ונירם. אמר רשע אין רם. אבד חשבון. אבד חשבונו של עולם. עד דיבון אמר הקב"ה המתן עד שיבא דין ונשים עד נפח.(1)עד שתבא אש שאינה צריכה ניפוח. עד מידבא עד שתדאיב נשמתן ואמרי לה עד דעבד מאי דבעי: א"ר יהודה אמר רב כל הפורש מד"ת אש אוכלתו שנאמר ונתתי פני בהם מהאש יצאו והאש תאכלם. כי אתא רב

רשב"ם

הימנו: שנקראו שיחין. אילנות: כדכתיב (תהלים צ"ב) צדיק כתמר יפרח כארז בלבנון ישגא וגו': ער מואב. כעיר שמהלך אחר תאותו: ואכלה נמי האש גסי הרוח. המגביהין דעתן כבמות ארנון הללו: בעלי במות בעלי גסות. דאמר מר כל המגיס דעתו כו' (ע"ז י"ט) אר"ל כל המתלוצץ נופל בגיהנם שנאמר זד יהיר לץ שמו וגו' וכל המתייהר נופל בגיהנם שנאמר זד יהיר לץ שמו עושה בעברת זדון ואין עברה אלא גיהנם: שנאמר יום עברה היום ההוא. אבד חשבונו של עולם כלומר לית דין ולית דיין. עד נופח. כלומר אש שתנופח מעצמו כדכתיב תאכלהו אש לא נפח (איוב כ'): שתדאיב נשמתו כמו ולדאבון נפש (איוב מ"א) ולא אדיב נפשיך (שמואל א' ב'). עד דעבד. קודשא בריך הוא מאי דבעי למעבד לרשעים לעולם הבא דאלו בעוה"ז דרכם לצלח כדי לטרדם מן עולם הבא. עד דריש לי' עד דעבד ומידבא דריש לי' מאי דבעי ובלשון קצר: מהאש יצאו. מן התורה שירשו דכתיב (ירמיה כ"ג) הלא כה דברי כאש וכתיב דברים

בי' הגר"א

ותאכל את שאינן מחשבין) כי הצדיק מחייב אותו לגיהנם ועי"ז יורש חלק עצמו ונוסף ע"ז יורש ג"כ חלק הצדיק שבגיהנם והוא דמיון בתוספת כמו להבה הוא תוספת לאש. (וז"ש ולהבה מקרית סיחון אלו הצדיקים) ר"ל חלק רע של הצדיק שנקרא קרית סיחון ולא סיחון. ונגד זה יש לו חלק בגיהנם. ואמנם אמר שהצדיק תאם ברע והרשע בחר ברע לכן נותנין לו ג"כ חלק הרע של הצדיק: (ואמר אכלה ער מואב זה המהלך אחר יצרו כעיר כו' בעלי במות אלו גסי הרוח כו') הם נגד ג' מדו' רעו' שמוציאין את האדם והם התאוה והכבוד מן התאוה בא לזנות ונגד זה אמר אכלה ער מואב שהפקירו בנותיהם לזנות. כי נחל שיטים מוליד תאוה באדם לזנות כמש"כ וישבו בשיטים ויחל לזנות. ולכן נגד אש התאוה יאכל אותו אש לא נופח בגיהנם ועל גסות הרוח אמר בעלי במות. נגד כי רם לבבו בגובה. נהפך הוא שיפול בגיהנם וז"ש נופל בגיהינם ואמר (ונירם אמר רשע כו') בנוסחות אחרות כתוב כאן עד דיבון אמר המתן עד שיבא דין ואח"כ כתוב ונשים עד נופח אמר הקב"ה עד שתבא כו' וגירסא זו עיקר והוא ע"ד אחז"ל א"ר ינחק אם ראית רשע שהשעה משחקת לו אל תתגרה בו שנאמר יחילו דרכיו בכל עת ולא עוד אלא שזוכה בדין שנא' מרום משפטיך מנגדו ולא עוד אלא שרואה בצריו שנא' כל צורריו יפיח בהם ונגד ג' דברים הללו אמר כאן אמר רשע אין רם ר"ל אין רם וגבוה תמני האף שמלת ונירם משמע רק אין רם ממילא משמע שר"ל אין זולתו וזה נגד יחילו דרכיו שהוא תמיד מצליח. (אבד חשבון אבד חשבונו של עולם) זה נגד שזוכה בדין כי אף שכל עולם בצער הרשע בנחת כמש"כ כי אין חרצובות כו' ובריא אולם בעמל אנוש איננו וזה נגד שאמרו ולא עוד אלא שזוכה בדין ר"ל אף בעידן ריתחא לא מגיע שום דין ויסורין על הרשע כמש"כ מרום משפטיך מנגדו: (עד דיבון המתן עד שיבא דין) זה מאמר הרשע על הצדיק המתן עד שיבא עליו דין ויסורין. וזה נגד מה שאמרו ולא עוד אלא שרואה בצריו כי הצדיקים הם מעונים ומדוכאים. כמש"כ כל צורריו יפיח בהם כי הרשע תולה הכל במקרה ומזל: (אמר הקב"ה ונשים עד נפח כו') אז"ל ב"שר "בושה "סרוחה "רימה וא"ד "בושה "שאול "רימה והענין כמ"ש במתני' מאין באת מטפה סרוחה ולאן אתה הולך למקום עפר רמה ותולעה ולפני מי אתה עתיד ליתן דין וחשבון כו' והם עבר והוה ועתיד מאין באת הוא עבר. ולאן אתה הולך הוא הוה כי הולך האדם לבית עולמו כי יום המות הוא תיכף מיום הולדו. ולפני מי אתה עתיד ליתן דין וחשבון הוא עתיד. ונגד זה אמרו בושה נגד הדין אוי לנו מאותה בושה. סרוחה נגד מאין באת. רימה נגד לאן אתה הולך. ולשון ד' הוא נגד ג' דינים כמש"כ ויצאו וראו בפגרי האנשים כו' כי תולעתם לא תמות ואשם לא תכבה והיו דראון לכל בשר והם ג' תולעתם הוא דין הקבר ברימה ותולע. ואשם לא תכבה הוא אש של גיהנם. והיו דראון הוא כף הקלע לעין כל בשר כאז"ל די ראון לכל בשר. ונגד זה אמרו. בושה נגד כף הקלע. שאול נגד דין גיהנם. רמה נגד דין הקבר. וז"ש אמר הקב"ה (ונשים) לשון תמהון כמו ושממו עליך רבים שיתמהו עליו כולם נגד והיו דראון לכל בשר. (עד נפח עד שתבא אש שאינה צריכה נפוח) נגד ואשם לא תכבה והוא דין גיהנם. (עד מידבא עד שתדאיב נשמתן) נגד תולעתם לא תמות שהוא קשה לנפש כמ"ש קשה רמה למת כו' שנאמר ונפשו עליו תאבל: (וא"ל עד דעבד מאי דבעי) פי' רשב"ם הוא דחוק דפשיטא מי יאמר לו מה תעשה ואמנם ר"ל שאומרים לנפש

בי' הגר"א

לבאר כאן ענין באסורים ובחשך. ונראה כוונתו כי האדם עץ השדה. וכמו שהדגן קשור בתבן. והתבואה במוץ. כן לב האדם קשורה בהרגילו הרעה כמ"ש כי יצר לב האדם רע מנעוריו. וכן אמר רק רע כל היום. **וגם** יכסה עיניו מראות דרך הישר. ושני דברים אלו מטים את האדם מדרך הטוב והישר והם. א' שעיניו טח מראות ומכה עיניו בסנורי' עד שנדמה לו עבירה לפעמים שהיא מצוה או נעשה לו כהיתר כ"ש רז"ל עבר ושנה נעשה לו כהיתר. **שנית** גם אם יודע האדם שהיא עבירה מתועבה ודרכה דרכי שאול ביתה ואחריתה מרה כלענה. רק שאי אפשר לו לסור מהרגילו ונעוריו. או שקשור בחבלת פועלי און ועושה חטאים. וקשה לו פרידתו מדרכם הרעה כי עזה כמות אהבתם. ועל שני אלו אמר ישעי' לאמר לאסורים צאו. כמה האסורים בעבותות אהבת העוה"ז ומוסרות הרגילות הרעה. לאמור להם צאו לנתק מוסרות הרגילות ולהשליך עבותות אהבת המדומה. ואשר בחשך הגלו. כוונתו לאשר טח עיניהם מראות האמת. וה"ל מסמיך עיניהם. להאליף עולם עובר בעולם קיים הגלו עיניכם. והביטו אור האמת. ושני אלו שאמר ישעי' הנה דרך חיים ותוכחת מוסר שאמר שלמה. כי ההבדל בין תוכחה ומוסר. כי תוכחה הוא בדברים להתוכח על מה שעשה כבר כמו הוכח תוכיח שהוא התוכחה על העבר. ומוסר הוא ליסר א"ע בדברים המכניעים ומשברים לבו בכדי שיתקן מעשיו להבא. ולהרחיק א"ע ממה שרגיל לעשות מחמת הרגלו הרע. וצריך להקדים א"ע במוסר. ואח"כ יוכל להתוכח בעצמו ולברר מעשיו שהם אינם על נכון. כי כ"ז שלא פירש א"ע מהרגלו הרע אזי לא יועיל לו מה שיתוכח ויברר לעצמו שעשה מעשה רשע וכסל. כיון שעדיין לבו אינו נכנע כמ"ש נירו לכם ניר ואל תזרעו אל קוצים. לכן אמר בתחילה לאמור לאשר באסורים צאו. לנתק מוסרות הרגילות הרע ולהשליך עבותות אהבת נפשו אשר אותה רעה. ולצאת ביד חזקה ורמה. כ"ש רז"ל לעולם ירגיז אדם יצ"ט על יצה"ר ויעשה נגד למה שלבו חפץ. ר"ל שיגלה ויתוכח ויברר לעצמו על מעשיו איזה דרך הישר שילך בה. וזה כוונת רז"ל בפרשה זו. (על כן יאמרו המושלים אלו המושלים ביצרם). כי בתחלה צריך האדם למשול ביצרו ולכובשו תחת רשותו והוא הנקרא מוסר. וכאשר הוא מושל ביצרו. אז יאמר לו (באו חשבון) והוא הוכחה (באו ונחשב חשבונו של עולם הפסד מצוה כנגד שכרה). והוא בעיון לגלות מסכת דרכו אשר דרך באפילה ולפקח עיניו אנה פניו מועדות בילך יותר. וידע במה יכשל. ואם אדם עושה כן שיקח מוסר תחילה ויסיר מהרגלו הרע ואח"כ יתוכח ויתחשב עמו חשבונו של עולם אז ישכיל ויצליח. וזהו שאמרו תבנה בעוה"ז ותכונן בעוה"ב כשרז"ל זכה נוטל חלקו וחלק חבירו בג"ע שנא' כי משנה חלקם יירשו לא זכה תבנה בעוה"ז. שתירש חלקך שבנית בעוה"ז במעשיך הטובים. ותכונן בעוה"ב מחלק חבריך יעשה כן לחלקך. כמו בחכמה יבנה בית ובתבונה יתכונן כי בתבונה שמוציא אל הכרם מה שמבין דבר מדבר יתוסף יסוד וקיום לביתו וכן להצדיק מוסיפין לו יסוד וכן מחלק חבירו בעוה"ב. מה שלא פעל בעצמו:

ואמנם ע"ז אמר עיר סיחון אם תשים אדם כו' שהוא הרשע. מתי תכונן (מעיר סיחון) כאז"ל זכה נוטל חלקו וחלק חבירו בג"ע וזה הוא דבר נוסף על חלקו וזה נקרא תכונן. כמ"ש בחכמה יבנה בית ובתבונה יתכונן כי ע"י התבונה שהוא דבר נוסף על החכמה עושה כן ובסיס לביתו שיהי' לו חיזוק. וזה"כ והכונן שיהי' לך דבר נוסף ומפרש מנין יבא לו התוספת ע"ז אמר עיר סיחון מן חלק הרשע שמשים עצמו כסיח שהולך אחר תאותו. (מה כתיב אחריו) כאן מתחיל ענין אחר מהרשעים שאינם מחשבים אחר (תצא אש ממחשבין) והוא ג"כ ע"ד שאחז"ל לא זכה נוטל חלקו וחלק חבירו בגיהנם. והענין כי בכל אדם יש חלק טוב וחלק רע וכנגד זה יש לכ"א חלק בג"ע וחלק בגיהנם. ואמנם הצדיק יגבר הטוב על הרע והרשע להיפך ונשאר מכל אחד חלק פנוי או בג"ע או בגיהנם ולכן נותנים לכ"א במה שבחר. ואחז"ל רשע בא לדין אומרים לו למה לא עסקת בתורה אם אמר נאה הייתי וטרוד ביצרי אומרים לו כלום נאה היית מיוסף כו' נמצא יוסף מחייב רשעים ולכן נקרא רשע שהולך אחר סיחה נאה. ונשמע מזה שהצדיקים מחייבים את הרשעים וז"ש (תצא אש מן המחשבין שהם הצדיקים ותאכל

שברה ושכר עבירה כנגד הפסידה. תבנה ותכונן אם אתה עושה כן תבנה בעוה"ז ותכונן בעוה"ב. עיר סיחון אם משים אדם עצמו כעיר זה שמהלך אחר סיחה נאה מה כתיב אחריו כי אש יצאה מחשבון וגו' תצא אש ממחשבין ותאכל את שאינן מחשבין ולהבה

רשב"ם

כנגד שכרה המרובה לעתיד: ושכר עבירה. שלא להשתכר בעבירה עכשיו כנגד הפסדה שיפסיד יותר לעתיד: אם אתה עושה כן. לחשוב הפסד כנגד שכר: כעיר זה שמתפתה ביצרו ובדברי אפיקורסי' ואינו מושל ביצרו: הלא אש מן המחשבין. הצדיקים ותאכל את שאינם מחשבין כדאמרינן בפרקין לעיל (דף ע"ה) כל אחד ואחד נכוה מחופתו של חבירו. חופתו של קטן מחופתו של גדול הימנו

ואמר רבב"ח זימנא חדא בו' א"ל תא אחוי לך היכא דנשקא ארעא ורקיעא אהדדי שקלתא לסילתאי אתנהתא בכוותא דרקיע' אדמצלינא בעיתא ולא אשכחיתא אמינא ליה איכא גנבי הכא אמר לי האי גלגלא דרקיעא הוא דהדר נטר עד למחר הכא ומשכחת לה:

אמר רב שמואל בר נחמן אמר יוחנן מאי דכתיב ע"כ יאמרו חמושלים וגו' המושלים אלו המושלים ביצרם. באו חשבון. באו ונחשב חשבונו של עולם הפסד מצו' כנגד שכרה

רשב"ם

היכא דנשקי ארעא ורקיעא. מקום גבוה הי' שם שנושקין יחד זה לזה ולאו היינו סוף העולם דהא מהלך חמש מאות שנה הוי וארץ ישראל אמצעיתו של עולם כדכתיב (יחזקאל ל"ח) יושבי על טבור הארץ. והיינו מקומו של רבב"ח. סילתא. סל לחם שלו: דהדר. חוזר כדאמרינן (פסחים צ"ד) גלגל חוזר ומזלות קבועים:

מאי דכתיב על כן יאמרו המושלים וגו'. פשטיה דקרא איירי כשנלחם סיחון במלך מואב הראשון ויקח את כל ארצו מידו נתנבא בלעם וחביריו שיכלה סיחון למואב. ומיהו פרשה יתירה היא דמה צריך לכתב זה אם להשמיענו דעמון ומואב טהרו בסיחון הרי כבר כתיב והוא נלחם במלך מואב הראשון ואין צריך יותר הלכך לדרשה כתבה משה רבינו: המושלים ביצרם. צדיקים כדכתיב ומושל ברוחו מלוכד עיר (משלי ט"ז) צדיק מושל ביראת אלהים (שמואל ב' כ"ג): הפסד מצוה. שמתבטל מריוח בשביל שעוסק במצוה או נותן צדקה ומחסר ממונו כנגד

בי' הגר"א

היכא דנשקא ארעא ורקיע אהדדי. פי' כי היצר נקרא סוחר דאפשר לגופא בזינין בישין כמ"ש בזוהר והוא מסיתו לפרוש מד"ת מפאת שמראה לאדם עיני הבאות הטוב מחמדת העולם ומלואה והאדם בהבקשה לתשובה לא יאבה שמוע אליו בזכרו יפה שעה אחת קורת רוח בעוה"ב מכל חיי העוה"ז אף הוא היצר ישוב אחריו לו הלא אמרו רז"ל גדול הנהנה מיגיע כפו יותר מירא שמים ואז תזכה לשתי שולחנות של עוה"ז ועוה"ב. וזה אומרו תא קום מן עסק התורה ואראה לך מקום שתזכה לשניהם הנה. וזה היכא דנשקא ארעא ורקיע אהדדי כנ"ל שתזכה לשתי שולחנות. הלכתי ופרשתי מן התורה ושמעתי לעצתו. וראיתי כי לא לאדם דרכו לא לכל אדם מועיל יגיע כפו בעוה"ז כמ"ש לא לחכמים לחם ולא לנבונים עושר. ונראה זאת לעין כי לא ביד האדם להתעשר ולא לשבוע מיגיע כפו. רק ה' נותן לחם לכל בשר כמ"ש דלתי שמים פתח וגו'. וכן יפתח ה' לך את אוצרו הטוב את השמים לתת מטר ארצך בעתו ולברך את כל מעשה ידיך. וכן אנחנו מתפללים שערי שמים פתח ואוצרך הטוב תפתח כי חלונות יש ברקיע שמשם הקב"ה מקבל תפילות ישראל ומשם משפיע להם מזונות בכל יום וזה אומרו ומזי דעביד כוי כוי (שקלתי לסלתאי ואנחת בכוותא דרקיע) פי' שהתפללתי לה' שיתן לי מזונותי. (אדמצלינא בעיתא ולא אשכחי) כמ"ש שאלו את ר"י מה יעשה אדם ויתעשר אמר להם ירבה בסחורה וישא ויתן באמונה אמרו לו הרבה עשו כן ולא הועילו אמר ר"ל יבקש ממי שהעושר שלו וכו' מאי קא משמע לן דהא בלא הא לא סגי. לזה עשה גם כן שהתפלל קודם למי שהעושר שלו ואח"כ חזר על פרנסתו אף על פי כן לא מצא. (אמינא גנבי איכא הכא) פי' שקליפת נוגה היא המונעת השפע מן הקודש והוא בעונותיהם של בני אדם שאינם נושאים ונותנים באמונה ומאנין את חבריהם כן היא עושה ומאנה את הקדושה וגונבת נשמות דסמכא לגבן: ע"כ נאמר כל ארחות בוצע בצע את נפש בעליו יקח. לכך כבר שהיא גנבה שפעו ומזונותיו. שלכך אמר ג"כ ישא ויתן באמונה ואלה לישא וליתן באמונה: א"ל לא תועיל כי גלגל הוא החוזר בעולם. לא בזכותא תליא מילתא אלא במזלא. כי שכר מצוה בהאי עלמא ליכא כמ"ש היום לעשותם ומחר לקבל שכרם וזה אמרו (גלגל רקיע דהדר) ע"כ לא תשמע לעצת היצה"ר לבטל מהתורה. ושכר מעשיך נשמר עד למחר. (נטר עד למחר הכא.) שתבא לכאן ומשכחת לה. ותמצא כל שכרך מוכן:

רבינו הגדול אמר על זה המאמר בקצרה. ואחר ופירש לנו בזקנותו באר היטב.
בדעתו הרחבה. ומי יוכל לשער רוחב לבבו. כחול אשר על שפת הים. אשא קצהו תהלה:

אמר ר' שמואל בר נחמן וכו'. המאמר הזה הוא קשה להבין. בתחלה אמר עיר סיחון אלו הרשעים. ואח"כ דרש מקרית סיחון מקרית לצדיקים שנקראו סיחון. וכן מ"ש ונירם אמר רשע אין רם. האיך נדרש זה וגם עיר סיחון מובן לשלפניו והם דרשו על של אחריו ועוד ואמרי לה עד דעבד אלי דבעי פירש דשנ"ם בקאי על הקב"ה והוא דסוק לפי הפשט. וגם למה הביא כאן עוד ג' מאמרים אחרים כל הפורש מד"ת את אוכלתו וכן כל הפורש עצמו מד"ת נופל בגיהנם: ונבאר בתחלה כוונת המאמר. ויתבררו כל הספיקות. על כן יאמרו המושלים באו חשבון. הבורא יתברך הורה לנו הדרך אשר נלך בה. בתורתו הקדושה. כי אמרו בזוהר פינחס על פ' לאמור לאמירים באו ואשר בספק הגלו אמרו שהם התנן והמיץ כוונתו לבאר

ביאור הגר"א

אלו בני אדם שהן פורצין גדעת ומשימים עצמם כבהמה. ולפי שפיתוי היצר אצל חסרון מזונות על דרך שדרשו בזוהר על ארץ הנגב נתתני לכן אמר לבני עורב אשר יקראו למי שנעשה אכזרי כעורב הקב"ה נותן להם לחם.

וסליק יתיב באילנא הא חזי כמה נפיש חיליה דאילנא אמר רב פפא בר שמ־אל אי לאו דהואי התם לא הימני: אמר

וזה אמרו אתא פוסקא ובלען לתכילא. וזה מדויק מה שפירש רש"י עורב נקבה כי משונה היא במנהגה נגד אם הבנים לכל בעל חי. והוא מליצה על ת"ח שנעשה אכזרי על בניו ועוסק בתורה יום ולילה: (וסליק ויתיב באילנא). פירש מה עושה לו הקב"ה מזמן לו אדם להחזיקו כיששכר וזבולון וכן אמר וינוחו מרחה וגו'. פירש שבא בעוה"ז במזל רע כי מזונא לאו בזכותא תליא אלא במזלא תליא ולא יכלו לשתות מים ממרה משום דושקם. ויורהו ה' עץ שהוא אחד ממחזיקי תורה כמו שאמרו עץ חיים היא למחזיקים בה ללומדיה לא נאמר אלא למחזיקים בה. וזהו כוונת אומרו סליק יתיב באילנא (הא חזי כמה נפיש חילא דאילנא.) פירש מה גודל כחו. לפי שמלאכו יעקב אבינו ומשה הקדימו ברכות זבולון ליששכר. וכן אמר אחרי ה' אלהיכם תלכו ובו תדבקון וכי אפשר לידבק וכו'. ומה שאמר נפיש חילא כוונתו על גודל צדקתו אשר יכול לכבוש את יצרו לחלק נכסיו כמו שדרשו על פסוק גבורי כח עושי דברו וכן הוא אומר אשת חיל מי ימצא וגו' כפה פרשה לעני וכן בבועז אמר גבור חיל על שם צדקתו וכבישת יצרו עם רות. וכן אמרו הני ברכי דרבנן דשלהי מינייהו הוי. ענין כוונת רז"ל הוא על מחזיקי התורה כי הם נקראים בירכי דרבנן כמו שאמרו בזוהר וכן אמר וירא כי לא יכול לו פי' שלא יכול לבטל ת"ח מעסק התורה מה עשה ויגע בכף ירכו פירש שהסית את מחזיקי ת"ח שלא יחזיקו עוד את הת"ח. וזה אמרו הכא ברכי דרבנן דשלהי מנייהו פירש מן הסטרא אחרא שהם מתישין כחן ומרפין לבנם ואל יאמרו מפני עול המסים והארנוניות הלא זה אמרם רז"ל כל הפורק ממנו עול תורה פי' להחזיק תלמידי חכמים נותנים עליו עול דרך ארץ שהוא המסים והארנוניות. וכן אמרו עשירי בבל יורדי גהינם הן פי' לפי שאינם מחזיקים ידי תלמידי חכמים: (אמר רב פפא בר שמואל אי לאו דהואי התם לא הימנא) פירש התם בארץ ישראל כמה שאמר מהתם להכא. לא הימנא לפי שבבבל לא ראה כלל מחזיקי תורה: ובזה יובן פי' כי תצור על עיר ימים רבים להלחם עלי' לתפשה ומפרש בזוהר בלק דף ר"ב שמזהיר הקב"ה למדת הדין המקטרג ואפרש קצת פרטים בדרך אחר ימים רבים הן ג' ימים הידועים היינו ראש השנה יוה"כ ונקראים רבים על שם של נער. ועיין מה שכתבתי במגילת אסתר. לא תשחית את עצה הוא עץ החיים הנ"ל המחזיק תלמידי חכמים. לנדוח עליו גרזן אלו הדינין. כי ממנו תאכל כמ"ש בזוהר דקאי על התורה שהוא חי ממנה רלה לומר שכל העולמות ניזונים בשביל התורה ולכן אותו לא תכרות. כי האדם עץ השדה. פי' הקיום של התלמיד חכם הוא ע"י עץ שמחזיק בו: לבא מפניך במצור פי' מפניך מפני מדת הדין שאתה מקטרג עליו שעל ידי העץ היא גורם מפניך שאילולי הוא הי' בולע אותו החמין בלחלו וזימקו. רק אשר תדע כי לא עץ מאכל הוא שאינו מחזיק ת"ח אותו תשחית בעלמא דין ובעלמא דאתי כמו שאמרו בזוהר ובנית מצור על העיר אשר היא עושה עמך מלחמה פי' כי הרשעים אפילו בשעת מיתתן מקשין ערפן ולוחמין עם מה"מ מה שאין כן הצדיקים כנתגלו ליונים שפושטין צוארם לשחיטה וזה אמרו אשר היא עושה עמך מלחמה. עד רדתה. פי' אל אדמה שאז נחת קטרוג מד"ה מעליו כמו שאמרו וישאו את יונה וכו' ויעמוד הים מזעפו עיין שם מה שכתבתי: וכוונת מאמר זה על מחוסרי אמנה שאין יכולין ללמוד מחמת עניות. כמו שאמרו (עירובין ס"ה) יכול אני לפטור את כל העולם כלו מן הדין שנאמר שמעי נא זאת עני' ושכורת ולא מיין וזה גרם בליעת תנין את הצפרדע כמו שאמרו (בסוטה דמ"ח) אמר רבי אלעזר מ"ד כי מי בז ליום קטנות מי גרם לצדיקים שיתבזבז שולחנן לעתיד לבא קטנות שהי' בהן שלא האמינו בהקב"ה עיין פי' רש"י ז"ל. וכן אמרו בחגיגה בא חבקוק והעמידן על אחת וצדיק באמונתו יחיה וכן קראו בתהלים ישוני ויועצו כשכיר וכל חכמתם תתבלע:

תלתא פרסי ובי מרבעתא דרישיה פרסא ופלגא. רמא כופתא וסכריה לירדנא: אמר רבב"ח לדידי חזי לי ההיא אקרוקת' דהוה כי אקרא דהגרוניא ואקרא דהגרוני' כמה הוי שתין בתי. את' תנינא בלעה אתא פישקנצא ובלעה לתנינא וסליק

רשב"ם

ב' מרבעתא דרישיה. מקום הנחת ראשו כשוכב על הקרקע: רמא כופתא. הטיל רעי: וסכריה. הרעי לירדנא לפי שעה: עד שמיקמקוהו המים מעט מעט:

אקרוקתא. צפרדע. כאקרא דהגרוני. גדול הי' כאותו כרך: ואקרא דהגרוניא כמה הוי שיתין בתי. תלמודא קאמר לה אתא תנינא. רבה קאמר ליה: פושקנצא. עורב נקיבה: באילנא. על ענף א' כדרך העופות: לא הימני. לא האמנתי: (מה שפירש רשב"ם על ואקרא דהגרוני תלמודא קאמר לה: אתא תנינא רבה קאמר ליה הוא ק"ל:)

היכא

בי' הגר"א

ואח"כ בן ארבעים לבינה להבין ולפלפל והם ג"כ ד' ימים עד שבעים שאז הוא ראוי לישיבה כמ"ש חז"ל זקן ויושב בישיבה. וזה אורזילא בר יומא ביום אחד הוא הולך מהלך ד' ימים לפי דעתו וז"א הר תבור כמה הוי ארבעין פרסה שהוא מהלך ד' ימים. (ומשכי דצוארי' תלתא פרסה) כמ"ש (יומא פ"ז. סנהדרין ז') רב כי הוה אזי אמבואה דאזיל אבתריה אמר הכי אם יעלה לשמים שיאו וראשו לעב יגיע כגללו לנצח יאבד רואיו יאמרו איו ואמרו (ב"ב ע"ה) אמר רב פפא שמע מינה האי עיבא תלתא פרסי תלי. ור"ל שנדמה לו כאלו כבר עלה לתכלית הגדולה: (ובי מרבעתא דרישא פרסא ופלגא) שמניח ראשו בין הגדולים אף שיהיו גדולים כמרע"ה שהיה חנייתו לפני המשכן באמצע מחנה ישראל ומחנה ישראל היה ג' פרסה נמצא מסוף מחנה ישראל עד האמצע פרסא ופלגי והאי אורזילא הוא מערב רב ועומד חוץ למחנה ישראל אמנם מניח ראשו במקום גדולים: רמא כופתא וסכר לירדנא) פי' כאשר הוא רואה שאינו יכול לנצח את ת"ח אז הוא מבזים ריסם. כי כן דרכי הקנאה כשאינו יכול להגביה את עצמו. אז הוא מבזים ומטנף את חבירו ואמרו כל הפוסל וכו'. וזה כוונת איוב כגללו לנצח יאבד כמו שחשב הוא על ת"ח כן יאבד בעצמו וזהו רמא כופתא וסכר לירדנא כי הת"ח נקרא ירדן וכל עניין המאמר הזה על קנאה שהוא אחד מג' מדות של בלעם הרשע שהיא עין רעה. וסדרן כמו שחשב כאן. מתחילה יתרומם נפש האדם על זולתו בזדון לבו וגאותו. ואח"כ יתאוה לתאוה וכבוד. ואח"כ יקנא לכל אדם. וכן כסדר דהמע"ה במזמור ק"ז נפשם ברעה תתמוגג. ברעה כוונתו בקנאת איש מרעהו וכן אמר תמותת רשע רעה והוא קנאתו ושונאי צדיק יאשמו כי רקב עצמות קנאה: או ר"ל ורמא כופתא. כי נהר דינור שם מטבילין הנשמות לעלות אל ארץ החיים ארעא קדישא. והוא נגד הירדן המפסיק בין א"י לח"ל. אבל הרשעים מתוך שזוהמתן מרובה נשארים שם ואינם יכולים לעלות מתוכה וזה אמרו כגללו לנצח יאבד ונשלם לו מדה כנגדה שהיה רמא כופתא ומבזים ביה ת"ח ועליהם אמר דוד נפשם ברעה שלהם תתמוגג שם בנהר דינור. והגאוה והתאוה והכבוד חשב בפסוקים הקודמים יעלו שמים וכו' כנ"ל:

ההיא אקרוקתא. אחז"ל במדרש שמות רבה. למה לקו המצריים בצפרדעים בשביל שבטלו את ישראל מלעסוק בתורה כשדין לצפרדע דלא שכיך יממא ולילה ולכן נקרא הת"ח לצפרדע. לכן אמר רבב"ח במליצתו שראה ת"ח א' (דהוה כי אקרא דהגרוניא ואקרא דהגרוניא כמה הוי שתין בתי) ועניינו כ"ש ששים המה מלכות וכו' אחת היא יונתי תמתי. ששים מלכות הנה ששים מסכתות אחת היא יונתי תמתי. היא היראה שהי' עומדת לעד כ"ש יראת ה' טהורה עומדת לעד וכן אמרו (שבת ל"א) והיה אמונת עתך כו' אמונת זה סדר זרעים כו' ואפ"ה אי יראת ה' כו'. וכוונתו שראה ת"ח בקי בכל הש"ס. אתא תנינא ובלעה ע"ד שכתוב (ישעי' כ"ז) ביום ההוא יפקוד ה' בחרבו הקשה והגדולה והחזקה על לויתן נחש בריח ועל לויתן נחש עקלתון והרג את התנין אשר בים. והעניין כמ"ש בזוהר כי שני תנינים הן אחד הוא על עפר משלו ונקרא נחש כמ"ש ונחש עפר לחמו: והשני בים ונקרא תנין. כמו את התנין אשר בים מפני ששם שני ילדין האחד בא משום בארץ ומתהלך סביב עמי הארצות שהולכן בארץ ולכן נקרא ע"ה. זה הילד נקרא נחש. והשני נקרא תנין השוחה בים סביב הת"ח שהולכן בים התלמוד ובמעייני החכמ' לבטלן מעסק התורה. כמו שדרשו בזוה' על פ' ויעלו בנגב. ואחז"ל לויתן נחש בריח ולויתן נחש עקלתון הם זכר ונקבה ואמרו (פסחים מ"ט) גדולה שנאה שסונאי' הע"ה כו' ונשותיהן יותר מהם תנא שנה ופירש קשה מכלן. וזה אמרו על לויתן נחש בריח ועל לויתן נחש עקלתון שהם ע"ה והרג את התנין אשר בים שהוא אשר שנה ופירש. וזה אמרו (אתא תנינא ובלעה) הוא השנה ופירש. (אתא פושקנצא ובלעה לתנינא) ענייני כמ"ש (עירובין כ"ב) שמצויות כעורב במי אתה מוצאן במי שמשים עצמו אכזרי על בניו כעורב. ועל זה אמר מי יכין לעורב צידו כי ילדיו אל אל ישועו. וכן נותן לבהמה לחמה לבני עורב אשר יקראו. והיא על דרך שאמרו רז"ל (חולין ה') אדם ובהמה תושיע ה'

בי' הגר"א

רשב"ם

בידיה ומריק מהאי להאי ולא נטפי מנידהו לארעא ואותו היום יעלו שמים ירדו תהומות הוה עד דשמעו בי מלכותא וקטליה:

אמר רבב"ח לדידי חזי לי אורזילא בר יומיה דהוה כהר תבור. והר תבור כמה הוי ארבע פרסי ובי משכי דצואריה תלתא

הים. ועומדים על ים העולם הזה כמו גשר וזה אמרו אגשרא דריגג. ושויר מהאי גישא להאי גישא ומהאי גישא להאי גישא. פי' קוטן ומשנה מלתו מכבוד לתאוה ומתאוה לכבוד כמ"ש (בביאורי על מגילה מה שאמרו ז"ל במגילה דף י"ב) אתנויי אתני בהדי הדדי אי מינן מלכי מינייכו אפרכי ואי מנייכו מלכי וכו' שהן תאוה וכבוד. שרים המתלאים זהב להם למלאת תאותם. ומלכי' מקום רגלם יכבדו. (ונקיט תרי מזגא דחמרא בידי' ומריק מהאי להאי ולא נטפא נטיפא לארעא) ענינו כמ"ש בזהר על שתי בנות לוט שאמרו. לכה נשקה את אבינו יין כו'. שהן ב' כחות והן התאו' והמתעורר שהן מסייעין זו לזו. התאוה באה מן המתעורר. והמתעורר לבדו בלא תאוה לשוא יעורר. ולא נטפא נטיפא לארעא. שלא עשו אחת מהן מעשה שלא נודעת חברתה וזה אמרו תרי מזגא דחמרא. ואמר נטיפה לארעא. פי' שלא נתן לו ה' לב לדעת שסופו לעפר: (וההוא יומא יעלו שמים ירדו תהומות) פי' יום הידוע. שהנפש ורוח השיכלית יעלו למעלה השמים. ונפש ורוח הבהמית ירדו תהומות כמ"ש מי יודע רוח בני האדם העולה היא למעלה ורוח הבהמה היורדת כו' ואעפ"כ לא שב ממעשיו הרעים (עד דשמעו בי מלכא) פי' מלכותא דרקיע (וקטלוהו.) מפני שכל הימים מה"ד מקטרגת ואין שומעין לה עד ההוא יומא שלכן נקרא הקב"ה נושא עון שסובל אותו עד ההוא יומא. וכל ענין סיפור המאמר הזה הוא על מדת התאוה והכבוד שעליו נאמר יעלו שמים ירדו תהומות. שעוסק בתורה ומצות שיכבדו אותו ויעלה לשמים שיאו. ואח"כ ירד תהומות במצולות התאוה ובאלות חומרי הילך. והוא על סדר הכתוב יעלו שמים ירדו תהומות נפשם ברעה תתמוגג אחר שאמר ותרומם גליו ונדת הגאוה אחר כך בא אל הכבוד ומתאוה:

אורזילא בר יומיה כמ"ש רז"ל אמרא אזיל למבעי קרני אודני דהוה לי' גזיזי מיני'. וענינו כי אמרו לגמור אינם והדר לסבור שנאמר שתה מים מבורך ואח"כ מנאלך. ונראה שזהו שכתוב בכור שורו הדר לו וקרני ראם קרניו. כי נאמר ורב תבואות בכח שור כמ"ש תנא דבי אליהו לעולם ישים אדם את עצמו כשור לעול וכחמור למשא. שור לעול לישא מה ששמע מרבו וזהו בכור שורו הדר לו. הדר הוא לגמר מרבו כשור לעול. ואח"כ וקרני ראם קרניו במשא ומתן של פלפול כמ"ש בעלי קרניים שמנגחים בתורה וכן בעלי תריסין הכל משל על הפלפול. והוא הדרה והוא זיוה של התורה שמתלא כריסו בתחילה מקרא משנה גמרא בבלי ירושלמי תוספתא מכילתא ספרא וספרי וכל הברייתות ואח"כ עוסק בשמוש ת"ח להסביר קראי בפלפול חברים. ועל המשנה סדר הלימוד ולומד בתחילה לידע האיך לפלפל ואינו יודע משנה אחת כלורתה אמרו רז"ל אמרא אזיל למבעי לי קרנא לידע היאך לנגח בקרני הברזל מתמת קניה. אודנא דהוי לי' גזיזא ויניי'. גם מקלת תורה ששמע בנערותו. אבד גם כן. וזה אמרו האי אורזילא בר יומא הוא הראש שעליו נאמר קרני ראם קרניו. בר יומא. פי' ביום הראשון שהתחיל ללמוד הוא נועק ומפרכס כמו הגדולים אשר בארץ: דהוי כהר תבור. שרוצה להגדיל עצמו כהר תבור וכמ"ש (מגילה כ"ט). עתידין בתי כנסיות כו' שנאמר (ירמיה מ"ו). כי כתבור בהרים וככרמל בים יבוא וכו' פי' רש"י למדנו שעבר כרמל ותבור את הים לתת עליהם התורה. דרש בר קפרא מאי דכתיב (תהלים ס"ח) למה תרצדון הרים גבנונים יצתה בת קול ואמרה להם למה תרצו דין עם סיני כלכם בעלי מומין אתם אצל סיני וכו' אמר רב אשי שמע מינה האי מאן דיהיר בעל מום הוא: (והר תבור כמה הוי ארבעה פרסה). שמראה בעצמו שאין ספר מן הקדושה כלום כמ"ש (סוטה דף כ"ב) ז' פרושין הן וכו' פרוש מה סובתי ואעשנה מה סובתי תו ואעשנה. ואמרו המקובלים שמיום הד' על השבת צריך להכין את עצמו לקדושה כל רגע וש"ק הוא עיקר הקדושה וכן אמרו חז"ל בן שלשים לכח כמ"ש ורב תבואות בכח שור שיחזור תמיד מה ששמע מרבותיו ואח"כ

כסא דחמרא שניהם מלאים יין והוה מוריק תרוייהו ביחד זה בתוך זה בהדי דקא משויר ואין נשפך אפילו טפה אחת ואעפ"י שהיה אותו היום רוח סערה שהיו עולים יורדי הים באניות עד לב שמים ויורדים עד תהומות מכח הרוח ואעפ"י כן לא נפלה טפה לארץ: יעלו השמים וגו'. פסוק הוא גבי יורדי הים בתהלים: שמעו בית מלכא וקטלו ליה. מלכא דשדא שאין דרכו של שד להראות לבני אדם והרגוהו מפני שהיה מגלה סודם. ואית דאמרי בו מלכא. קיסר שהיה ירא שלא יטול מלכותו שהיה אותו שד מאד' שבא על שדה והיה רב בנין האנשים: **אורזילא** בר יומיה. ראם בן יום אחד דאותו היום נולד: כהר תבור. כן נולד גדול:

הוטא דחלא לית דעבר שנאמר (ירמיה ה) האותי לא תיראו נאום ה' אם מפני לא תחילו אשר שמתי חול גבול לים חק עולם לא יעברנהו:
אמר רבב"ח לדידי חזו לי הורמין בר לילתא דהוה קא רהיט אקופיה דשורה דמחוזא ורהיט פרשא כי רכ"ב סוס'א מתתאי ולא יכול ליה זמנא חדא הוה מסרגן ליה תרתי חיותא וקיימן אתרי גשרי דדונג ושוור מהאי להאי ומהאי להאי ונקיט תרי כסא דחמרא בידיה

רשב"ם

הורמין בנו של לילית. ממשפחת שלא שידי: ולפי שמעתי הורמיז בזיין ושר הוא כדאמרינן בסנהדרין מפלגן לספלי דהורמיז: של קופיה דשורא. על פיני החומה. והאי עובדא להודיע לדקותו של הקב"ה שמרחם על בריותיו ואינו נותן רשו' לאלו להזיק וגם שלא ללסם בדבק יחידי. והריש פרש'. לפי תומו: ולא יכיל ליה. שהיה רץ ביותר ואיהו הפרש לא היה מתכוין לכך: מסרגן. שהיה אוכף ומרגא כמוכין על הפרדים אסרי גשרי דדונג. שם אותו הנהר והיו רחוקים זה מזה והשד מדלג מגרידה זו לגרידה זו: תרסי כסא

בי' הגר"א

לדיקים שהם מלודים עאכ"ו. ואמרו (בסוכה נ"ב.) א"ל אפי' יצה"ר בתחלה דומה לחוט של בוכיא וכו' אבל הצדיקים אינם מגיעים להשפעות מיצה"ר אפילו כשים. ואמרו (שם:) יצרו של אדם מתגבר עליו בכל יום והקב"ה עוזרו. וזה אמרו חוק מזי בגורתיה דמריך. שנאמר האותי לא תיראו נאום ה' אם מפני לא תחילו אשר שמתי חול גבול לים חוק ולא יעברנהו. פי' מדוע לא תיראו מיצר ואו"ת יצה"ר אינו מגיע אותנו. והלא שמתי חול גבול לים. בצדיקי' אינו שולט אפי' כחוט של בוכיא: וספור של רבב"ח זה הוא על מדת הגאוה וסופו הלת בכעס: וסדר אותו על סדר הפסוקים הספור שראשון ע"ש ויאמר ויעמד רוח סערה שהוא משבר ומשבע לספינה כמ"ש בפי' יונה ויהי הסער והאניה חשבה להשבר כו' וע"ש. וספור השני על פסוק שלאחריו ותרומם גלין וכו':
לדידי חזי לי. הורמיז בר לילתא. ענינו כנאמר והבדילה הפרוכת לכם בין הקודש ובין ק"ק ואמרו בזוהר שהוא אלו הכנד שהוא מבדיל בין כלי הקול שהוא ק"ק המיוסד לתורה ולתפלה ובין כלי המאכל שהוא ג"כ קודם כמאמר הילל בזמו ובגמל חסד להדא עלובתא נב"ח (שבת ד' ל"ב.) שהוא מינא מפלגא ולמתאי דאהורמיז כלומר ש"ל מפלגא ולעילא הודה שהוא מיוחד להקב"ה אבל מפלגא ולתתא דאהורמיז כת"ש בזכריה וכי תאכלו וכי תשתו כו'. אמר ליה אי אפשר דא"כ לא שביק ליה לאשבוריה מיכלי ומשתי. והנה האכילה והשתיה מגשמין הפלגא ולמטה אלא בתוך מינה שגם הוא קודש. אבל יש בני אדם שגם תורתם ומעשיהם אינם אלא להתפאר ואמרו בזוהר שהן תכ"ע דערב רב ועבי ליבית האומדי' כבשה לנו שם בציון בי כנישתא וכו' ואנו היתה כלו של הורמיז אף מפלגא ולעילא דאהורמיז. (וזהו הורמיז בר לילתא דהוה קא רהיט אקופא דשורא דמחוזא) ע"ד שאמרו (בר"ה דף י"ז) ועליהם אמרה שנה ה' יחתו מריביו א"ר יצחק בר אבין ופניהם דומין כשולי קדירה ואמר רבא ואינון משפירי שפירי בני מחוזא ומקריין בני גיהנם. פי' שפירי. כל מעשיהם אינם אלא להתנאות בהם וקורדום לספור בהם. ואמרו (בב"ב דף ח') אני חומה זו תורה ושדי כמגדלות אלו ת"ח. וזהו אומרו (דרהיט אקופא דשורא דמחוזא) ר"ל בני ת"ח של מחוזא בני גיהנם המעסקים בתורה להתגאות בהם. (ורהיט פרשא כי רכיב סוסיא מתותיה ולא יכיל ליה) שהצדיקי' ות"ח נקראים רוכבים כמ"ש (בחלק ל"ו). את רגלים רצתה ואיך תתחרה את הסוסים ותה נסגיל שכר ד' פסיעות שפסעתי לנבוכדנצר פרץ המר כבודי אתה תמים כשאני משלם שכר לאברהם יצחק ויעקב שרצו' לפני בסוסי' עאכ"ו ואמרו (עירובין נ"ד.) תנא דבי רב ענן מ"ד רוכבי אתונות למורות אלו ת"ח שהולכים מעיר לעיר וממדינה למדינה ללמוד תורה ומתבארין אותה כצהרים. כמ"ש (איוב ל"ה) מלפנו מבהמות הארץ. פי' ביגמוד האדם מן הרשעים שדומים במעשיהם לבהמה. כמו שהם לומדים תמיד שלא לשם שמים בשקידה רבה ככה תלמוד בנגד שלם לשם שמים. כי קשה לאדם מאוד לנהוג בספק וספק לש"ש כמ"ש (ברכו' כ"ח.) יהי רצון שתהא מורא שמים עליכם כמורא ב"ו ואמר הדע וכו'. וזה אמרו ורהיט פרשא כו' ולא יכיל ליה: שהלומד לשמה קשה לו ללמוד כ"כ בשקידה יתר ככ"ל. (זמנא חדא הוה מסרגן לי' תרתא חייתא וקיימן אתרי גשרא דדונג). כי היצה"ר וכל שליחיו נקראים על פי הדותיי פריסים כמ"ש בזוהר שהרם ליתן את הזכר וכו'. וכן מדותיו נקראין כודנייתא דלא מולידין וזה מנין בנות לוט כמש"כ בזוהר ובגמ' לקמן שאמרו ואיש אין בארץ לבוא עלינו וכו'. ועקרי של הורמין על ב' מדות הללי שהן מפלגא ולמטה באדם. ומפלגא לעילא יש רוח גבוה שהיא תאות הכבוד כמו שפי' הרמב"ם על עין רעה הוא הקנאה. ונפש רחבה הוא התאוה ורוח גבוה הוא הכבוד. וכל עיונו של הורמין רק על נפש ורוח הבהמית של האדם כמ"ש במדרש על כליון וערפה ששניהם עתידין למחות מן העולם כמ"ש כ"ינג מפני האש

ש' פרסא זמנא חדא הוה אזלינן באורחא ודלינן גלא עד דחזינן בי מרבעת' דכוכבי זוטא דהוי כמבזר ארבעין גריוי ביזרא דהרדלא ואי דלינן טפי הוה מקלינן מהבלא. ורמיא לה גלא קלא להברתא ואמר לה הברתי מי שבקת מידי בעלמא דלא שטפתי' וניתי אנא ונהרבי' אמר לה פוק חזי גבורתיה דמריך דאפילו במלא חוטא

רשב"ם

גלא. יותר משיעור גבהו השליכנו למעלה עד לרקיע א"כ הגלא דרקיע נפיש עד מהלך קרוב לת"ק שנה שיש מן הרקיע לארץ: מרבעתי' שכיבו: דכוכבא זוטא. ככב קטן שבכוכבים: ביזרא כו'. בית זרע ארבעים כור של חרדל דנפשי מכל שאר זרעים: מקלינן מהבליה. נשרפים מחום הכוכב: ורמא לה גלא. נתן קולו כלומר צעק. כדוגמת תהום אל תהום קורא לקול וגו' ושמא המלאכי' הממונים עליה' הם: שבקת מידי בעלמא וכו'. מפני שהגביה כל כך היה סבור שיצא חוץ לשפת הים ושטף את העולם: ונהרביה. מפני עון הדור: אמר לה. גלא לחבריה. פוק חזי גבורתי' דמרך וכו' כלומר אין לי רשות לצאת: כמלא הוטא דחלא. כמלא רוחב החוט אינו יכול לצאת חוץ מן החול: שנאמר האותי לא תיראו. אלמודא קאמר לה:

הירמין

בי' הגר"א

ומתגבר תמיד שאין לך כל יום ויום שאין קללתו מרובי' מחבירו. וכמ"ש בעובדי' זדון לבך השיאך אם תגביה כנשר כו'. ושיעור הילוכו הוא ג' מאות פרסה. בכל יום עשרה פרסאות ובחודש שהן שלשים יום גומר מהלכו תלת מאה פרסה. כי הילוכו אינו אלא כפי הילוך בני אדם בעוונותיהם כך הם מתגברים ומתרוממים בעוה"ז למעלה וזהו אומרו בין גלא לגלא תלת מאה פרסי כלומ' משיתחיל ממשלת האחד עד תחלת ממשלת הגל השני (ורומא דגלא תלת מאה פרסי) כנ"ל כמ"ש מרום שבתו אומ' כו' (עובדי' שם): (זמנא חדא הוה אזלינן באורחא ודלינן גלא כו'). פי' ענין התרוממות הגלים והצרות בלים ומגאוה שמתחיל' היצר מגביה את לב האדם ואח"כ שוברו כמ"ש (משלי י"ו) לפני שבר גאון. והענין הוא. כשמתחיל האדם לילך בדרך הטוב והמסילה העולה בית אל. אז יתרומם ויתגאה לבו מאד ואמרו בזוהר. על פסוק (שם ד') וארח צדיקים כאור נגה הולך ואור עד נכון היום ודרך רשעים באפילה לא ידעו במה יכשלו. מה שהזכיר אצל רשעים דרך ואצל צדיקים ארח. מפני שדרך רשעים כבושה. ליסטים כמותם כבושה לא כן אורח צדיקים אי אפשר להשיג דרך החיים ברגע א' אלא כאור נגה הולך ואור עד נכון היום. וזהו אמרו זימנא חדא. נחותי ימא ספרו לו שכל ימיהם היו בים ומלוות עיה"ז. פעם אחת התחיל לילך בדרך הטוב. והגביהו אותו שלוחי השטן בגאות לבו: (עד דחזינן מרבעתא דכוכבי זוטא) מפני שישראל נמשלו לכוכבים כמ"ש (מגילה דף ט"ז) כי נפל תפול לפניו דרש ר' יהודא ברבי אלעאי שתי נפילות אלו למה מלמד שאמרו לו אומה זו משולה לעפר ומשולה לכוכבים כשהן יורדין יורדין עד עפר. וכשהן עולין עד לרקיע. וכ"ש הצדיקים שנאמר (דניאל י"ב) ומצדיקי הרבים ככוכבי' לעולם ועד. ונדמה לנחות ימא הקטן שבהם גדול מאד: (הוי כמבזר ארבעין גריוי בזרה דהרדלא). כמ"ש (ב"ק דף י"ז) א"ר יוחנן משום רשב"י מאי דכתיב (ישעי' ל"ב) אשריכם זורעי על כל מים משלחי רגל שור וחמור כל העוסק בתורה וג"ח זוכה לנחלת שני שבטים וכו'. ולכאורה בפשטא דקרא וכן בדרשא מלת כל הוא מיותר הל"ל זורעי על מים. ונראה שתורה נמשלה למים מפני שמטהרת את האדם כמים כ"ש (ברכות דף ט"ז) ואמר רב חמא בר חנינא למה נסמכו אהלים לנחלים דכתיב (במדבר כ"ד) כנחלים נטיו כגנת עלי נהר כאהלים נטע ה' לומר לך מה נחלים מעלים את האדם מטומאה לטהרה אף אהלים מעלים את האדם מכף חובה לכף זכות. ולפעמים עולה בדעתו של אדם. תיכף כשמתחיל האדם ללמוד הוא נטהר. והיצה"ר כבר נפרד ממנו. לכך נאמר על כל מים כמו שמים אינן מטהרין אלא בארבעים סאה. מים שכל גופו עולה בהם. כך בתורה עד שכל גופו יוכתש כאמרם נמשל לחרדל. מה חרדל מר ואינו יכול לאכול אלא ע"י כתישה. כן התורה מתשת כחו של אדם כ"ש רז"ל למה נקרא שמה תושיה שמתשת כחו של אדם וכן דרשו על שמן זית זך כתית וזהו אמרם כמבזר ארבעין גריוי ביזרא דחרדלא. חרדל רמוז על כתישת מרירת היצר בעול התורה ומובדל שמן של היצר מפני עול התורה וארבעי' גריוי הוא שיעור של מי טהרה והתורה נמשלה למים: (ואי דלינן טפי הוי מקלינן מהבליה). כי סופו ומדריגה העליונה של הגאוה היא מדת הכעס. ואמרו כל הכועס שכינה מסלקת ממנו ואמרו בתענית האי צורבא מרבנן דרתח אורייתא דרתחת בי'. וז"א אי דלינן טפי בגדלת הגאוה היינו נשרפין מאש הכעס: (ורמי לי' גלא קלא וכו' שבקת מידי דלא שטפת ניתי אנא ונאבדי'.) פי' כשמתחיל הגל למשול א"ל לגל שעבר כלום הנחת לשום אדם שלא הפכתו לרע: (א"ל פוק חזי גבורתיה דמריך דאפי' כמלא חוטא דחלא לית דעבר.) מפני שהצדיקים נמשלים לחול שעל שפת הים כ"ש (ב"ב דף ז') רבי יהודא נשיאה רמא דשורא אדרבנן א"ל רשב"ל רבנן לא צריכי נטירותא דכתיב (תהלים קל"ט) אספרם מחול ירבון אלא אלו מעשיהן של צדיקים שאספרים מחול ירבון וק"ו ומה חול שמועט מגין על הים מעשיהם של

צדיקים

אמר רבה בב"ח אשתעי לי נחותי ימא האי גלא דמטבע לספינתא מתחזי כי צוציתא דנורא חיוורתא ברישא ומחינן לה באלותא דחקיק עליה אהיה אשר אהיה יה יה ה' צבאות אמן אמן סלה ונייח:

אמר רבב"ה אשתעי לי נחותי ימא. בין גלא לגלא ש' פרסא ורומא דגלא ש'

פי' רשב"ם

אמר רבה וכו'. כל הני עובדי דקא חשיב משום מה רבו מעשיך ה' ויש מהן להודיע מתן שכרן של צדיקים לעתיד לבוא. או לפרש מקראות האמורים בספר איוב המדברים בעופות גדולות ובהמות ודגים גדולים שכל שיחת תלמי' חכמים צריכה תלמוד (דמטבע) שרוצה לטבעו: (ברישא). שהולך לפניה: (צוציתא דנורא חיורתא) אש לבנה ומלאך מזיק הוא: (אלותא) מקלות כמו לא באלה ולא ברומח במס' שבת: אמן אמן סלה גרסינן: ונייח מזעפו: (בין גלא לגלא כו') משום דאמרינן בסמוך ורמא גלא קלא לחברתה אצטריך לאשמועינן דמשלש מאות פרסה שמעו קולו של חבירו: (דלינן גלא

בי' הגר"א

אמר רבה וכו'. נראה לפרש דכל אלו המעשים מספר סדכן על פסוק תהלים ק"ז יורדי הים באניות וכו' המה ראו מעשה ה' כי כבר ביארתי בביאורי על יונה שהעולם הזה נקרא ים והגוף נקרא אניה. ועל ידם הנשמה יורדת בים בעוה"ז ואותם שכל מעשיהם תמיד בעסקי עוה"ז נקראים יורדי הים. מפני שמתבוננים' בתהפוכ' עוה"ז. ונקראם עושי מלאכה במים רבים ע"ש שהם של נפר נקרא רבים כמ"ש בביאורי' על המגילות. המה ראו מעשי ה' ונפלאותיו במצולה. שרואים תמיד האיך זן כל אחד ואחד לפי מעשיו מדה במדה כמדתו וקמסדר כל מדות רעות ותשלומיהן של כל אחד ואחד. ויאמר ויעמוד כו'. וכן מסדר כאן רבב"ח. (אשתעו לי נחותי ימא). הם המתבוננים בתהפוכות עוה"ז כנ"ל. (האי גלא דמטבע לספינתא). ידוע שהגוף נקרא ספינה. וכל הצרות שעוברים עליו נקראים גלים. כמ"ש (תהלים מ"ב) כל משבריך וגליך עלי עברו והמה באים ומוליך המות הממית לאדם. ונקרא דמטבע לספינתא כמ"ש בפי' על יונה. והוא היצה"ר הממית לאדם בתחלה כמ"ש הוא יצה"ר הוא מה"מ ויורד ומסית עולה ומקטרג יורד ונוטל נשמה. (דמתחזי כצוציתא דנורא). כמעשה דרב עמרם חסידא בפרק עשרה יוחסין. אשבעיה ליצריה די נפק מיניה נפק מיניה בעמודא דנורא: (חיוורתא ברישא). כי בתחלה כשמסית. מראה לו חמשים שמני טהרה שמותר כמ"ש (משלי ה') כי נופת תטופנה שפתי זרה וגו' ואחריתה מרה כלענה חדה כחרב פיות. שהוא סרבא דת"ח וטיפות מרם תלוין בה. ורגליה יורדות מות. וכל זה גורם לנו שעבוד מלכיות והצרות כמאמר רבי אלכסנדרי בתר צלותי' (ברכות י"ז) רבון כל העולמים גלוי וידוע לפניך שרצונינו לעשות רצונך ומי מעכב שאור שבעיסה ושעבוד מלכיות. פי' כי לולא שעבוד מלכיות לא היו מניחין השאור להחמיץ כמ"ש ויאפו את הבצק מצות כי גורשו ממצרים. ולכן אפו מצה (והאריך בזה בעל ב"א בפי' הגדה) ובגלות מזכו שתי אלו השאור שבעיסה. כמ"ש (הושע י') מלוש בצק עד חמצתו. וגם שעבוד מלכיות. ויש לנו על זה שתי הבטחות. א' שאף בגלות יציל אותנו מכל צרה כמ"ש ואף גם זאת בארץ אויביהם לא מאסתים וגו' וכן עמו אנכי בצרה. והשנית שהבטיח לנו לגאלינו מן הגלות. הבטיח לנו במצרים אהיה אשר אהי'. אהי' עמהם בשעבוד זה ואהי' עמהם בשעבוד מלכיות. ועל השני לגאלינו מן הגלות. יש לנו משכון שנאמ' כי יד על כס יה ואחז"ל שאין השם שלם ואין הכסא שלם עד שיגאלנו. וענין השם כמ"ש רז"ל (עירובין דף י"ח ב') וא"ר אלעזר בר יעקב מיום שחרב בהמ"ק די לעולמו שישתמש בשתי אותיות שנאמר כל הנשמה תהלל יה וענין כסאו ג"כ ידוע כי גדולת הקב"ה ומלכותו עם ישראל הוא. וכהן בשפלות ובגלות אין מלכותו שלימה ולכן בים אמרו ה' ימלוך לעולם ועד. כי אין מלך בלא עם. ואין נקרא ה' צבאות עד שיגאל את צבאו וימלוך עליהם. כמ"ש גואלינו ה' צבאות ע"ש שאמר (ירמי' מ"ו י"ח) גואלם חזק ה' צבאות שמו. וכן כי ה' צבאות מלך. וזהו אומרו (ומחינן לי' באלותא דחקיק עליה אהי' אשר אהי' ה' צבאות). ובאיזה זכות אנחנו מלפין כל זאת מפני שכל התעוררות צריך להיות מלמטה. ואמרו (סוטה דף מ"ט) אמר רשב"ג מיום שחרב בהמ"ק אין לך יום ויום שקללתו מרובה מחבירו ועל מה עלמא קיים אקדושא דסדרא ואמן יהש"ר. וכן מצלת אותנו לעוה"ב כמ"ש (שבת קי"ט:) אר"ל כל העונה אמן בכל כחו פותחין לו שערי ג"ע שנאמר פתחו שערי' ויבא גוי צדיק שומר אמנים אל תקרי שומר אמנים אלא שאומרים אמן ואמרו כל העונה אמן בעוה"ז זוכה ועונה לעה"ב שנאמר אמן ואמן. וזהו שומר אמנים פי' שני אמנים והו אומרו כאן אמן אמן סלה:

בין גלא לגלא תלת מאה פרס'). דע כי כל הגלים הם צרות המתרגשות לבוא בעולם כמו כל משבריך וגליך עלי עברו. והם שלוחי השטן. וראשיהם הם י"ב נשיאים. כל אחד מושל חודש אחד. ובכל יום ויום הולך

ומתגבר

הקדמה

מלאו הבאים אחריהם. לחבר תורה שבכתב ושבע"פ בלוליאת התבונה והאמת. בתוך נתיבות משפט. ויש שמלאו ונתיבותיהם עקשו להם. ובדור אחרון ז"מ במשך אורינו ואפילתינו כלהרים. ה' הדריכו בנתיבות לא ידעו וכל נתיבותיו שלום. נכונה בשלום ויצא בשלום. מן יום ראשון בן תשע שנים אשר נתן לבו להבין כל חלקי התורה בנגלה ובנסתר. לקח מקח טוב לעצמו. מלא את כריסו מעדנים. תלמוד בבלי וירושלמי שונה להמו. ממגד התוספתא ומילואה. ממגד שמים תלמידי חכמים בפלפול הפוסקים ראשונים ואחרונים. וירא כי עת להכנה כי אין תומך. ובא מועד שהניחו לו אבותיו להתגדר בהן. להגיה על נכון השבושים שנפלו בתוספתא ומכילתא וספרא וספרי וירושלמי ה' סדרים וסדר עולם ופרקי ר"א ובברייתות הנעלמות אין מספר כמו חלקי הזהר ותקוניו. להכין אותם ולסעדם ורק מתלמוד בבלי וירושלמי. לאמור להשבושים אשר באו מידי הסופרים והמדפיסים לאו. ולאשר בחשך לא ידעו איש מקומו איה. הגלו. אין דבר נעלם ממנו. ואין נסת"ר מנגד עיניו. הלא זה רוכב שמים בתבונתו. ובגאותו שחקים. הוא עלה שמים וירד עוז מבטחה. והבין נסתרות שמבראשית לגר בחפניו. אותותיו ראינו. לאות עולם אל תאמר מה הי' שהימים הראשונים היו טובים מאלה. הן אתה בדור אחרון שבאחרוני' הראנו ה' את כבודו ואת גדלו. איה סופר איה שוקל ערך קלה רוחב לבבו. אין קץ לחידושי תורתו תורת ה' תמימה הכל סלת נקי כמתכנתה תמיד. מי יתן בספר ויוחקו. יבואו הזכאים ויתגלגל זכות על ידם. אי בדור יזכה את כל הדור.

ולפי שפירוש רבנ"ח וקבא דבי אתונא הזכיר בכל מקום. כמ"ש בביאורי על יונה. וכמ"ש בביאורי על ה' מגילות מפני שבסגנון אחד ביאר את שניהם. ולהדפיסן בצירוביא על מקרא ואגדות לא הי' אפשר בזה. לכן עשינו חלק ראשון מאגדות. וח"ב על המגילות ועל יונה:

וגם ההקדמה שעשה הרב הגאון דק"ק וולאזין יצ"ו. נדפס באחרונה ולא הגיע לידינו רק שלשית. לכן הדפסנו כאן. אחת משלנו. אולי ימצא המעיין. איזה מקום לפקפק. יתלה בחסרון ידיעה. או בהשגרתא דלישנא. וגם מפני שעם ה' אין דעתם דומות זו לזו. יש מהן נפשם חפיצה שיודפס כרך אחד מחומשים ניירות. ויש שבחרו במועט. והנה הנס על משניות נדפס יותר משלשים ניירות הדפסנו כעת מועט המחזיק מרובה למביני העם. ה' יזכינו ללמוד וללמד מתורתו. וזכות תורתו וצדקתו יעמוד לנו ולכל ישראל המפלים דעת את ה' בתורתו התמימה:

דברי **יהודה ליב** ודברי **אברהם** בני הגאון האמתי קדוש ה'. חסידא ופרישא המנוה מו' **אליהו** זצללה"ה נשמתו עדן:

הקדמת

בניו הרבנים המופלגים זרע ברך ה׳ המפורסמים נ״י:

פתח פיך הקורא. ביאוריו הנעימים מעיד תמלא. ובענק האכל. ממוסריו אשר ראוים הם למי שאוהב. והיה פריו למאכל. ועליהו לתרופה. ועתה לתת את נקבת רבים וכן שלמים העושים את אזנם כאפרכסת לשמוע באגדה מפיו דעת ותבונה. אכפתי מלא קומץ. גם שנדפס בראשונה ביאורו על משלי מתלמיד הגון אשר למד אתו כפי השגתו. ואם קרא לא שנה ולא שלש אתו עמו. ובבית גנזיו מלאנו כהנה וכהנה. וגם פירושו על משניות זרעים נדפס על ידי גיסינו הרב החריף מוהרר משה מפינסק. גם הוא לא יצא ידי חובת הביאור במקומות שצריך להאריך כפי שנתנו לו נכתב. ורצוננו היה לדפוס בווין על נייר יפה. הדר הוא לכבודו ותורתו. והר״ש מנד א׳ כדי שיבינו הכל כוונתו לתרץ את הלשון אשר נמצא במשניות וירושלמי לפי פירושיו והוא בעל רצוננו והדפים בק״ק לבוב.

וגם פה בליקוטים חלק ראשון לא עשינו עיקר כי אלהא שפתותינו שבח כמרמזי רקיע. אין חקר לרוחב לבבו כלבן של ראשונים. כפתחו של אולם. ויקם עדות קלא מפי כתביו שהניח אחריו ברכה. כי אזן חקר ותיקן ביאורים על הסדר על מקרא משנה גמרא בבלי ירושלמי תוספתא מכילתא ספרא ספרי סדר עולם פרקי ר״א. זהר. תקוני זהר כמה כרכים. ספר יצירה. היכלות רעיא מהימנא ספרא דצניעותא. על ארבע ש״ע. על כמה מסכתות. על אבות דר״נ. מסכתות קטנות. מסורת. דקדוק טעמי אמת. יותר ממאה כללים חדשים וגם ישנים. על תכונה ואלגיברא ומשולשים כמה כרכים. וליקוטים יותר משלשים כרכים יש מהן ארבעה ניירות ועד עשרה ועד עשרים ניירות. מי יתן ידעו ויראו ויבינו על לבבם ויאמרו כלם. לא ידענו בחייו מיוחד מה הוא. לא הוגד לנו החצי לעת כזאת ראינו על אחת שבע.

ואל תתמהו על החפץ איך נחק האפשרי. היות אדם לבדו ימי שנותיו שבעים שנה. יכול עשותו ספרים הרבה. הכל ברורים כסלת נקי. אמת כאמיתן של תורה. כבר למדנו רבינו ז״ל הלומד תורה לשמה זוכה לדברים הרבה. נעשה כמעין המתגבר. וה׳ עמו גלה לו אוצרות אורות. ומטמוני מסתרים. הוא יצא לפניו להשכילו בינה. הוא היה מלמדו להועיל מדריכו בדרך ילך. על כן עשה והצליח. כי לא אבד זמנו כהרף עין. עינינו ראו גם בעת דבר אתנו דבור ומלי דיבור כדרכו ורק בעת ההכרח. לא פסק פומי׳ ולבו מגרסי׳ לזאת תמכו כ׳ ביד ימינו. והשמיעו חדשות אשר לא שערו אבותינו. שיקוס (בדור אחרון יתמי דיתמי. את שני קצותיו אכלה אש ותוכו ניכר) איש עומד בפרץ. לבנות חרבות עולם. לקומם מוסדי דור ודור להשיב עטרת תפארת התורה על יושנה. לגדור המלות שנשכחו לשוב וליכון. לשונג נתיבות החכמה לשבת. להשביע בלחלוחות העלומות נפשינו ועלם האמת לאמתו יחליץ. וע״פ ביאוריו ופירושיו נהי׳ כגן רוה וכמוצא מים אשר לא יכזבו מימיו. להוליד ע״פ הנחותיו. בכל מקום אשר נפנה נצליח ונשכיל. עד שלא בא איש חמודות. איש אלהים מו״ר מ״ה הגאון אליהו זכור לטוב. הי׳ דרכי ה׳ בתורה שבכתב ושבע״פ שוממה מכמה דורות לפניו. וה׳ אהבו הנחילו דברים הרמים והנשגבים. מעיני כל החכמים. כאחד מלבא מכוס במרום. כי מעת רבנן סבוראי והגאונים. נתיבותיהם לא

מצאו

הערת

כבוד

הרב הגדול אור ישראל והדרו גאון יעקב צבי ישורון החכם הכולל כו'. המפורסם כש"ת מוהר"ר יעקב צבי מעקלענבורג נ"י בעהמ"ח הכתב והקבלה ועיון תפילה האב"ד דפ"ק.

ב"ה

האי צורבא מרבנן המופלג כו' מוהר"ר אברהם משה רא"ש כלר מטעי קודש כין ונכד להגאון החסיד המפורסם מו"ה **אברהם** זללה"ה בעהמ"ח ס' **מעלת התורה**. התאזר חיל להוציא לאור כמה מכתבי כ"י קודש מד"ז עיר וקדיש איש אשר רוח אלהים בו רבינו הגדול הגאון אור העולם רבן של כל בני הגולה מרנא ורבנא כ"ה **אליהו** חסידא קדישא מווילנא נ"ע.

וראיתי כי נאמן הוא מאד במלאכת הקדש ומתיגע יגיעות הרבה להגיהם כשורה ולהביאם לבית הדפוס. וכעת הוא נכון ג"כ להדפיס ביאוריו על אגדות רבב"ח וסבי דבי אתונא שהי' כבר בדפוס ונוסף עוד עליהם לקוטים על אגדות ומקראי קדש. וכאשר לפעלא טבא יישר. ומהראוי לכל איש ישראלי לעמוד בימין עזרו בזה לקחת אותו ממנו. בכדי שבמחירם יוכל להפיץ את יקרות מיתר חבורי קדש אשר הוא נכון להאיר בם עיני ישראל. והנה כל איש ישים אל לבו לזכור אלות הר עיבל וישמור נפשו מהשיג גבולו ומלהדפיס בלתי רשותו משך עשרה שנים. וזכות הגר"א יגן על כל מי שיעמוד בעזרת הנ"ל להפיץ דברי קודש על פני תבל. וברכה כפולה ומשולשת לכל המחזיקים ותומכים בימינו.

קעניגסבערג. יום א' ר"ח מנחם התרכ"ג ליצירה.

יעקב צבי ב"ר גמליאל מעקלענבורג.

פירוש

על כמה אגדות

מאת אדונינו. מאור עינינו. גאון עוזינו מורינו ורבינו א"א הגאון החסיד האמתי המפורסם גדול שמו בישראל. בדורו ובכמה דורות שלפניו. כבוד קדושת תורתו וחסידותו וגודל ענוותנותו רבינו הגדול קדוש ישראל ואורו רבינו **אליהו** זלל"ה מווילנא:

הביטו וראו בעיון היטב. ותדעו ותבינו דבר דבור על אפניו. אבת לאמתתן של תורה. כנתינתן מסיני ויהנו כולם מאורו ולדתענג ברוב טיבו. אשר הניח אחריו ברכה. ואשרי העם שלו ככה. אשר זכינו להגות מאורו בדורנו דור אחרון.

יצא לאור בשנת ישרים ע"י בניו זרע ברך
ה' היקרים הרבנים המופלגים המפורסמים נ"ע

ועתה יצא לאור עם הוספות כמה מאורות חמודות וגנוזות

ע"י **אברהם** משה נ"ר **אהרן** רא"ם כ"י נכד הרב הגאון החסיד כר ישראל מו"ה **אברהם** זלוק"ל בעהמ"ס ס' מעלות התורה אחי הגר"א זלה"ה: פה קעניגסבערג כמו שנדפס

בווילנא

בשנת יראו ישרים וישמחו לפ"ק

פירוש על כמה אגדות
לרבנו אליהו מווילנא זצוק"ל

(דפוס קניגסברג דף א-יא)

Explanation of Several Aggaddos

by the Vilna Gaon

(Koenigsburg edition, folios 1-11)